OXFORD TEXTUAL PERSPECTIVES

Last Words

Last Words

The Public Self and the Social Author in Late Medieval England

SEBASTIAN SOBECKI

OXFORD
UNIVERSITY PRESS

OXFORD
UNIVERSITY PRESS

Great Clarendon Street, Oxford, OX2 6DP,
United Kingdom

Oxford University Press is a department of the University of Oxford.
It furthers the University's objective of excellence in research, scholarship,
and education by publishing worldwide. Oxford is a registered trade mark of
Oxford University Press in the UK and in certain other countries

First Edition published in 2019

Impression: 1

Published in the United States of America by Oxford University Press
198 Madison Avenue, New York, NY 10016, United States of America

British Library Cataloguing in Publication Data
Data available

Library of Congress Control Number: 2019941578

ISBN 978–0–19–879077–8 (hbk.)
978–0–19–879078–5 (pbk.)

DOI: 10.1093/oso/9780198790778.001.0001

Printed and bound by
CPI Group (UK) Ltd, Croydon, CR0 4YY

ACKNOWLEDGEMENTS

This book has incurred many debts over the last five years. I will not be able to recall all exchanges with those who have shaped my thinking about late medieval manuscripts and literature, whether at conferences or over a glass of wine. It would take a volume entirely made up of acknowledgements to express my gratitude.

Greg Walker and Elaine Treharne encouraged this project from the beginning. Rory Critten and Sonja Drimmer read most of the material in this book in the course of the last few years. They have been among my frankest and most incisive readers. Linne Mooney, Kees Dekker, and Jonathan Hsy went with a fine comb through the article that would become Chapter 1, while Bob Yeager diligently audited my thinking on all things Gower. John Scattergood and Bobby Meyer-Lee, covering between them some of the finest scholarship on fifteenth-century literature, robustly tested the reasoning in the Ashby chapter. Fiona Somerset generously lent her erudition and fine judgement in aid of my essay on Lydgate; she also saved me from flogging a dead horse. I am grateful to Shannon McSheffrey for having studied the chapter on the *Libelle* and sharing with me her extensive knowledge of Richard Caudray's remarkable life. Hoccleve was the last to join the book, and I am grateful to Lawrence Warner for his eagle-eyed insights and exquisite company. The Hoccleve chapter has greatly profited from Liza Strakhov's perceptive scrutiny, forcing me to articulate the *so what*. No discussion of the *Series* could be had without David Watt, and I remain in his debt for the care with which he read my chapter.

Many others have helped to move this project along through conversation and ready help, whether by offering their time or sharing their resources with me: Euan Roger, Gwilym Dodd, Emily Steiner, Zach Stone, Helen Killick, Kathleen Kennedy, Marion Turner, Elliot Kendall, Dan Wakelin, Anthony Bale, Matthew Boyd Goldie, Misty Schieberle, Derek Pearsall, Simon Horobin, Matthew Giancarlo, Isabel Davis, Paul Strohm, Noa Nikolsky, James Simpson, Peter Nicholson, and Orietta Da Rold. As always, my Groningen colleague Alasdair Macdonald provided me with advice and encouragement.

The team at Oxford University Press have been wonderful throughout the time it took for this book to see publication. I am especially grateful to Jacqueline Norton for supporting my idea and to Aimee Wright for once again navigating me with a steady hand through the pitfalls of the production process. I would also like to thank the editors of the journals in which two of the chapters have appeared: Susanna Fein and David Raybin at the *Chaucer Review*, and Sallie Spence at *Speculum*. I am indebted to the anonymous readers for both journals and for Oxford University Press. I would like to thank Penn State University Press and the Medieval Academy of America for permission to reuse my articles from the *Chaucer Review* and *Speculum*, respectively.

This book would hardly have materialized without the ready help of research libraries and academic institutions, with their superb staff and fine reading rooms. I am grateful to the Bibliothèque nationale de France, the Bodleian Library, the British Library, Cambridge University Library, the John Rylands Library, the Bavarian State Library, McGill University Library, and the National Archives. I would also like to thank the New Chaucer Society and the Early Book Society for giving me the space and occasion to talk about my work. The material in this book was earlier presented at conferences and gatherings in Cambridge, Dublin, Leiden, Oxford, and Toronto; I am grateful to the audiences for the ensuing exchanges.

The Institute for the Study of Culture at Groningen's Arts Faculty supported my research stays and conference trips. A visiting fellowship at All Souls College, Oxford, gave me the time to crystallize my argument, and the Codrington Library proved an excellent venue in which to scheme a book. I would like to thank the John Gower Society for awarding me the John Hurt Fisher Prize for the essay that is now Chapter 1.

Finally, I would like to thank Nadia for helping me with the research on Ashby and for seeing things I didn't notice. As ever, Alicja has been my most fearless critic and staunchest ally.

CONTENTS

LIST OF FIGURES

LIST OF ABBREVIATIONS

EETS	Early English Text Society
LALME	*A Linguistic Atlas of Late Mediaeval English*, eds. Angus McIntosh, M. L. Samuels, and Michael Benskin (Aberdeen: Aberdeen University Press, 1986), 4 vols
MED	*Middle English Dictionary*, eds. Hans Kurath and Sherman M. Kuhn (Ann Arbor, MI: University of Michigan Press, 1954–2001): <https://quod.lib.umich.edu/m/med/>
NIMEV	*A New Index of Middle English Verse*, eds. Julia Boffey and A. S. G. Edwards (London: British Library, 2005)
ODNB	*Oxford Dictionary of National Biography* (Oxford: Oxford University Press, 2004): <http://www.oxforddnb.com>
STC	A. W. Pollard and G. R. Redgrave, eds, *A Short-Title Catalogue of Books Printed in England, Scotland and Ireland, and of English Books Printed Abroad 1475–1640*, 2nd edn, revised and enlarged, begun by W. A. Jackson and F. S. Ferguson, completed by K. F. Pantzer (London: Bibliographical Society, 1976–91)
TNA	The National Archives, London

The Indexical Self

An Introduction

Contextual Authors

There are many ways that I could have begun this book. At first, I envisioned a vindication that would have come to the rescue of those fifteenth-century poets who have been, in my view, misrepresented as devoted Lancastrian propagandists. I had thought that if I could show that John Gower, Thomas Hoccleve, John Lydgate, and George Ashby were still more conflicted in their political thinking than we already tend to grant them and, the reception of their writings more fluid and mercurial, that somehow 'Lancastrian' could be reclaimed as a neutral period marker, much as 'Elizabethan' or 'Victorian'—terms devoid of any trace of political position, let alone allegiance. Instead of saddling these writers with an unquestioned deference to the regime under which they happened to live and write, I had hoped to contend that their personal aspirations would surface as the defining properties of fifteenth-century narrative poetry written in the first person—at once carving out for themselves poetic identities while also paying lip service to existing social, political, and ecclesiastical hierarchies. That was an optimistic beginning.

The more I thought about these writers, the more I recognized that I was asking the wrong question. The point is not whether their

Last Words: The Public Self and the Social Author in Late Medieval England.
Sebastian Sobecki, Oxford University Press (2019).
DOI: 10.1093/oso/9780198790778.001.0001

aspirations were of greater consequence to them than their surrounding political and, hence, social contexts, but whether they were able to imagine their personal aims and desires as distinct from, and hence not necessarily aligned with, the de facto hegemonies structuring their social selves through parishes, wards, and hundreds. Were they able to view themselves as social agents capable of effecting foundational change, of derailing systemic processes, of shaping publics? The question is not whether such events occurred—they certainly did. Rather, was it possible to visualize and desire them beforehand? It is one thing to imagine, plan, and execute a revolution; it is quite another to stumble into one, as William Langland and the disgruntled commoners of 1381 realized. To borrow a household term from sociology and clinical psychiatry, fifteenth-century persons were quintessentially *sociocentric* in their self-perception, that is, they viewed themselves primarily as embedded in society and thus delimited by it, rather than as independent agents free to attach or detach themselves from societal constructs.[1] But this question appeared to controvert the very tenets of my training as a literary medievalist with its privileging of the singular subject—text, work, or writer—over what surrounded it and formed its background. I sensed that the rituals of literary criticism ran counter to the sociocentric position of medieval writers. So I first needed to come clean about my methodology, about how I approach medieval texts as a researcher and a teacher.

It became increasingly clear to me that in recent years the gap between how I teach literature in the classroom and how I approach it in my own research had widened to the extent that I often assumed contradictory positions in my almost binary academic roles. My teaching has been shaped by the formative training I received at Cambridge's English Faculty in the 1990s, where manuscript studies peacefully coexisted with a dual devotion to, on the one hand, an institutionally sanctioned, rigorous practical criticism and its attendant exercises in close reading and, on the other, to the determined pursuit of a text's intellectual context. In my case, the critical position that resulted from this twinning of two often antagonistic schools of reading, with

[1] It is for this reason, I believe, that Paul Strohm's influential study *Social Chaucer* continues to generate productive responses, thirty years after its publication (*Social Chaucer* (Cambridge, MA: Harvard University Press, 1989)).

manuscript studies hovering in a neutral zone, led to an excision of the writer *qua* author or agent altogether. A medieval text, however unstable, however much exposed to *mouvance*, always took centre stage—on this focal point both manuscript studies and practical criticism seemed to converge. The text, or the incarnated text in a manuscript instance, was always central and therefore its own self-sustaining subject. A text did not exist in a vacuum of course, but with its author long dead and buried by both time and Roland Barthes, the social configuration surrounding it could certainly be deployed, if studied and observed carefully enough, to extract more meaning from the text, to let it speak for itself, bypassing the author along the way. This is why, I believe, New Historicism has been particularly appealing to those trained in practical criticism, since texts often appear to resist their contexts, of which the author was a part. Critics see in a text's resistance to its historical context often an anachronistic projection of the modern reader's own standpoint: we thus believe that we see our contemporary concerns foregrounded in historical texts.

This is how I found myself approaching texts in the classroom. By contrast, my research on manuscripts and archival material brought a pragmatic dilemma into sharp relief. With time, I came to the persuasion that medieval manuscripts, and therefore the texts they articulate, are essentially deictic artefacts. The further they are removed from their author and their originating context, the more fragmented and less satisfactory their meaning becomes. This holds true on a textual level as much as on a material level. Through variant textual readings each written-out text refers to those copies it is not: to understand the significance of a variant reading or scribal change, we need to see at least two divergent instances. This tension is particularly noticeable in illuminators' and copyists' difficulties in extending self-referential texts to secondary audiences.[2] Similarly, to understand how a text was read, or was meant to be read, we need to examine what is often referred to as the 'manuscript context', that is, its physical proximity to the other texts with which it has been paired or bound. This form of codicological

[2] Sonja Drimmer's term 'ambigraph' captures this bipolarity, inherent in many if not all non-holographic manuscripts, of being at the same self-referential and trying to reach a secondary audience ('The Manuscript as an Ambigraphic Medium: Hoccleve's Scribes, Illuminators, and Their Problems', *Exemplaria*, 29/3 (2017), 175–94).

deixis is famously illustrated by *Beowulf* and its manuscript context. Given the lack or perhaps loss of other copies of this poem, the sole surviving physical text of *Beowulf* in London, British Library Cotton MS Vitellius A XV acquires especially compelling interpretive value in its manuscript context. This is not just a question of subsequent compilation: every medieval text, each copy of a work, was crafted by a scribe or scribal author for a particular manuscript instance or, as I prefer to call it given the author's deictic presence, incarnation.

The upshot of this practice of reconstructing authors through manuscript study has reinvented the author not as a textual or paratextual phenomenon but as a contextual one, allowing the writer to exercise indirect intentionalism over the text from the inscrutable position of being outside the medieval manuscript. But in practice this aspect of manuscript studies often amounts to reverse-engineered authorial intentionalism: if we can recover the purpose, occasion, or reception of textual witnesses that were overseen by the author or produced in their lifetime, then we can infer their original or first meaning, particularly if a text was subsequently revised or rededicated. As medievalists we tend to get away with this intentionalism because it lies buried deep beneath our outwardly arcane practices of codicology and palaeography, and because our texts are profoundly unstable, porous, and semantically tampered with by all who handled or owned them. Even if a medieval writer could be said to be an author and intellectual proprietor of a text, then what is it exactly that he or she is an owner of? For all the difficulties we have with defining medieval authors, delineating the boundaries of a medieval text—even one that has reached us only in a single autograph copy—is intellectually frustrating. We are not afforded any textual stability; not by manuscript *mouvance*, not by scribal interference, and certainly not by a seemingly wilful rejection of *auctoritas* on the part of the writer.

Given the medieval text's unwanted semantic instability, the paucity of corroborating information on the purpose, occasion, or reception of a text invariably led me to sifting through records and other archival materials. Such work, certainly in my own practice, often follows a pattern of concentric circles, starting from the known biological originator of a text, its author. Gradually these circles become wider, extending to a writer's known contacts, persons, or events mentioned in the text, and so on. My desire to pursue textual or authorial references in archival contexts is not rooted in historicism but in my formalist commitment to practical criticism and the primacy of the text as text. To my mind, the study of manuscripts and other written records is as much a part of close reading as is the attention we pay to the lineation of a poem. There is no qualitative difference between, on the one hand, consulting other textual witnesses to establish the meaning generated by variants and, on the other, to locating evidence for a text's occasion in a historical record. As far as the text in question is concerned ('text', that is, as contained and defined by a single manuscript instance), both techniques—collation with other manuscripts or the use of historical records—are external to the text and therefore in need of further interpretation. Collation and archival search are both interpretive tools based on a careful comparison of the subject of study to the available external evidence.

For all its ingenuity, the cumbersome practice of reverse-engineering authorial intention appears to brush aside the many attempts of medieval writers to inscribe themselves in their manuscript texts, whether as dreaming personae, spectral presences, or petitioners asking for prayers for the soul. This is best brought out by the manuscript palinode, as I discuss in Chapter 4 on Lydgate's *Testament* and Chaucer's Retraction. The manuscript palinode or retraction is built around a deictic joke: there's no more where this came from. It is as if the author was saying: 'dear reader, please pray for me because I am discarding the *idea* of my work, while you are holding a *physical copy* of it'. The author retracts their authorship of a work without withdrawing the physical copy that transmits this information and, paradoxically, itself. Every palinode, every literary testament, every personal dedication is an attempt by the writer to travel with the text, to be remembered together with their work or perhaps despite it. To read a medieval palinode as self-censorship is to misread the premodern person as delimited and detached from its environment, as renouncing its sociocentric identity.

An even more potent indicator of our habitual misreading of the premodern person and its authorial function is the interpretive value we attribute to anonymity. More often than not, modern readers view anonymity as a position assumed by an author not only where it is a strategy to avoid, say, persecution, but as a default stance, a literary tradition, so much so that the anonymous condition of medieval vernacular literature becomes a deferential gesture, expressive of a denial of *auctoritas*.[3] Yet any reader of Chaucer's *House of Fame* is aware of the token value of many authorial gestures of faux humility. And to my knowledge no one has remarked that these deferential gestures of crediting classical or earlier medieval *auctores* with an idea or the work in question as a rule only occur in self-identifying texts in which we already know who the author is. The deferential argument even appears to confirm itself through its own circularity: surely, so the reasoning goes, such deferential gestures are only provided *because* the author has identified him or herself, unduly claiming *auctoritas* for themselves. But this circular reasoning is the result of mistaking anonymity for disguise, of confusing the loss of a presence with a calculated absence, of turning deictic authors into incognito writers. Medieval vernacular literature and, specifically, autograph poetry is not anonymous for any ideological reason. (I refer to 'vernacular' in England as writing produced in English and certain varieties of Anglo-French.)[4] It is anonymous to anyone but a text's primary audience who knew the author's identity. There is no anonymity in medieval vernacular poetry, there is only deictic presence. Anonymity was the result of the widening of a text's audience beyond its primary target. In this sense all medieval texts are performative, whether or not they are constructed around the conventions of orality. Such texts are only anonymous by choice as far as they never needed to encode their author's identity because it was already known. This is not to deny the validity of translational approaches to medieval authorship in the tradition of Rita Copeland's trailblazing work,[5] but to point to a tension between the intellectual models developed by medieval scholarship and those generated by vernacular writing with its personal and limited manuscript dissemination. As a principle,

[3] By contrast, on the medieval tradition of authorship in learned, non-vernacular discourses, see Alastair Minnis, *Medieval Theory of Authorship: Scholastic Literary Attitudes in the Later Middle Ages* (London: Scolar Press, 1984).

[4] I explain my understanding of 'vernacular' in *Unwritten Verities: The Making of England's Vernacular Legal Culture, 1463–1549* (Notre Dame, IN: University of Notre Dame Press, 2015), 11–12, and, specifically in relation to the varieties of Anglo-French in use in England, 43–69. On Anglo-French as an English vernacular, see Ardis Butterfield, *The Familiar Enemy: Chaucer, Language, and Nation in the Hundred Years War* (Oxford: Oxford University Press, 2010).

[5] The starting point for this vital critical strand is Rita Copeland's *Rhetoric, Hermeneutics, and Translation in the Middle Ages: Academic Traditions and Vernacular Texts* (Cambridge: Cambridge University Press, 1995).

audiences knew their authors, and authors knew their audiences. This is why so many 'anonymous' texts do not give their author's name yet seem to make no particular attempt to conceal his or her identity. That's because the identity of the author was obvious to the text's primary audience.

The Indexical Self

So far I have used the word 'deictic' to speak of texts that cannot be understood without recourse to their contexts, primarily that of the author. Deixis, however, is more properly at home in linguistics where it denotes words and phrases such as 'I', 'here', and 'now' that can only be understood in a particular context. My understanding of the speaking 'I' in a medieval text is primarily informed by clinical psychiatry and philosophy of the mind where self-referential meaning is circumscribed by the term 'indexical'.

The underlying contention of this book is simple: as a rule, medieval vernacular literature, specifically homodiegetic writing (that is, writing that features an authorial persona as part of its narrative), is indexical. Therefore, the narrative 'I' in such texts is deictic and thus contingent on its biological author. By 'indexical' I mean that such texts were created for a specific audience with direct access to the author and a full understanding of a text's fabric of allusions. This is why I have recently argued that the General Prologue to Chaucer's *Canterbury Tales* relies for much of its humour—the pastiche of the historical Harry Bailey, the jokes at the expense of the Prioress, etc.—on an intimate audience familiar with specific persons, places, and conditions in late fourteenth-century Southwark.[6] This does not mean that the characters in the *Canterbury Tales* are accurate reflections of specific individuals, but they are accurate *enough* to elicit jokes that only an in-the-know audience could have appreciated. By the same token, Chaucer the pilgrim is equally deictic, otherwise the jokes about his lack of poetic skill at either end of the Tale of Sir Thopas would fall flat. The indexical nature of these references rests on Chaucer's awareness

[6] Sebastian Sobecki, 'A Southwark Tale: Gower, the Poll Tax of 1381, and Chaucer's *The Canterbury Tales*', *Speculum*, 92/3 (2017), 630–60.

that the audience knew at least some of his other work and was familiar with his abilities as a writer. If it was common even in the late pre-Enlightenment period for writers to imagine a hearing, silent audience and, hence, to 'create a fictive persona who can address that reader in the physical absence of the writer',[7] then that persona must be deictic in an indexical manuscript written for an audience who knew the author.

In recent years, A. C. Spearing has done much for our understanding of the first-person speaker, the 'I' in medieval poetry. Spearing imports the term *autography* into the study of medieval poetry, and defines it as 'extended, non-lyrical, fictional writings in and of the first person'.[8] He acknowledges the pitfalls of anachronistic readings, astutely observing instead that 'medieval writings rarely *represented* the distinct subjectivity of a text's fictional speaker, and their habit was to encode subjectivity in textual form by means such as deixis—subjectivity not usually that of a specific, self-consistent person but broadly and variously diffused throughout the text'.[9] The notion of a purely fictional speaker in a literary text, he continues, became the norm 'long after the Middle Ages'.[10] And although first-person speakers in medieval texts are therefore not fictional or predominantly fictional, they need not be identical with their biological alter egos since *autography* 'is first-person writing in which there is no implied assertion that the first person either does or does not correspond to a real-life individual'.[11] Spearing is correct, I think, to note that the normativity of the fictional self is firmly post-medieval, yet his model of the 'real-life individual' from whom the literary self in *autography* springs strikes me as equally post-medieval. Spearing's idea of the author, as far as it is articulated, does not account for the specific epistemological condition of sociocentric persons. But how would a theory of the sociocentric person inform the medieval author and constructs of the 'I' in homodiegetic texts?

[7] Elspeth Jajdelska, *Silent Reading and the Birth of the Narrator* (Toronto: University of Toronto Press, 2007), 11.

[8] A. C. Spearing, *Medieval Autographies: The 'I' of the Text* (Notre Dame, IN: University of Notre Dame Press, 2012), 1.

[9] Spearing, *Medieval Autographies*, 5. For Spearing's broader theory of subjectivity in medieval literature, see *Textual Subjectivity: The Encoding of Subjectivity in Medieval Narratives and Lyrics* (Oxford: Oxford University Press, 2005).

[10] Spearing, *Medieval Autographies*, 5.

[11] Spearing, *Medieval Autographies*, 7.

My starting point is Charles Taylor's notion of the *porous self* before the Enlightenment, articulated in a series of essays that culminated in his 2007 work *A Secular Age*.[12] Taylor, a philosopher of religion, circumscribes the premodern self as contextually dependent, porous, without the ability to sever itself from its enchanted environment. In this world, the physical is never just the physical and the self is not protected from the social and spiritual forces that exercise pressure on it. In the premodern world, Taylor argues, it is not the individual who assigns meaning; instead 'meaning is already there in the object/agent, it is there quite independently of us; it would be there even if we didn't exist'.[13] In contrast to the modern, post-Enlightenment self, the porous medieval self has no independent means of protection from its physical and spiritual surroundings, it does not enjoy the option of a protective secular buffer that renders the acceptance of metaphysical reality a matter of personal choice:

> And so the boundary between agents and forces is fuzzy in the enchanted world; and the boundary between mind and world is porous, as we see in the way that charged objects can influence us. Our modern way of being has rendered this condition weird and inconceivable for many of us.[14]

Taylor's analysis of the porous self and the enchanted world in which it is defencelessly embedded explains the powerful role played by religious and worldly orthodoxy: 'sin was playing the role which we would attribute today to a failure of the immune system'.[15] That is because the struggle against harmful spiritual forces in the enchanted world becomes a communal, social effort since there is nothing to buffer the self from its context:

> So we're all in this together. This has two consequences. First, it puts a tremendous premium on holding to the consensus. Turning 'heretic' and rejecting this power, or condemning the practice as idolatrous, is not just a personal matter. Villagers who hold out, or even denounce the common rites, put the efficacy of these rites in danger, and hence pose a menace to everyone.[16]

[12] See especially Charles Taylor, 'An Issue about Language', in *Language, Culture, and Society: Key Topics in Linguistic Anthropology* (Cambridge: Cambridge University Press, 2006), 16–46; and *A Secular Age* (Cambridge, MA: Belknap Press of Harvard University Press, 2007).

[13] Taylor, *A Secular Age*, 37.

[14] Taylor, 'An Issue about Language', 45.

[15] Taylor, *A Secular Age*, 39.

[16] Taylor, *A Secular Age*, 42.

If the self is porous, it can never fully demarcate its boundaries from its environment. By hypostatizing sin as a material phenomenon, it is exposed to metaphysical forces. Such a self cannot individuate itself from its social and physical situation.

But Taylor's powerful theory of buffered and porous selves has independently existed in clinical psychiatry since at least 1982. In that year, in an attempt to understand the divergent results in the psychiatric treatment of ethnic minorities in the United States, Atwood Gaines published an influential essay in which he speaks of the 'indexical' and 'referential' selves, borrowed from previous studies in the field.[17] On the one hand, he argues, Western psychiatrists see the individual as a 'bounded, unique, more or less integrated motivational and cognitive universe, a dynamic centre of awareness, emotion, and action organised into a distinctive whole and set contrastively both against other such wholes and against a social and natural background'.[18] Such an individual, Gaines continues, is 'capable of instituting personal change',[19] a vital predisposition for the efficacy of any therapeutic measure. Not only does Gaines's understanding of the referential self correspond to Taylor's 'buffered self', but it is the boundedness of both entities that permits change. After all, for Taylor, 'the buffered self can form the ambition of disengaging from whatever is beyond the boundary, and of giving its own autonomous order to its life. The absence of fear can be not just enjoyed, but seen as an opportunity for self-control or self-direction.'[20] By distancing itself from its context, both the referential self and the buffered self can modify its view of its situation and effect change.

Gaines traces the emergence of the referential self somewhat triumphantly to 'the Great Tradition of Protestant Europe'.[21] By contrast, the Latin European self is 'indexical', not an

> abstract entity independent of the social relations and contexts in which the self is presented in interaction. Notions of the self as a

[17] Atwood D. Gaines, 'Cultural Definitions, Behavior and the Person in American Psychiatry', in *Cultural Conceptions of Mental Health and Therapy*, ed. Anthony Marsella and Geoffrey White (New York: Springer, 1982), 181.

[18] Clifford Geertz, quoted in Gaines, 'Cultural Definitions', 181.

[19] Gaines, 'Cultural Definitions', 18.

[20] Taylor, *A Secular Age*, 38–9.

[21] Gaines, 'Cultural Definitions', 182.

> discrete, unique social entity are far less important [to the Latin European self] as an explanatory construct used to interpret the behaviour of persons across situations. Rather, the self is perceived as constituted or 'indexed' by the contextual features of social interaction in diverse situations.[22]

This, then, is Taylor's porous self, which cannot view itself as constituting a separate entity from the enchanted world surrounding it, or, as Gaines puts it 'the boundary of the Latin self is not drawn around a single biological unit, but around the "foyer". The self consists in part of significant others, primarily family.'[23] Although both Gaines and Taylor view the origins of the indexical/porous self as lying in premodern Christianity, they differ in locating the moment of the emergence of the referential/buffered self, with Taylor's model more accurately identifying this development not with Protestantism, and thus with an institutionalized rift within a metaphysical system, but with the radical emergence of secularity in the Enlightenment.[24]

Taylor's model of the porous self is an instrument or foil against which to explain the development of the buffered self; consequently, his theory serves to exemplify the shift from a religious, or enchanted view of the world, to a secular one. By contrast, the clinical notion of the indexical self has been enlisted to assist practitioners in treating patients from ethnic minorities shaped by enchanted and sociocentric cultural contexts. At the same time, Gaines's model demonstrates for clinical psychiatrists the diagnostic pitfalls when assessing the indexical self; these pitfalls, in turn, can be translated into interpretive limitations for some forms of literary criticism, for, after all, the indexical self is not a discrete entity capable of existing independently from 'social relations and contexts in which the self is presented in interaction'.[25] Indeed, it is comprised of social interactions, contexts, and relationships. It could even be argued that the indexical self is not strictly a *self* in that it cannot exist outside of its social context, just as the porous self is not self-contained. But this is not to say that medieval persons lacked self-awareness in the sense in which Jacob Burkhardt portrayed them.[26]

22 Gaines, 'Cultural Definitions', 182. 23 Gaines, 'Cultural Definitions', 184.

24 My thoughts on authorship take a different paths from those of Robert Edwards whose argument remains invested in periodisation and 'the Renaissance' (*Invention and Authorship in Medieval England* (Columbus, OH: Ohio State University Press, 2017), 317–25; online pagination).

25 Gaines, 'Cultural Definitions', 182.

26 Jacob Burckhardt, *The Civilization of the Renaissance in Italy: An Essay*, trans. S. G. C. Middlemore (London: Allen and Unwin, 1878).

Rather, many of the attributes defining Burkhardt's notion of the 'Renaissance' individual strike me as more securely at home in the Enlightenment.

Clinical psychiatry has further refined Gaines's model of the indexical self, explaining more fully, I believe, the porous premodern self, the starting point for Taylor's journey into secular modernity. Hope Landrine recognizes that the various indexical constructions of the person she has studied and identified have in common that 'the self is not construed to be the centre of cognition, affect, or action, and so is not the explanation for behaviour'.[27] As even a brief perusal of medieval wills and testamentary arrangements demonstrates, the indexical self

> seeks to maintain, fulfil, actualize, and develop not itself, but the relationships and community through which it exists. One seeks to advance the family rather than the self, to assure the achievement and happiness of the relationship rather than the self, to please the gods, or to assure the autonomy of the relationship, not of the self.[28]

As with Hoccleve's recovery, an indexical self engages in *secondary control*: 'The individual is changed, adjusted, and acted on until he or she fits more harmoniously within the family, relationship, or community'.[29]

Consequently, an identifiable named textual self that is entirely dissociated from the medieval author in which it originates and whom it enacts lies beyond the reach of an indexical self. Spearing, too, grants that, 'although the textual "I", consisting of ink on parchment or paper, not of flesh, blood, and consciousness, cannot be literally identical with the author, that does not mean that it must represent a self-consistent imaginary person distinct from the author'.[30] Therefore, in Hoccleve's *Series*, Spearing notes, 'it seems justifiable to refer to the "I" simply as "Hoccleve". That is less misleading, at any rate, than to call the "I" a "narrator" or "persona"'.[31] But I would go further than Spearing: because the axioms of the world surrounding the indexical self were absolute, the same principles

[27] Hope Landrine, 'Clinical Implications of Cultural Differences: The Referential versus the Indexical Self', *Clinical Psychology Review*, 12/4 (1992), 411.

[28] Landrine, 'Clinical Implications', 412.

[29] Landrine, 'Clinical Implications', 412.

[30] Spearing, *Medieval Autographies*, 14.

[31] Spearing, *Medieval Autographies*, 173.

governed the narrative world of an author's literary deictic 'I'. If the latter was generated to facilitate the needs or wishes of the author, then it was bound by the same reality, the same liturgical year, and the same political tenets as the originating indexical self of the author. Hoccleve's Thomas, Langland's Will, and Chaucer's Geoffrey are extensions of their writers' biological selves, animate simulacra that may depart in the mode of representation but not in the identity of the self they represent. Not everything they see, do, or feel must have happened that particular way, but the substance of what they see, feel, or experience must be true if their deictic selves are to extend their efficacy beyond the narrative and alter their author's reality, whether this is Hoccleve's Thomas ascertaining stability for his biological self or Ashby's persona pleading for his author's social rehabilitation. This is how I understand the Latin gloss early in Book 1 of John Gower's *Confessio Amantis*: 'Hic quasi in persona aliorum quos amor alligat, fingens se auctor esse Amantem' ('Here the author, fashioning himself to be the Lover').[32] It seems to me that Gower is carefully signposting here that he is enfolding his biological self into a literary 'I', to prepare an unprepared audience for a fictionalized guise, not a fictionalized narrator. Perhaps this was a necessary measure because the *Confessio Amantis* is not a dream poem, even though the framework narrative is cast in the mould of a homodiegetic dream sequence. As if it were an elaborate pun, in the *Confessio* Gower may be gesturing toward the realization that a waking 'I' sees more than a sleeping one. Just as a text cannot be divided from its originating self, so the narrative self released into a homodiegetic narrative cannot be severed from its authorizing biological self—the narrative 'I' is deictically contingent on the author insofar as its meaning is dependent on the authorial self to which it is umbilically tied. And if Spearing is right in positing that 'the change to fictional speakers

[32] The translation is by Andrew Galloway, *Confessio Amantis*, ed. Russell A. Peck (Kalamazoo, MI: Medieval Institute Publications, 2006). On this passage, see Sonja Drimmer, *The Art of Allusion: Illuminators and the Making of English Literature, 1403–1476* (Philadelphia, PA: University of Pennsylvania Press, 2018), 90; Matthew W. Irvin, *The Poetic Voices of John Gower: Politics and Personae in the* Confessio Amantis (Cambridge: D. S. Brewer, 2014), 82–4; and Alastair Minnis, 'The Author's Two Bodies? Authority and Fallibility in Late-Medieval Textual Theory', in *Of the Making of Books: Medieval Manuscripts, Their Scribes and Readers: Essays Presented to M. B. Parkes*, ed. P. R. Robinson and Rivkah Zim (Aldershot: Scolar, 1997), 259–79.

as the norm occurred long after the Middle Ages',[33] then the 'I' in medieval texts, unlike their post-Enlightenment counterparts, is more likely to be deictic than not.

Because the narrative 'I' is a deictic function of the indexical self of the author, the closer we bring the biological, historical Hoccleve or Ashby to their named narrative selves in their poems, the more meaning we restore to the deictic 'I' in the text. 'Meaning' is not meant to be singular—in fact, this process leaves room for ambiguity if only because we can never fully collapse the deictic self in the text with its biological referent, just as a writer will never be able to fully collapse his or her narrative and biological selves into one, because doing so would amount to an individual's absolute diagnostic self-awareness of all their actions, fears, and motivations. The space between the deictic self in the text and its underwriting authorial referent remains an interpretive space for us, but in the majority of cases it is not the product of a willed distancing by the author but rather a function of what Paul Strohm calls the text's subconscious.[34]

Narratives of Extraction

Medieval vernacular poetry is quintessentially indexical, while most poems and manuscripts presuppose familiarity with their authorial or scribal maker. Vernacular texts, therefore, are never at an arm's length from their originator. At the very least, they are written as if they were not supposed to be. And this condition created difficulties not only for subsequent copyists but also for illuminators. In her study of fifteenth-century illuminations in English literary manuscripts, Sonja Drimmer reframes the indexical nature of medieval literature as a challenging creative space for those trying to extend a text's audience beyond its original readers: 'whatever authority is allowed the rhetorical "I" of the text is a contingent authority, drawn not from the virtuosity of language, truth of content, prestige of its author but rather from

[33] Spearing, *Medieval Autographies*, 5.

[34] Paul Strohm, *Theory and the Premodern Text* (Minneapolis, MN: University of Minnesota Press, 2000), xiii.

copy-specific features of the manuscript itself'.[35] Consequently, this book will concentrate on the primary audiences and authors of the following works: Gower's *In Praise of Peace* and *Henrici Quarti primus*, Hoccleve's *Series*, *The Libelle of Englyshe Polycye*, Lydgate's *Testament*, and Ashby's *Active Policy* and *A Prisoner's Reflections*. Each of these texts is homodiegetic, with the authorial 'I' being either central or participatory. My contention is that as indexical sociocentric selves medieval poets were not in a position to imagine surrogate narrative deictic selves—first-person 'I's—as detached from their biological selves. It seems to me that the optimal moment at which to measure or capture the written self of a sociocentric writer (as all medieval writers were) occurs when authors attempt to extract themselves from the enmeshed context of a lived life, material book objects, and a reality that is refracted through literary conventions. For sociocentric individuals such withdrawals cannot be willed acts of fragmentation or extraction. If we misread these writers as referential, buffered selves, we will see these events as ruptures, breaks, or collapses. These moments of extraction may appear to be attempted deletions or withdrawals, but only to us; for the indexical self they are opportunities to redefine their social place, to fulfil their roles. This is why the book will focus on moments of extraction from public life (Ashby, Caudray), from biological and social life (Lydgate, Hoccleve), or from both (Gower). It is their last public words, spoken through their deictic literary selves, that allow us to reconstruct the degree to which medieval authors are shaped by their sociocentric selves.

All five poets inscribe themselves in their poetry through indexical selves in various ways. The first chapter, '*Ecce patet tensus*: The Trentham Manuscript, *In Praise of Peace*, and John Gower's Autograph Hand', examines how in 1400 Gower oversaw and ultimately withdrew his last ambitious project, the Trentham manuscript (British Library Additional MS 59495), conceived for the recently crowned Henry IV. I show that the Trentham manuscript remained in Gower's possession at the monastery of St Mary Overeys in Southwark, where he lived and died. It started out as a trilingual collection for the king, offering the new ruler robust advice on foreign policy, yet Gower chose not to

[35] Drimmer, *The Art of Allusion*, 60.

present this work, instead withdrawing from public life. *Henrici Quarti primus*, the final poem in this manuscript, which I argue is written in Gower's own hand, features the poet's most personal deictic self. The trilingual Trentham manuscript, just as Gower's trilingual tomb in Southwark Cathedral, is an indexical work, explained only through recourse to Gower himself. This is a revised version of an article published in *Speculum* in 2015.[36]

Chapter 2, 'The *Series*: Thomas Hoccleve's Year of Mourning', introduces a new life record on Hoccleve that demonstrates his ties to the Bedfordshire village of Hockliffe and shows that he owned property there in the 1420s. The new document, a will by Hoccleve's fellow Privy Seal clerk John Bailey, provides a revised context for the *Series*, which I read as the poet's attempt to mourn the death of a friend and contemplate his own mortality. I adjust the dating of the *Series* to November 1420 to Spring 1421 and consider this cycle of poems as an attempt to fulfil Hoccleve's indexical self spiritually and socially, through his textual alter ego Thomas, and in preparation of his own death. The structural emphasis on *Learning to Die* in the *Series* is crucial for understanding the spiritual aspiration of the porous self to achieve a harmonious balance with its surrounding metaphysical reality.

In Chapter 3, 'Parting Shots: Richard Caudray's *Libelle of Englyshe Polycye*', I argue that the *Libelle* (1436–7), was written by Richard Caudray, clerk of the council until 1435, thereafter secretary to John Holland, admiral of England, and dean of St-Martin-le-Grand in London. The *Libelle*, I maintain, is not an attempt to mask his identity; on the contrary, the intended recipients were council members and, together with the approving authority, Walter Hungerford, all of them were familiar with the author. The deictic 'I' of the *Libelle* is Caudray, and the poem is an example of an instance of indexical writing misread as deliberately anonymous.

In Chapter 4, 'Lydgate's Kneeling Retraction: *The Testament* as a Literary Palinode', I show that John Lydgate's *Testament* is not a rejection of his secular career but a literary palinode that attempts to impress a sense of coherence onto a diverse body of work. As the language of conversion, the repetitive litaneutical code (reminiscent

[36] Sebastian Sobecki, 'Ecce Patet Tensus: The Trentham Manuscript, *In Praise of Peace*, and John Gower's Autograph Hand', *Speculum*, 90/4 (2015), 925–59.

of a litany) at the end of the poem is vindicated by the earlier performance of poetic bravado. Lydgate's textual piety, which I show to be indebted to the devotion to the Holy Name of Jesus, is paradoxically sustained by the displacement of prior secular forms. In a central gesture, the kneeling monk-poet presents his life's work to God, who acts as his patron. Finally, I demonstrate that manuscript illuminations depicting a kneeling Lydgate confirm the reception of such a pose as simultaneously pious yet secular. The *Testament*, then, is not about Lydgate's 'self-erasure'—a position not available to the indexical self—but, just like Hoccleve's *Series*, is about reconciling his porous self with the spiritual demands of preparing for his own death. An earlier version of this chapter appeared in the *Chaucer Review* in 2015.[37]

Chapter 5, 'The Signet Self: George Ashby's Autograph Writing', identifies the autograph hand of the Signet clerk and poet George Ashby across eleven documents, five of which bear his scribal signature. I also demonstrate that the Cambridge manuscript of his *Active Policy of a Prince*, Cambridge University Library, Mm.4.42, is a holograph intended for Prince Edward of Westminster. At the same time, this work marks Ashby's withdrawal from public life, and I date the poem to 1461–2. I also show that Ashby's *A Prisoner's Reflections* was composed between Michaelmas 1463 and 24 March 1464. Ashby's deictic self dominates the *Prisoner's Reflections*, and his defining context is that of the Signet clerk, constantly attached to the person of the king or queen. The exile from this situation in 1461 triggers the poetic impulse that leads to his two known works—two narratives that signal the uprootedness of his sociocentric self in an attempt to realign himself with his environment.

Other texts and writers could have been chosen for this book, of course. John Audeley would be another author worth considering, less so perhaps Margery Kempe, not least because her *Book* is not a narrative of extraction. My selection concentrates on writers who at one stage in their lives wrote for and about the most visible public and political audiences, and this holds true for all five poets in this volume.

As a whole, this book incorporates literary criticism, close reading, historical enquiry, palaeography, and the study of manuscripts and

[37] Sebastian Sobecki, 'Lydgate's Kneeling Retraction: The *Testament* as a Literary Palinode', *Chaucer Review*, 49/3 (2015), 265–93.

archival records. Individual chapters, however, foreground one or more of these methodologies: Chapter 1, on Gower, uses the close study of a manuscript to reread its texts and historical setting, followed by a palaeographical focus on one of its scribes. Chapter 2 (Hoccleve) draws on a new archival record to offer an alternative reading of the *Series*, while Chapter 3, on Caudray and *The Libelle of Englyshe Polycye*, attempts to reconstruct the poem's author using the historical information contained in the poem. Chapter 4, on Lydgate, is a formalist critique of a poem, followed by a discussion of manuscript illuminations, whereas Chapter 5, on Ashby, is mostly concerned with a palaeographical identification of his hand and a re-examination of the circumstances under which Ashby's poems were written.

No medieval text was designed to be read hundreds of years later by an audience unfamiliar with its language, situation, and author. By ascribing to these texts purposive anonymity or a willed distancing of author and textual 'I', we romanticize the reach of their foresight while misjudging the craft of their social pragmatism. Through its investments in archival study, book history, and literary criticism, this book is an attempt to chart the extent of this pragmatic public self in England's fifteenth-century literature.

1

Ecce patet tensus

The Trentham Manuscript, In Praise of Peace, *and John Gower's Autograph Hand*

Among those witnesses of John Gower's works that are known to have been produced during his lifetime, the Trentham manuscript (London, British Library Additional MS 59495) stands out for its remarkable design as a seemingly planned trilingual collection.[1] The manuscript, usually dated to the first year of Henry IV's reign, exclusively contains Gower's poetry—showcasing his virtuosity in English, French, and Latin. A number of its poems are either addressed to or invoke Henry, yet nothing is known about the history of this manuscript

[1] The manuscript formerly belonged to the now demolished Trentham Hall in Staffordshire. On this manuscript, see R. F. Yeager, 'Politics and the French Language in England during the Hundred Years' War: The Case of John Gower', in *Inscribing the Hundred Years' War in French and English Cultures*, ed. Denise Baker (Albany, NY: University of New York Press, 2000), 127–57; Lynn Staley, *Languages of Power in the Age of Richard II* (Philadelphia, PA: Pennsylvania State University Press, 2006), 346–9; Siân Echard, *Printing the Middle Ages* (Philadelphia, PA: University of Pennsylvania Press, 2008); Candace Barrington, 'The Trentham Manuscript as Broken Prosthesis: Wholeness and Disability in Lancastrian England', *Accessus*, 1 (2013), 1–33; and Arthur W. Bahr, 'Reading Codicological Form in John Gower's Trentham Manuscript', *Studies in the Age of Chaucer*, 33 (2011), 219–62 (reprinted with changes in Arthur Bahr, *Fragments and Assemblages: Forming Compilations of Medieval London* (Chicago, IL: University of Chicago Press, 2013)).

Last Words: The Public Self and the Social Author in Late Medieval England.
Sebastian Sobecki, Oxford University Press (2019).
DOI: 10.1093/oso/9780198790778.001.0001

before the seventeenth century. As a result, scholarship on the Trentham manuscript (henceforth: Trentham) tends to foreground the question whether this compilation was ever presented to Henry.[2] I will adduce fresh evidence to establish the early provenance of Trentham, and show that the manuscript remained in Southwark until the middle of the sixteenth century. Second, I will offer a new context for its composition by reading the collection against the background of Anglo-French relations during the first months of Henry's rule. Finally, I will argue for Gower's personal involvement in and continued ownership of this manuscript.

The Provenance of the Trentham Manuscript

The earliest known owner of Trentham is one Charles Gedde, who presented the codex to Thomas, third Lord Fairfax of Cameron (1612–71) in 1656.[3] From that point onward, the ownership history of the manuscript has been documented.[4] On fol. 2v the signature 'rychemonde' appears in a sixteenth-century hand, followed by the annotation 'Liber Hen: Septimi tunc Comitis Richmond manu propria script', identified in the current record of the British Library catalogue as written in Fairfax's hand.[5] However, the claim that Trentham may have been in the possession of Henry VII when he was Earl of Richmond cannot be verified.

There is another inscription in Trentham that has been hitherto unidentified but which contains vital information for the early provenance of this manuscript. In the top-right corner of the last folio (41r) the following inscription appears: 'Will Sanders vn Just' (Fig. 1). George Macaulay tentatively described this as a fifteenth-century hand, adding that the writing appears to be 'cut away'.[6] The current record in the

[2] Bahr, 'Reading Codicological Form', 222, n. 10.

[3] Add. MS 59495, fol. 5r.

[4] Echard, *Printing the Middle Ages*, 110–13, and the description in the British Library Catalogue of Archives and Manuscripts (http://searcharchives.bl.uk/, under vol. 1 for Add. MS 59495).

[5] This inscription is discussed by Echard, *Printing the Middle Ages*, 110 and 112 (Echard mistakenly gives 'fol. 6v').

[6] G. C. Macaulay, ed., *The Complete Works of John Gower*, 4 vols (Oxford: Clarendon Press, 1899–1902), 1:lxxxi. Michael Livingston, in his edition of *In Praise of Peace*, reiterates Macaulay's impression that the writing has been cut off (Michael Livingston and R. F. Yeager, eds, *The Minor Latin Works with In Praise of Peace* (Kalamazoo, MI: Medieval Institute Publications, 2005), note to l. 47.).

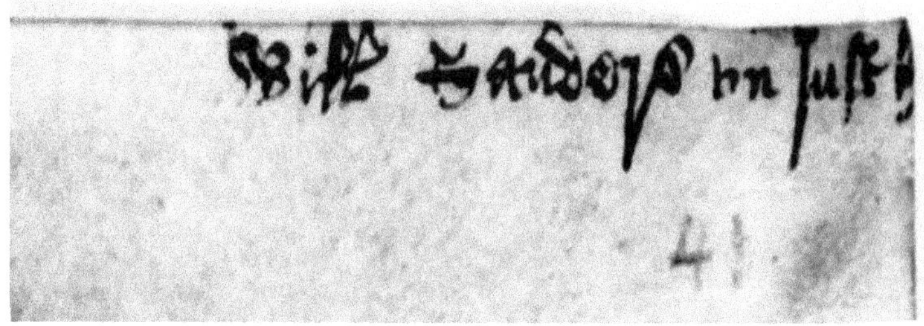

FIG 1 London, British Library Add. MS 59495, inscription on fol. 41r.

British Library corrects Macaulay's dating, identifying the handwriting as belonging to a sixteenth-century legal hand.[7] But the inscription features not one but two hands: the portion 'Will Sanders' is indeed written in a mid-Tudor legal hand with mixed features and Chancery forms. By contrast, 'vn Just' is written in a later italic hand of the seventeenth century. As an abbreviation, *un Just* is commonly accompanied by *de P.*, and stands for *un justice de peace*, law French for 'Justice of the Peace'.[8] The remaining text, surmised by Macaulay as cut away and denoted by '(?)' in the British Library record, can be read, too. Given its location at the very top-right edge of the folio, the inscription extends into the corner which is slightly curled to the inside, producing almost a dog-ear effect. If the corner is peeled back by 2–3mm, a capital superscript D above a capital subscript P. emerges, yielding the reading

Will Sanders vn Just	D
	P.

The same page contains further evidence. Below and to the left of the signature a faint outline of a coat of arms can be seen (Fig. 2), showing an escutcheon containing a chevron.

[7] The British Library Catalogue of Archives and Manuscripts (http://searcharchives.bl.uk/, under vol. 1 for Add. MS 59495).

[8] See, for instance, the 1659 printing (STC 1253:15) of John Rastell's standard work, the bilingual *Les termes de la ley* (on 284v, under the entry for 'Sessions', the law French column has 'Just de P').

FIG 2 British Library Add. MS 59495, outline of escutcheon with chevron, fol. 41r. © The British Library Board.

'Sanders' is not an uncommon name in Tudor England, and a small number of individuals with this combination of first and surname occur in sixteenth-century records. However, the search becomes much easier when looking for a William Sanders JP in the mid-Tudor period. William Saunders (1495–1571) of Ewell in Surrey served as justice of the peace for the county from 1541 to 1564. The blazon of the Saunders family of Ewell reads 'Sable a chevron Ermine between three bull heads cabossed Argent',[9] which translates as a white or silver chevron set against a black background with tails and three bulls'

[9] *Surrey Coats of Arms I–Z*, based on work done by Robert S. Boumphrey and available from the Surrey County Council; https://www.surreycc.gov.uk/culture-and-leisure/history-centre/researchers/guides/coats-of-arms; accessed: 5 June 2019. More on the coat of arms of the Sanders family in Surrey can be found in Ralph Sanders, Peggy Sanders Van der Heide, and Carole Sanders, *Generations: A Thousand-Year Family History* (Philadelphia, PA: Xlibris, 2007).

heads cut off at the neck. The outline on fol. 41r, therefore, matches that of the various Saunders families of Surrey.

As part of the dissolution of the monasteries, Henry VIII's administration set up the Court of Augmentations to regulate the sequestration of ecclesiastical lands and moveable goods. On 1 February 1539, Saunders was appointed one of the seventeen receivers for this court, and by the middle of the following year he was firmly established in that post, which he held until 1547.[10] As he was receiver for Surrey and Sussex, Saunders's portfolio included St Mary Overeys (also 'Overie' or 'Overy') in Southwark, the Austin priory where Gower had lived for roughly the last thirty years of his life.[11] In fact, Saunders oversaw the long process of dissolving the priory. This was a cumbersome task because the priory enjoyed the status of a mitred abbey and was valued at between £624 and £656 at the time of its dissolution—the prior alone received a pension of £100, which he had negotiated up from an original £80.[12] It was Saunders's task to pay the six-monthly pensions of ten former monks and the prior after the dissolution of Gower's parish.[13] Saunders appears to have been chosen for this assignment

[10] S. R. Johnson, 'Saunders, William (by 1497–1570), of Ewell, Surr.', in Stanley T. Bindoff, ed., *The History of Parliament: The House of Commons, 1509–1558*, 3 vols (London: Secker and Warburg for the History of Parliament Trust, 1982), 3:276–8, and Michael L. Walker, 'The Manor of Batailles and the Family of Saunder in Ewell during the 16th and 17th Centuries', *Surrey Archaeological Collections*, 54 (1955), 76–101, at 87. Walter Cecil Richardson, *History of the Court of Augmentations, 1536–1554* (Baton Rouge, LA: Louisiana State University Press, 1961), 50, gives 5 July 1540 as the date of Saunders's appointment.

[11] On Gower and St Mary Overeys, see John Hines, Natalie Cohen, and Simon Roffey, 'Iohannes Gower, Armiger, Poeta: Records and Memorials of His Life and Death', in *A Companion to Gower*, ed. Siân Echard (Cambridge: Brewer, 2004), 23–42, especially 28–41.

[12] The lower figure for the value of the priory is the result of calculations made by William Dugdale, *Monasticon Anglicanum: A History of the Abbies and Other Monasteries and Cathedral and Collegiate Churches with Their Dependencies in England and Wales*, 6 vols (London: Bohn, 1846), 6/1:173; the higher figure is John Speed's (Charlotte G. Boger, *Southwark and Its Story* (London: Grattan, 1881), 216). The prior's pension is given in J. S. Brewer and James Gairdner, *Letters and Papers, Foreign and Domestic, Henry VIII*, 18 vols (London: H. M. Stationary Office, 1862–1901), 14/2:142 (no. 401).

[13] Brewer and Gairdner, *Letters and Papers*, 13/2:503 (no. 1196). For the names of the monks and the pensions list, see also Brewer and Gairdner, *Letters and Papers*, 14/2:142 (no. 401), and William Dugdale, *Monasticon Anglicanum: A History of the Abbies and Other Monasteries and Cathedral and Collegiate Churches with Their Dependencies in England and Wales* (London: Bohn, 1846), 6/1:173.

because his family had deep ties with St Mary Overeys. The last prior, Bartholomew Linsted (*alias* Fowle),[14] was an executor of the will of Saunders's mother and he seems to have been a family friend: in his will Saunders's father makes bequests to the prior, to the priory itself, and to the church of St Mary Magdalene.[15] In addition, Saunders inherited from his father property in Southwark, some of which was located in the parish of St Saviour, which after 1540 became the amalgamated new parish comprising St Mary Overeys as well as the nearby Southwark churches St Mary Magdalene and St Margaret.[16] Saunders also owned the Three Crowns Inn, and he may have possessed further property in Southwark.[17]

William Saunders sympathized with the Catholic cause (he saved crosses and vestments on occasion), and he appears to have been assigned to St Mary Overeys because of his family connections, which permitted him to pay out the pensions of his parents' friends and conduct the dissolution in a manner that minimized conflict with the affected monks. Perhaps the authorities' choice of Saunders for the sequestration of a distinguished mitred abbey provides an explanation for why the dissolution of the monasteries operated relatively smoothly and successfully in some areas. Despite his religious views, Saunders was very good at regulating the sale of former church property, and he made a career of it: throughout the 1540s and 1550s he collected related posts, including the office of commissioner for the sale of church goods in east Surrey. Saunders also joined the Chantry Commission for Surrey in February 1546 and became escheator in Surrey and Sussex three years later.[18] His skills were valued even under Mary, when he was employed in her household, probably in a financial capacity.[19]

[14] On Linsted, see David Knowles, C. N. L. Brooke, Vera C. M. London, eds, *The Heads of Religious Houses: England and Wales*, 3 vols (Cambridge: Cambridge University Press, 1972–2008), 3:523.

[15] Walker, 'The Manor of Batailles', 84.

[16] Early inventories of St Saviour, dating from the 1550s, are given in J. R. Daniel-Tyssen, 'Inventories of the Goods and Ornaments of the Churches in the County of Surrey in the Reign of Edward VI', *Surrey Archaeological Collections*, 4 (1869), 81–91. Some of the items listed as belonging to the church were given by Linsted (who was also known as Fowle).

[17] On the Saunders's connections with Southwark, see Walker, 'The Manor of Batailles', 83–6.

[18] Walker, 'The Manor of Batailles', 87.

[19] Johnson, 'Saunders, William'. Walker, without demonstrating any support, claims that Saunders was a cofferrer under Mary ('The Manor of Batailles', 87).

But Linsted only surrendered St Mary Overeys on 14 October 1541,[20] that is, after Saunders had also been appointed a justice of the peace for Surrey. In all likelihood, therefore, Saunders may have received Trentham as part of his role in the dissolution of the priory between 1541 (when he became JP for Surrey) and 1547, the end of his receivership at the Court of Augmentations.[21] In theory it is conceivable, though highly improbable, that the manuscript had left St Mary Overeys and returned to it before it was acquired by William Saunders at the time of the priory's dissolution.[22] Saunders certainly obtained items of value for himself during his role as receiver: his will of 1570 mentions two gold crosses which he gave to his children.[23] *London Lickpenny* tells us that it was possible by the early afternoon to buy a hat on Cornhill market that had been stolen at Westminster only that morning,[24] but the illegal sale and appropriation of sequestered church goods continued to be a serious offence throughout the sixteenth century—as the hanging of Bardolph in Shakespeare's *Henry V* demonstrates.[25] Yet for many Catholics who were actively involved in the dissolution of the

[20] Boger, *Southwark and Its Story*, 216. James Storer, *Select Views of London and Its Environs*, 2 vols (London: Vernor, Hood, Storer, and Greig, 1804–5), 1:no pagination; section beginning 'St Mary Overies' gives the date as 14 October 1540, whereas H. E. Malden, *A History of the County of Surrey*, 4 vols (London: Constable, 1902–12; reprint 1967), 2:107–12, gives 27 October 1539. But since Linsted was still alive in 1553, and Saunders oversaw the dissolution over a number of years, the manuscript did not have to reach him at the beginning of the process if Trentham was in the possession of Linsted or one of the monks.

[21] Since a later hand added 'vn Just DP' to his name on fol. 41r, it is not necessary for Saunders to have acquired Trentham during his time as JP. He may have obtained the manuscript during his first year in office as receiver for Surrey and Sussex.

[22] Nothing in Trentham overtly associates the manuscript with the priory, so it is unlikely that it would have found its way back to St Mary Overeys once it had left Southwark. There is the remote possibility that the book was indeed in the possession of Henry VII when he was Earl of Richmond: Richard Foxe, Henry's secretary at the time and Bishop of Winchester from 1501, was a friend and tutor to Henry Saunders, William's father. Both were involved in the Savoy Hospital, and Foxe was the main executor of Henry Saunders's will (Sanders et al., *Generations*, 110–16). But this theory would require Foxe to have known about Trentham's association with the priory, in addition to being familiar with the Saunders's ties to St Mary Overeys.

[23] TNA PROB 11/53/491. Walker, 'The Manor of Batailles', 87, speculates that these crosses were church property before 1550.

[24] James M. Dean, *Medieval English Political Writings* (Kalamazoo, MI: Medieval Institute Publications, 1996), l.97–104.

[25] *Henry V*, act 3, scene 6.

monasteries, the occasional keeping of items that belonged to a church with which they and their families had been associated must have been a matter of faith as well as institutional preservation. There is ample evidence from Mary's reign for the enormous difficulties the queen encountered when trying to convince parishioners to return stolen objects despite assuring them that these would be put back to their traditional use.[26]

The discovery of William Saunders's ownership holds three significant corollaries for the study of the Trentham manuscript. First, the manuscript most probably remained in the possession of the priory between Gower's death (if not before then) and the middle of the sixteenth century. Second, if Trentham was kept at St Mary Overeys until the priory's dissolution, then this book was never presented to Henry IV. Third, we now know of a manuscript that in all likelihood was owned by Gower until his death in 1408. It is true, of course, that the poet's will does not mention the book, but neither are his writing materials or drafts included in the document.[27] Presumably his blindness and advanced age made him part with such belongings in the years after he had stopped composing. Also, it would be a mistake, I think, to interpret a will as the full inventory of the testator's belongings. A second error is to assume that the items listed in a will are the only items of value in the possession of the testator. A common pattern in medieval and early modern wills is to pass on the most significant manors, holdings, or estates to the main heir, followed by a list of other holdings and often individual items given to lesser heirs and servants.[28] Moveable goods are usually allocated only to this second category of

[26] Ethan H. Shagan, *Popular Politics and the English Reformation* (Cambridge: Cambridge University Press, 2003), 289–91.

[27] The will has been printed by Richard Gough, *Sepulchral Monuments of Great Britain*, 2 vols (London: the author, 1786–96), 2:15–26. A corrected version was edited by a certain W. H. B. as 'Will of John Gower the Poet, anno 1408' in *Gentleman's Magazine* 3 (1835): 49–51. For a translation, see Macaulay, ed., *The Complete Works of John Gower*, 4:xvii–xviii.

[28] Wealthy people who owned land often produced two wills for use in different courts, one document relating to property and rents from property, and the other giving personal bequests of moveable goods. See, for instance, the wills of John Carpenter and his wife Katherine, described by Thomas Brewer, *Memoir of the Life and Times of John Carpenter* (London: Taylor, 1856), 91–102, and the texts of one of his wills together with those of both of Katherine's wills, in appendices 2–4 on pp. 131–65. I am grateful to Linne Mooney for this information.

heirs, but those possessions that belong to or are contained in manors and houses granted to the main heirs are not inventoried. Gower must have owned writing utensils, parchment, drafts, and, perhaps, manuscripts that would not be deemed significant enough to be listed in his will. The *Martyrology* that he bequeaths to St Mary Overeys is a religious work and therefore deserves to be singled out as a bequest to his priory.[29] Trentham, together with his writing materials, may have passed to St Mary Overeys during his last years or it may have reverted to the priory together with his quarters and other personal belongings.[30]

Anglo-French Relations and *In Praise of Peace*

Seemingly too humble to be a royal presentation copy, yet too well executed to gather dust on a shelf, Trentham has puzzled readers for quite some time. John Fisher saw in it a present fit for a king. He deems that 'both the script and initials appear to be up to the standard of the best Gower manuscripts', whereas R. F. Yeager finds Trentham to be 'plain, unlike most royal presentation copies', adding elsewhere that the manuscript is not 'of the quality usually associated with presentation copies prepared for monarchs'.[31] But if Trentham was never given to Henry IV, could it be a copy or perhaps a master of a text that was?

[29] W. H. B., 'Will of John Gower', 50.

[30] It is also possible that he obtained his writing materials from the priory should it indeed have had a scriptorium. Although Malcolm Parkes has argued against the existence of a facility at St Mary Overeys (M. B. Parkes, 'Patterns of Scribal Activity and Revisions of the Text in Early Copies of Works by John Gower', in *New Science out of Old Books: Manuscripts and Early Printed Books: Essays in Honour of A. I. Doyle*, ed. Richard Beadle and A. J. Piper (Aldershot: Scolar, 1995), *passim*, especially 81–2), as a mitred abbey the priory had significant holdings and therefore administrative needs. At its dissolution the last prior received a pension of £100, a sum usually designated for a bishop. If the monastery did not have its own scriptorium, it surely must have had frequent and ready access to such facilities nearby. At the New Chaucer Society Congress in Reykjavik, held in 2014, Martha Carlin and Caroline Barron revealed new documentary evidence that points to a concentration of scribes in the Southwark area.

[31] John H. Fisher, *John Gower, Moral Philosopher and Friend of Chaucer* (New York: New York University Press, 1964), 72; R. F. Yeager, 'John Gower's French', in *A Companion to Gower*, ed. Echard, 137–52, at 145; and Yeager, 'John Gower's Audience: The Ballades', *Chaucer Review*, 40 (2005), 81–104, at 89.

The latter possibility can be excluded, I think, because among the five early copies of Gower's works that show signs of corrections, Trentham is the only manuscript that contains no major revisions.[32] Yet if Trentham is a copy of a manuscript that was presented to Henry,[33] then why does it display a standard of craftsmanship that puts it on a par with presentation copies? Ralph Hanna astutely notes the extraordinary lengths to which the main copyist, M. B. Parkes's Scribe 5, goes in the manuscript:

> the scribe shows extreme specialisation of script, and uses two stylings of anglicana for English and Latin, a script like that of the London Herald MS [University of London Library, MS 1] for the French items only. He has a rather uneasy go of it; for nearly a full leaf at the point of transition (fols 11v–12v), he inconsistently tries to convert his script from its Anglo-Latin anglicana to his Anglo-Norman secretary letter-forms. Both script and the texts it communicates are distinctly 'modern'—Anglo-Norman poems almost contemporary and presented in an innovative writing style. But equally, their cultural bases are old-fashioned, and their script's lengthy history is appropriately a French one, associated with Edwardian imperialist adventure.[34]

In other words, the care taken in executing Trentham, together with the various decorated initials and occasional marginal annotations, suggests that the manuscript contains some of the features of a presentation piece, whereas we now know that it most probably did not leave St Mary Overeys during Gower's lifetime. A modest book need not be too lowly a gift, especially if the author knew the recipient personally.[35]

At the same time, the many allusions to Henry internally emphasize the palaeographical and codicological nature of a presentation copy, whereas other stretches of the manuscript do not seem to concern themselves with the king. All the while, however, there is consensus that from beginning to end the Trentham manuscript reveals a

[32] Parkes, 'Patterns of Scribal Activity', 82.

[33] Yeager, 'John Gower's Audience', 88.

[34] Ralph Hanna, *London Literature, 1300–1380* (Cambridge: Cambridge University Press, 2005), 227.

[35] One such example is Skelton's gift of *A Lawde and Prayse Made for Our Sovereigne Lord the Kyng* to Henry VIII in 1509. See my discussion of Ashby's *Active Policy* in Chapter 5, p. C5. P43.

conscious design and careful organization. In the précis to his substantial discussion of Trentham, Arthur Bahr puts the conundrum as follows: 'The manuscript thus presents its modern readers with an interpretive quandary. Its suggestions of purpose are too numerous and fundamental to ignore, but they are sufficiently complicated by literary ambiguity and material uncertainty that we cannot extract from the manuscript a single goal, audience, or agent.'[36] In the ensuing discussion Bahr resolves this problem by positing that Trentham

> is an artfully constructed meditation on the multiple natures and implications of kingship, and the very complexity of its construction serves to acknowledge both the visceral pleasure of using aesthetic modes to grapple with such vitally important questions and the impossibility of creating clear-cut 'propositional content' as answers to them.[37]

To some extent, then, the ambiguity of form in Trentham is seen as willed, as a productive constituent of the complex work in which this compilation engages. With the benefit of knowing that Trentham was unlikely to have been presented to Henry, I would venture a simpler answer: Gower's objective lost its urgency during the production of the manuscript. I will argue that he started the manuscript probably in December 1399 or January 1399/1400 to advocate a renewal of Richard's truce with France, but when the king surprisingly confirmed the twenty-eight-year truce on 18 May 1400, Gower's project was no longer acute. After all, if most readers agree that much of this manuscript was directed at Henry IV, then why should the composition of this collection not reflect the rapidly changing political situation surrounding the new king? By the time the poet added the final poem, which only nominally makes reference to Henry, Trentham had become Gower's book. Since it stayed with Gower until his death, it is fair to assume that he approved of its final form. And there is indeed scholarly consensus that the poet oversaw the production of this copy.[38]

Setting the modest oblong format of the volume (232 × 155 mm) against the high quality of the main scribe and his specialized execution

[36] Bahr, 'Reading Codicological Form', 223.

[37] Bahr, 'Reading Codicological Form', 261.

[38] Barrington, 'The Trentham Manuscript as Broken Prosthesis', 1.

of scripts in three different languages, Trentham creates the impression of a rushed presentation copy.[39] This sense is enhanced by the fact that a number of the poems in the manuscript, such as 'Ecce patet tensus', recycle lines and themes from Gower's other works. In fact, as Candace Barrington notes, except for *In Praise of Peace* and the *Cinkante Balades*, 'the manuscript's poems appear fully or partially elsewhere'.[40] In addition to these two works, some of the short poems may also have been composed at the time. Much of the quandary surrounding Trentham can be explained when thinking of a deadline Gower had wished to meet. And the fact that *In Praise of Peace* and the *Cinkante Balades* are unique to Trentham might suggest that they hold particular clues for the purpose of the collection. Since the English poem opens the manuscript, I will concentrate my discussion on its contents.[41]

In Praise of Peace is Gower's only other extant English poem beside the *Confessio Amantis*. The poem consists of 385 lines of English decasyllabic rhyme royal, most of which consistently scan as iambic pentameter.[42] In the manuscript the poem is divided into ten sections, nine of which are rubricated by flourished initials.[43] The content of the poem, however, features seven discernible movements. The first spans the preamble (stanzas 1–4), which praises Henry IV and confirms his claim to the throne, and stanzas 5–16, which are dedicated to the cultural history of peace and concentrate on the *exempla* of Solomon and Alexander. The second and third juxtapose war and peace in two addresses to Henry: the first lists the shortcomings of

[39] Another instance of a writer preparing a last-minute manuscript of advice for a king—this time Henry V—is discussed by Linne Mooney, 'A New Holograph Copy of Hoccleve's *Regiment of Princes*', *Studies in the Age of Chaucer*, 33 (2011), 263–6. For a challenge to Mooney's identification, see Lawrence Warner, 'Scribes, Misattributed: Hoccleve and Pinkhurst', *Studies in the Age of Chaucer*, 37/1 (2015), 55–100.

[40] Barrington, 'The Trentham Manuscript as Broken Prosthesis', 2.

[41] I treat the opening Latin remarks as an introduction to *In Praise of Peace*.

[42] Besides a number of nineteenth-century editions, *In Praise of Peace* has been edited by Macaulay in *The English Works of John Gower*, vol. 2; Livingston and Yeager, eds, *The Minor Latin Works with In Praise of Peace*; and Kathleen Forni, ed., *The Chaucerian Apocrypha: A Selection* (Kalamazoo, MI: Medieval Institute Publications, 2005). All quotations from this poem are taken from Livingston and Yeager.

[43] Livingston and Yeager, *The Minor Latin Works*, introduction, and Candace Barrington, 'John Gower's Legal Advocacy and "In Praise of Peace"', in *John Gower, Trilingual Poet: Language, Translation, and Tradition*, ed. Elizabeth Dutton (Cambridge: D. S. Brewer, 2010), 119–20.

war (stanzas 16–21) and the second enumerates the advantages afforded by peace (stanzas 22–4). With the fourth movement the poem leaves behind its mostly secular discussion of peace, explicating instead the religious significance of peace in the books of the Bible (stanzas 25–39). The fifth movement again turns to Henry, asking him to change the course of history and surpass the Nine Worthies (stanzas 40–4). Next, the poem enumerates the Christian properties of peace, concentrating on charity and *pite*, or compassion (stanzas 45–51). The seventh and final movement, occupying stanzas 52–5, acts as a conclusion to the poem and contains a final appeal to Henry.

Traditionally *In Praise of Peace* has been treated as a Lancastrian panegyric for the new king that is interlaced with occasional cautionary notes on domestic policy. However, my reading will place the poem in the context of Anglo-French relations. More specifically, I argue that *In Praise of Peace* was composed between Henry IV's coronation in October 1399 and his confirmation of the truce with France on 18 May 1400. The immediate occasion for this poem and for the compilation of the manuscript was the prospect of imminent war with France in early 1400. Essentially, in this poem Gower is asking Henry to confirm Richard II's twenty-eight-year truce with France. More broadly, however, Trentham is conceived as an Anglo-French collection to showcase the cultural ties—and love—that bind the two countries together. By asking Henry to adopt Richard's policy of appeasement and rapprochement with France, Gower is pursuing a daring strategy in this poem and collection as a whole. As a consequence, I suggest that Gower emerges in his relationship with Henry as an assertive and bold poet who does not shy away from taking political risks.

In Praise of Peace carries no title in the manuscript but the authorial explicit refers to the work as 'carmen de pacis commendacione, quod ad laudem et memoriam serenissimi principis domini regis Henrici quarti suus humilis orator Iohannes Gower composuit'.[44] The first English title, *The Praise of Peace*, was not assigned by Walter W. Skeat, as is commonly stated, but was the idea of Edward

[44] '[A] hymn in peace's commendation that John Gower, his own humble orator, composed in praise and honor of his highness, prince, and lord, King Henry IV'. The translation is from David R. Carlson, *John Gower: Poetry and Propaganda in Fourteenth-Century England* (Cambridge: D. S. Brewer, 2012), 204.

W. B. Nicholson, Bodley's Librarian between 1882 and 1912. Macaulay states as much in his 1901 edition of the text, but a year earlier Heinrich Spies connected the English title with Nicholson in *Englische Studien.*[45] Even though Skeat used the title *The Praise of Peace* in the list of contents to his 1897 edition of various Chaucerian works, a different title, 'Unto the worthy and noble Kinge Henry the Fourth', actually precedes the text in his edition.[46] In his 1901 edition for the Early English Text Society Macaulay amalgamated both of Skeat's editorial titles into *To King Henry the Fourth in Praise of Peace.*[47]

Over the last thirty years, *In Praise of Peace* has attracted the attention of some of the most discerning readers in the field. In 1987, R. F. Yeager scrutinized the poem in a perceptive survey of Gower's and Chaucer's approaches to proto-pacifism, and in the same year David Lawton even suggested that *In Praise of Peace* may have influenced the political position taken by John Lydgate in his *Siege of Thebes.*[48] Five years later, Paul Strohm exposed the poem's affinity with Lancastrian propaganda and, in particular, with *The Record and Process of the Renunciation and Deposition* of Richard II, a document that furnished the blueprint for officially sanctioned accounts of Henry's *coup d'état.*[49] Strohm dates *The Record and Process* to 1400 at the earliest, thereby pushing back the composition date for Gower's poem, which had been traditionally linked to Henry's coronation.[50] On the basis of the volatile domestic situation with which Henry had to grapple during the early

[45] Gower, *The English Works of John Gower*, 2:481; Heinrich Spies, 'Bisherige Ergebnisse und weitere Aufgaben der Gower-Forschung', *Englische Studien*, 28 (1900), 163–208, at 181.

[46] *The Complete Works of Geoffrey Chaucer: Chaucerian and Other Pieces*, ed. Walter W. Skeat, 7 vols (Oxford: Clarendon Press, 1894–7), vol. 7. See v and vi for the description and list of contents and 205 for the opening of the text of the poem. Macaulay states that Skeat's title was suggested by Nicholson (*The English Works of John Gower*, 2:553).

[47] *The English Works of John Gower*, 2:481.

[48] R. F. Yeager, 'Pax Poetica: On the Pacifism of Chaucer and Gower', *Studies in the Age of Chaucer*, 9 (1987), 97–121, and David Lawton, 'Dullness and the Fifteenth Century', *English Literature History*, 54 (1987), 761–99, at 781. More recently, Robert Meyer-Lee took Lawton's observation a step further, and proposed that *In Praise of Peace* may also have been a model for Lydgate's coronation poem for Henry VI (*Poets and Power from Chaucer to Wyatt* (Cambridge: Cambridge University Press, 2007), 37.

[49] Paul Strohm, *Hochon's Arrow: The Social Imagination of Fourteenth-Century Texts* (Princeton, NJ: Princeton University Press, 1992), 89–90.

[50] Strohm, *Hochon's Arrow*, 90. Henry was crowned on 13 October 1399.

days of his reign, Strohm suggests 1401–4 as a plausible range for the poem's composition.[51] Frank Grady, in an influential reading of *In Praise of Peace*, advances a slightly earlier *terminus ad quem*, again using domestic criteria. He argues that it was written 'certainly before the Percys' revolt of the summer of 1403 and probably before Henry's troubles with the Franciscans of Leicester in 1402'.[52] Subsequent treatments of the work have accepted Grady's and Strohm's post-1400 dating, though recently, for a number of different reasons, Jenni Nuttall, David Carlson, and Michael Livingston have again recommended moving the poem nearer to Henry's coronation.[53] A post-1400 dating can be excluded on purely codicological grounds: Parkes has shown that *In Praise of Peace* was written by the earlier of two scribes; the hand of the second scribe added the last poem in Trentham before 1401, the second year of Henry's reign.[54]

In a study of Gower's political context Carlson has recently elaborated on his reading of the poem.[55] He argues that *In Praise of Peace* is not about peace or '*pax per se*'; instead, he maintains that peace 'figures in Gower's poem only as a topic, in subordination, amongst others, by which a locally particular panegyric for a particular ruler is constructed'.[56] For Carlson, peace in this poem is a symbol of control.[57] He therefore views *In Praise of Peace* essentially as 'Lancastrian propaganda, even because of the occasionally critical-admonitory remarks it incorporates'.[58] This is not to say that the poem is critical of Henry for, Carlson maintains, Gower praises 'peace to argue in favour of Lancastrian domination'. In other words, *In Praise of Peace* is an 'official verse panegyric... written *ad laudem regis*'.[59] Because it is a laudatory work,

[51] Strohm, *Hochon's Arrow*, 90.

[52] Frank Grady, 'The Lancastrian Gower and the Limits of Exemplarity', *Speculum*, 70 (1995), 552–75, at 572.

[53] Jennifer Nuttall, *The Creation of Lancastrian Kingship: Literature, Language and Politics in Late Medieval England* (Cambridge: Cambridge University Press, 2007), 57, and David R. Carlson, 'Gower *pia vota bibit* and Henry IV in 1399 November', *English Studies*, 89 (2008), 377–84, at 377. This is also a position taken by James Dean, 'Gower, Chaucer, and Rhyme Royal', *Studies in Philology*, 88 (1991), 251–75, and by Michael Livingston in his introduction to Livingston and Yeager, *The Minor Latin Works*. On the dating see also Livingston's note 4 and Livingston's note to line 208.

[54] On the manuscript's scribes, see Parkes, 'Patterns of Scribal Activity'.

[55] Carlson, *John Gower*, 203–10 and 216.

[56] Carlson, *John Gower*, 204.

[57] Carlson, *John Gower*, 205–7.

[58] Carlson, *John Gower*, 205.

[59] Carlson, *John Gower*, 209.

Carlson dates the poem nearer to Henry's coronation, suggesting that it was written 'simultaneously with the arrival of the Lancastrian dynasty itself, just at the moment of Henry's acquisition of the kingship and the patronal resources that it disposed'.[60]

This reading of the poem as a panegyric is at odds with Bahr's reappraisal of Trentham as a compilation that balances laudatory sentiments with cautionary verses.[61] Bahr's approach is refreshing because he views the poem in the context of the entire manuscript. His analysis leads him to state that *In Praise of Peace* as well as the manuscript itself is marked by a sobering tone:

> The cautionary undertones of *In Praise of Peace* are sufficiently subtle that they require a substantial level of active apprehension from the reader. In this they begin the Trentham manuscript's gradual construction of ambivalent patterns whose initial outlines . . . seem significant, and potentially threatening, only in retrospect. Here those outlines, if we choose to perceive them, suggest a recognition that whatever our idealistic wishes, the possibility remains that Henry's reign will slide off in the other direction: not peace but war; not ancestry or acclamation or any of the various Lancastrian claims alluded to in the poem's opening stanzas, but conquest—like Alexander's—pure and simple.[62]

However, Bahr's reading overlaps with existing approaches in taking for granted that this poem is domestic in focus. Whilst agreeing with Bahr on the poem's cautionary tone and on the need to read it in its (sole) material context, I wish to inflect this reading trajectory with a synchronic historical angle that makes *In Praise of Peace* not so much a word of advice on domestic matters from poet to king but a stern warning about leaving in place the fragile peace with France that has characterized Richard's reign.

Whereas the poem has been read as an early instance of pacifism, as an invitation for the king to seize religious jurisdictions,[63] and as

[60] Carlson, *John Gower*, 216.

[61] Bahr, 'Reading Codicological Form'. In 2011, when Bahr's article appeared, Carlson's book presumably was already in press.

[62] Bahr, 'Reading Codicological Form', 232.

[63] Greg Walker, *Writing under Tyranny: English Literature and the Henrician Reformation* (Oxford: Oxford University Press, 2007), 92–4.

implicitly shaped by internalized legal conventions,[64] the virtually exclusive focus on the domestic political situation has remained unchanged. But when Yeager first drew attention to Gower's vision of a *pax poetica* in this poem, he viewed *In Praise of Peace* as addressing both domestic and foreign politics.[65] I would like to take the path less travelled and delve into England's precarious relationship with France between Henry's coronation and his confirmation of the truce in the following spring.[66]

The first four stanzas of the poem assert Henry's right to rule. This unqualified embrace of the official Lancastrian version of events appears to pose a dilemma for Gower: how does one vindicate usurpation by violent means in a poem that advocates the renunciation of precisely such violence? And indeed, Gower first justifies Henry's appropriation of the crown by force before he urges the king to renounce violence and espouse a policy of conciliation. Strohm has shown that in toeing the line—as laid down in *The Record and Process*—Gower inherited some of the flaws built into the vindication of Lancastrian rule.[67] This apparent conundrum has caused Frank Grady—somewhat ingeniously—to resolve the contradiction by discerning an almost subversive layer in Gower's tone: the poet uses the Lancastrian language of propaganda just as he demonstrates the limitations of such language by exposing 'both the difficulties inherent in imagining a pacific Lancastrian monarchy and the problem at the heart

64 Ben Lowe, *Imagining Peace: A History of Early English Pacifist Ideas, 1340–1560* (University Park, PA: Pennsylvania State University Press, 1997), and Candace Barrington, 'John Gower's Legal Advocacy and "In Praise of Peace"', in *John Gower, Trilingual Poet*, ed. Dutton, 112–25. Lowe, a historian whose reading trajectory follows the early history of pacifism, does not even notice the domestic dimension but reads the poem as an accession address to Henry with the objective of encouraging peace with France.

65 Yeager, 'Pax Poetica', 99.

66 An early date for the poem does not invalidate Strohm's observation that *In Praise of Peace* is indebted to *Record and Process*. In his recent edition David Carlson gives a date of 1399 for the latter work (*The Deposition of Richard II: The Record and Process of the Renunciation and Deposition of Richard II (1399) and Related Writings* (Toronto: Pontifical Institute of Mediaeval Studies, 2007), introduction). Furthermore, as Chris Given-Wilson notes, G. O. Sayles had suggested that *The Record and Process* was only the culmination of an iteration of documents ('The Manner of King Richard's Renunciation: A "Lancastrian Narrative"?', *English Historical Review* 108 (1993): 365–70, at 388).

67 Strohm, *Hochon's Arrow*, 89–90.

of his own historical method'.[68] However, this only becomes an ethical dilemma if we read the poem as confining itself to offering Henry advice on domestic affairs.

Given its violent birth, Henry's reign did not get off to a good start. Quite rightly Grady characterizes the early years of Lancastrian rule as marked 'by an environment of wars, rebellions, tax revolts, administrative incompetence, inflation, and Lollardy'.[69] Yet none of these developments presented Henry with much of an alternative; these problems simply had to be confronted. Making peace with rebels may not have been an option, but peace with France was a different matter altogether. Renewing hostilities with France and thereby risking a violation of the fragile truce in place since 1389, on the other hand, was an action that left Henry's administration with a choice. And there are good grounds to believe that the poem makes such a distinction between domestic needs ('lond') and international options ('world'), the former stressing royal imperative, the latter choice.

When Gower rehearses the Lancastrian defence of Henry's usurpation in the opening stanzas, he clearly refers to England and its inhabitants three times as 'this lond', 'the lond', and 'the londes folk' (ll. 5, 17, and 13). Clearly there is no need to argue with a premodern monarch's need to maintain quiet and stability at home—still less if Henry's right to rule is divinely sanctioned. Somewhat obsessively, 'God' is mentioned nine times in the course of the first four stanzas to establish beyond any doubt that Henry is God's choice: 'God hath thee chose in comfort of ous alle' (l. 4). But then the poem shifts gear. Gower slips in the concept of political choice. First comes a stanza on Solomon, who was guided by wisdom in his policies. This inspired choice is then contrasted with a minatory sequence on Alexander the Great, who opted for conquest, not of his 'lond' but 'Of all the world to winne the victoire' (l. 38). The spectre of Alexander reveals an acute fear of territorial aggression. Michael Livingston, the poem's most recent editor, stresses Gower's use of Alexander as a negative exemplum, although he too sees *In Praise of Peace* largely as domestic advice for Henry.[70] But as a historical *exemplum*, Alexander set the benchmarks for

[68] Grady, 'The Lancastrian Gower', 558.
[69] Grady, 'The Lancastrian Gower', 555.
[70] Livingston and Yeager, *The Minor Latin Works*, introduction.

international conquest and imperial expansion. This is, after all, what justified his inclusion in the canon of the Nine Worthies, to whom stanza 41 is dedicated.

The Alexander sequence initiates a long passage of sustained criticism of war, in which Gower repeatedly invokes princes and kings, clearly in reference to Christian rulers at odds with one another, as in stanza 9:

> So mai a kyng of werre the viage
> Ordeigne and take, as he therto is holde,
> To cleime and axe his rightful heritage
> In alle places wher it is withholde.
> Bot otherwise, if God Himsilve wolde
> Afferme love and pes betwen the kynges,
> Pes is the beste above alle erthely thinges.

One has to ask, however, whether the incessant emphasis on international war is appropriate for a poem with an apparently domestic focus. Gower envisages that a king may wage war to enforce his rightful heritage 'in alle places wher it is witholde', yet he should, nevertheless, 'afferme love and pes betwen the kynges' everywhere else (I am more inclined to place a comma after 'wolde' so that 'otherwise' does not lose its sense). It is clear that 'in alle places wher it is witholde' does not restrict itself to domestic matters; rights must be pursued relentlessly—as well as everywhere. These lines point to the actual objective of the poem: Gower is asking Henry to confirm Richard's twenty-eight-year truce of 1396 and affirm peace with France.

The spatial, geographic dimension circumscribed by the deictic 'places wher' is a thinly veiled allusion to Gascony, and the Duchy of Aquitaine of which it is part. Gascony may have presented Henry with a public as well as personal pretext for renewing hostilities with France. In 1390 Richard II made Henry's father, John of Gaunt, duke of Aquitaine for life. But Henry may well have believed—as did Froissart—that the title had been granted in hereditary tenure. A number of historians maintain that the roots of the conflict between Richard and Gaunt lie with the latter's recall from Gascony (in fact, it has been suggested that Richard's demise was accelerated by the widespread opposition to the truce of 1396).[71] On his return from France,

[71] Anne Curry, *The Hundred Years War* (London: Macmillan, 1993), 89.

John of Gaunt 'was received by the King', as Thomas Walsingham puts it, 'with honour, as was fitting, but not, so some said, with love'.[72] After his domestic ambitions had exhausted their potential and his quixotic Castilian enterprise had resulted in spectacular failure, Gaunt fixed his eyes on Gascony, which he went on to secure with a small force in 1394.[73] This commitment to Aquitaine became a family affair after Gaunt's death: less than two weeks after Henry's coronation, on 23 October 1399, the new king made it clear that Gascony was one of his priorities by appointing his son, the future Henry V, duke of Aquitaine.[74] Whereas, as a concession to France, Richard had appointed John of Gaunt to the duchy as a vassal of the king of France, Henry IV made Gascony a direct fief of the English crown. This focus on France is substantiated by stanza 11, where Gower almost overtly refers to the hostilities that would later form part of the Hundred Years' War: 'The more he myghte oure dedly werre cesse, / The more he schulde his worthinesse encresse' (ll. 76–7). Livingston, too, concedes that this passage refers to the conflict with France. The insular risings and rebellions were Henry's personal wars to establish his sovereignty, but 'oure dedly werre' denotes a collective effort, an Anglo-French conflict that is as yet unresolved. Although the truce of 1396 has been in place since 1389, when it was sealed by Richard's marriage to Princess Isabel of France, the Anglo-French war was by no means over and can therefore still be concluded ('cesse').

A closer look at the months between Henry's accession and his delayed confirmation of the truce reveals that in the winter of 1399/1400 just about everyone in Westminster believed that war with France was imminent. It was only a lack of resources that prevented Henry from moving into action.[75] What may have prompted Gower to write this poem and produce the Trentham collection, however, is the position publicly assumed by Henry toward France in the first three

[72] *The Chronica Maiora of Thomas Walsingham, 1376–1422*, ed. D. Preest and J. G. Clark (Woodbridge: Boydell, 2005), 295.

[73] Curry, *The Hundred Years War*, 72–4.

[74] Curry, *The Hundred Years War*, 92–3, and G. L. Harriss, *Shaping the Nation: England, 1360–1461* (Oxford: Clarendon Press, 2005), 426–7.

[75] Curry, *The Hundred Years War*, 78. Gower received a grant of two pipes of Gascon wine a year on 21 November of that year (Fisher, *John Gower*, 68). It would be interesting to evaluate Henry's gift in this context.

months of his reign. The *Recueil des croniques et anciennes istories de la Grant Bretaigne*, written between 1465 and 1475 by the pro-English Burgundian chronicler Jean de Waurin, assigns a speech to Henry that he is alleged to have made during a procession in London in January 1400: 'I swear and promise to you that neither his highness my grandfather King Edward, nor my uncle the prince of Wales, ever went so far in France as I will do, if it please God and St George, or I will die in the attempt'.[76]

The problem of the Lancastrian regime change proved to be a monumental setback for Anglo-French reconciliation.[77] As Jonathan Sumption notes, many of Richard's supporters fled to France and brought with them their version of events.[78] Their reports styled Richard as a friend of France and Henry's usurpation as a revolution. Jean Creton, who served as valet to the Earl of Salisbury, spoke of Richard as a king who 'loved the French people with all his heart'.[79] He would later write *La Prinse et mort du roy Richart*, a poem on Richard's martyrdom. In this work, Creton helps establish Henry's belligerent reputation: 'And, certes, the only reason why he was deposed and betrayed, was because he loyally loved his father-in-law, the King of France, with a love as true and sincere as any man alive'.[80] Similarly, in the anonymous *Chronique de la traison et mort de Richart Deux Roy d'Engleterre*, as the heads of the Earl of Gloucester and of Richard's brother, the Earl of Huntington, are placed on London Bridge, an English mob, no longer checked by a Francophile Richard, shouts: 'God save our lord King Henry, and my lord the Prince! Now we will wage war with all the world except with Flanders.'[81] Reflecting on

[76] Jean de Waurin, *A Collection of the Chronicles and Ancient Histories of Great Britain, Now Called England: From* AD *1399 to AD 1422*, trans. William Hardy and Edward Hardy (London: Longman, Roberts, and Green, 1887), 42–3.

[77] Curry, *The Hundred Years War*, 89. The French never accepted Henry, 90.

[78] Jonathan Sumption, *The Hundred Years War*, 3 vols (London: Faber and Faber, 1990–2009), 3:863. See also Craig Taylor, 'Weep Thou for Me in France': French Views of the Deposition of Richard II', in *Fourteenth Century England III*, ed. W. M. Ormrod (Woodbridge: Boydell, 2004), 207–22.

[79] Sumption, *The Hundred Years War*, 3:863.

[80] John Webb, 'Translation of a French Metrical History of the Deposition of King Richard the Second', *Archaeologia*, 20 (1824), 1–423, at 221.

[81] Benjamin Williams, ed., *Chronique de la traïson et mort de Richart Deux Roy d'Engleterre* (London: English Historical Society, 1846), 258.

Henry's usurpation, the mid-fifteenth-century chronicler Robert Blondel states that the English population tainted themselves with collective guilt by supporting Henry:

> Et n'est point de doubte que toute l'isle d'Angleterre qui approuva cellui meffait se rendit infecté et coulpable de si grant crime que non pas seulement le roy françois ne sa parens, affins et alliez, maiz aussie tous chevalliers vaillans qui comme zelateurs de justice, de tous crimes publicques mesmement qui sont perpetrez contre la roial majesté.[82]

Blondel continues that

> que encores viendra aucum prince de hault courage qui sera si amoureux de justice et de la chose publicque qu'il entreprendra par armes a pugnir soubz la main de Dieu si horrible cas, et que, ainssi que Scipion l'Auffricain pugnit jadis Cartaige, il repetera les despoilles dont les pillars d'Angleterre ont a grant tort et par trop de foiz despoillié le royaume françois.[83]

Sumption lists a number of other examples of works in support of Richard, written in French, that created the perception of English Francophobia.[84] What is even more significant from the perspective of French policy was 'the widespread misconception', as Sumption puts it, that 'Richard had been deposed because of his support for peace with France'.[85] Sumption summarizes the situation as follows:

> in France men were convinced that he was accused of abandoning Brest and Cherbourg to their former owners and of entering into the twenty-eight-year truce without the consent of his subjects. Charles VI's ministers had for years regarded Richard II as the solitary barrier against the tide of English francophobia. They were obsessed by the English King's dispute with the Duke of Gloucester, which had received extensive publicity in their country. They assumed that Bolingbroke's supporters must have hated Richard for the same

[82] Alexandre Héron, ed., *Oeuvres de Robert Blondel*, 2 vols (Rouen: Lestringant, 1891–93), 1:440.
[83] Héron, *Oeuvres de Robert Blondel*, 1:441.
[84] Sumption, *The Hundred Years War*, 3:863.
[85] Sumption, *The Hundred Years War*, 3:864.

> reasons as Gloucester had. For many years the received opinion on the continent was that the deposition of Richard II was a declaration of war.[86]

Even Christine de Pizan, as late as 1403 and 1404, praised Richard II in the highest terms.[87]

On learning that Henry's coronation was confirmed, the French immediately reinforced their garrisons on the marches of Calais and Aquitaine.[88] Charles VI was exceptionally hostile to the new English king. The military historian Anne Curry even calls the first fifteen years of the fifteenth century a 'cold war',[89] and to some extent the truce of 1396 had never been properly observed.[90] There were English raids on the Norman coast as well as plenty of mutual, officially sanctioned acts of piracy in the months and even years after Henry's accession.[91] Then there was the problem of Isabel, Richard's widow and daughter to Charles. A. J. Pollard sees Isabel's marriage to Richard as the cornerstone of the fragile truce between England and France.[92] Much depended on how Henry would treat Charles's daughter: after a series of diplomatic incidents, Isabel was sent back to France in May 1401, but without her dowry.

A glance at privy council meetings between the end of 1399 and the following spring reveals that the inner circles of England's royal administration were preoccupied with Gascony and the anticipated outbreak of war with France. In the winter of 1399/1400 the council conducted much administrative and legal business in Gascony to bolster English interests there.[93] On Christmas Eve Henry took the unusual step of

[86] Sumption, *The Hundred Years War*, 3:864.

[87] Taylor, 'Weep Thou for Me in France', 213–14.

[88] Sumption, *The Hundred Years War*, 3:864.

[89] Curry, *The Hundred Years War*, 62.

[90] Christopher Allmand, *The Hundred Years War: England and France at War, c. 1300–c. 1450* (Cambridge: Cambridge University Press, 1988), 26.

[91] Allmand, *The Hundred Years War*, 26–7. Much of this continued after the truce: the French threatened invasion of Gascony in 1401 and again in 1402.

[92] A. J. Pollard, *Late Medieval England 1399–1509* (London: Longman, 2000), 30–1. John A. Wagner believes that Henry's decision not to send back Isabella until August expressed his fundamental hostility to Valois France (*Encyclopaedia of the Hundred Years War* (Westport, CT: Greenwood, 2006), 148).

[93] Thomas Rymer, *Foedera*, ed. George Holmes, 10 vols, 3rd edn (The Hague: Neaulme, 1739–45), 3.1–2:171–4.

appointing a Gascon, Gaillard de Durfort, to the office of grand seneschal of Aquitaine,[94] presumably to secure the loyalty of the Gascon barons, who were being wooed by the French court at the time. In January, following the Revolt of the Earls, Henry closed all ports because he feared that once 'reports of [the revolt] began circulating on the continent, they could precipitate a foreign invasion'.[95] And even when Charles confirmed the peace with England on 31 January in an attempt to renew diplomatic relations, which had been severed since November,[96] Henry's new tone toward France became abrasive: 'Instead of referring to Charles as *carissimo consanguineo nostro Franciae* as he had done in November...he now addressed him as *adversario nostro Franciae*'.[97] Matters took a dramatic turn for the worse in February: two high-ranking English ambassadors—the bishop of Durham and the Earl of Worcester—were denied an interview by Charles, who had the English herald imprisoned in what amounted to a diplomatic scandal. Ian Mortimer believes that 'Henry's priority in January 1400 should have been the defence of the realm'.[98] He continues,

> Charles VI of France had refused to recognise him as king, and had refused even to meet his ambassadors...Nor would he confirm the truce. Instead he had strengthened the castles on the borders of Picardy, forbidden all trade with Englishmen, and had gathered a fleet at Harfleur ready to invade South Wales and take possession of Pembroke and Tenby castles.[99]

In response to the French reaction, Henry called a council meeting for 9 February. A confirmation of the truce was unexpectedly presented by William Faryngton, Charles's envoy, but there were still no letters of safe conduct that would permit English envoys to meet Charles.

[94] Rymer, *Foedera*, 3.1–2:174.

[95] S. P. Pistono, 'Henry IV and Charles VI: The Confirmation of the Twenty-Eight-Year Truce', *Journal of Medieval History*, 3 (1977), 353–6.

[96] Pistono, 'Henry IV and Charles VI', 357.

[97] Pistono, 'Henry IV and Charles VI', 362. Only the outbreak of the Franco-Burgundian feud following the assassination of Louis of Orleans in 1407 by John the Fearless gave England peace (Maurice Hugh Keen, *England in the Later Middle Ages: A Political History* (London: Methuen, 1973), 255).

[98] Ian Mortimer, *The Fears of Henry IV: The Life of England's Self-Made King* (London: Random House, 2013), 210.

[99] Mortimer, *The Fears of Henry IV*, 210.

The councillors believed that war was imminent and proceeded to raise troops at their own expense. The minutes of the council meeting concede that 'war with France was [deemed] inevitable'.[100] The council agreed to mobilize on land and sea over the coming three months,[101] and in March they decided to send a force to Gascony.[102]

As if aware of the negotiations between the two countries, Gower speaks of the possibility that peace can be acquired, purchased even: 'And do the werre awei, what so betide. / Pourchace pes, and set it be thi side' (ll. 123–4). At a time when the privy council was busy warmongering Gower's poem has something remarkable to say:

If eny man be now or ever was
Agein the pes thi prevé counseillour,
Lete God ben of thi counseil in this cas,
And putte awei the cruel werreiour.
(ll. 127–30)

This international dimension is further intensified by the appeal for a political solution that transcends a mere armistice: 'To make pes, acord, and unité /Among the kinges that ben now devised' (ll. 234–5). Clearest of all, perhaps, the closing stanza of *In Praise of Peace* reaches out beyond Henry and to an international audience:

Noght only to my king of pes Y write,
Bot to these othre princes Cristene alle,
That ech of hem his oghne herte endite,
And see the werre er more meschief falle.
(ll. 379–82)

Despite Gower's outspoken stand, the allegation that the poet was a political sycophant does not seem to go away. For many years, this charge was encapsulated by the image he paints of himself in the preface to the first edition of the *Confessio Amantis.* The poet places

[100] Harris Nicolas, ed., *Proceedings and Ordinances of the Privy Council of England*, 7 vols (London: Record Commission, 1834–37), 1:xi, of the chronological catalogue (102–6 for the actual record).

[101] Pistono views the situation as follows: 'Since war against France seemed imminent, the lords present at the council agreed for the nobility to supply the king with ships, men and money during the following three months' ('Henry IV and Charles VI', 361).

[102] Nicolas, *Proceedings and Ordinances of the Privy Council*, 1:xii–xiii.

himself in a boat, rowing in the Thames, when he chances upon King Richard's barge:

> In Temse whan it was flowende
> As I be bote cam rowende,
> So as fortune hir tyne sette,
> My liege lord par chaunce I mette.[103]

The king then invites Gower to board the royal barge before asking him to write a substantial work ('boke'), or 'som newe thing' (l. 51). This little vignette of poetical ambition—the paddling poet who happens to meet the cruising king—has fired the critical imagination. If this was not evidence enough of a self-congratulatory prince pleaser, then the subsequent alleged two re-dedications of the poem to Henry IV (the first of which was believed to have been made still during Richard's reign and addresses Henry as the Earl of Derby) only exacerbate Gower's reputation as the literary equivalent of a weather vane.[104] And it was Fisher who stamped the stigma of sycophancy on Gower: 'Has there ever been a greater sycophant in the history of English literature?'[105] Although some qualifications follow, it is never hard to guess whether Fisher saw in Gower an 'opportunistic timeserver or a poet-philosopher of depth and integrity'.[106] For Robert Myer-Lee, Gower 'wore a Lancastrian collar' and was 'an early and widely disseminated Lancastrian apologist'.[107] Much of this reputation has been dismantled by, as Georgiana Donavin puts it, 'corrective analyses',[108] and a recent editor of *In Praise in Peace* states that 'Gower, too, has been redeemed from later scholarship's not-wholly-accurate depictions of him as a sycophant'.[109]

[103] Macaulay, *The English Works of John Gower*, 1:3, ll. 39–42. All references to the *Confessio* will be to Macaulay's edition.

[104] Terry Jones offers intriguing evidence for two instead of three redactions, the second of which was made after Henry IV's usurpation. See 'Did John Gower Re-Dedicate His *Confessio Amantis* before Henry IV's Usurpation?', in *Middle English Texts in Transition: A Festschrift Dedicated to Toshiyuki Takamiya on His 70th Birthday*, ed. Simon Horobin and Linne R. Mooney (Woodbridge: York Medieval Press and Brewer, 2014), 40–74.

[105] Fisher, *John Gower*, 133.

[106] Fisher, *John Gower*, 134.

[107] Meyer-Lee, *Poets and Power*, 49 and 91.

[108] Georgiana Donavin, 'Rhetorical Gower: Aristotelianism in the *Confessio Amantis*'s Treatment of "Rethorique"', in *John Gower: Manuscripts, Readers, Contexts*, ed Malte Urban (Turnhout, Belgium: Brepols, 2009), 155–73, at 166, n. 43.

[109] Livingston and Yeager, *The Minor Latin Works*, introduction, n. 9.

Strohm considers *In Praise of Peace* a piece of Lancastrian propaganda.[110] His reading places the poem close to 'official' Lancastrian arguments.[111] Strohm's classification of Gower as a Lancastrian polemicist takes as a foundation *The Record and Process*: in the anti-Ricardian and jingoistic *Cronica tripertita* Gower 'had no reason . . . to withhold mention of conquest', whereas the 'more conciliatory *In Praise of Peace* aspires to surmount conflict and hence relies upon the blurred and contradictory but ultimately reassuring formulations of the *Record and Process*'.[112] *In Praise of Peace* has thus become an important building block in the theory of Gower as a Lancastrian sycophant. If here as elsewhere in Strohm's discussion of Lancastrian propaganda *The Record and Process* becomes the basis for assessing whether a given work conforms to the criteria of 'Lancastrianism', then it must follow that 'blurred and contradictory' formulations form a part of this definition. But *The Record and Process* is an anguished document, a 'wounded text' in Strohm's own usage. He applies this term to some of John Fortescue's writings, but the definition hauntingly invokes *The Record and Process*:

> These texts straddle and embrace contradiction, irreconcilable postulates and doxa, and invest in irrational prejudice, unexamined hierarchies, and even protonationalist jingoisms. The further, and deeper, contradiction of these texts inheres in their very gesture toward self-stabilization. This is, of course, their attempt to firm up their politics by professing loyalty to a single dynastic philosophy or a particular royal incumbency.[113]

Although Strohm does not appear to be thinking about *The Record and Process*, his concept of the 'wounded text' reads like a summary of the troubled proto-text of Lancastrian writings. And if *The Record and Process* is the reservoir on which Lancastrian writers draw (in addition to being the origin myth of the Lancastrian dynasty), then it is unsurprising that subsequent works betray the same nervous acceptance of a dynastic incumbency that showed unease with the circumstances of its own inception. But this argument could be inverted: if 'blurred and

[110] Strohm, *Hochon's Arrow*, 75–94.
[111] Strohm, *Hochon's Arrow*, 89.
[112] Strohm, *Hochon's Arrow*, 90.
[113] Paul Strohm, *Politique: Languages of Statecraft between Chaucer and Shakespeare* (Notre Dame, IN: University of Notre Dame Press, 2005), 147.

contradictory' formulations circumscribe the narrative of Lancastrian usurpation, any text written at the time that does not distance itself unequivocally from Henry yet dabbles in public matters must appear blurred and contradictory. This is not to say that I reject Strohm's project of moving *The Record and Process* into the centre of our thinking about Lancastrian literature and the concomitant language of power; rather, I would like to suggest that because this text reflects the complicated and indeed contradictory, if not repressed, nature of Henry's accession, its use as the basis for evaluating whether a writer is Lancastrian in sympathy is limited.[114] There can be no doubt that Gower was a Lancastrian writer, but I would argue that he was a Lancastrian writer in the same sense in which Shakespeare was an Elizabethan writer or Dickens a Victorian writer: Gower happened to live through a significant political transition and he happened to live at a time when poetry relied on courtly endorsements instead of ticket revenues or book sales.

The poem emphatically confirms Henry's entitlement to the throne, yet it also warns the king against using the same justification to enforce his claims to Gascony and France on the grounds that conquest constitutes a choice by going beyond the defence of one's divine birth right. As Carlson correctly notes, '[T]o a ruler recently come to the throne by violence, or to people near him, some such remarks as Gower makes might seem critical, in the sense that they might be taken to pass judgment, in retrospect, negatively, on what had been done'.[115] Advising a nervous, new ruler to exercise restraint in domestic affairs is certainly risky, but to urge him to abandon his claims to France after he had so spectacularly enforced his claim to the English throne borders on bravery. After all, until Henry confirmed the truce in May 1400 England and France were, as one historian puts it, 'on the verge of open war'.[116]

[114] For other approaches to writers working in the service of the Lancastrian cause at the time, see Gwilym Dodd, 'Was Thomas Favent a Political Pamphleteer? Faction and Politics in Later Fourteenth-Century London', *Journal of Medieval History*, 30 (2011), 1–22, and the discussion of Richard Frampton in Linne R. Mooney and Estelle Stubbs, *Scribes and the City: London Guildhall Clerks and the Dissemination of Middle English Literature, 1375–1425* (Woodbridge: York Medieval Press and Brewer, 2013), 107–18.

[115] Carlson, *John Gower*, 205.

[116] Pistono, 'Henry IV and Charles VI', 363.

The Purpose of the Trentham Manuscript

In its manuscript context, two aspects of *In Praise of Peace* are particularly striking. First, this is the only English poem in a compilation that otherwise gathers Gower's French and Latin poetry; second, the poem occupies the prominent initial position. Codicologically, Trentham is of course self-consciously multilingual. Tim Machan, who believes that this manuscript was prepared for Henry's coronation, notes the colour rubrication throughout that marks the different languages of the codex.[117] It is noteworthy that the majority of the texts in Trentham are written in Gower's Anglo-French. A manuscript that brings together the three languages of later medieval England and that is dominated by French draws attention not only to the single English poem it contains but also to the very idea of what 'English' means. As Ardis Butterfield puts it, 'Gower, as no other English writer of the fourteenth century, makes us question Englishness'.[118] He does this in Trentham more openly than in any of his other poetic or material contexts. This is vitally important because Gower's French was much less insular—and therefore less 'English' in a cultural sense—than other contemporary Anglo-French texts. His *Cinkante Balades*, which also survive only in Trentham, have prompted Brian Merrilees to argue that Gower's command of French verse 'reflects the newest trends in continental French'.[119] And, as mentioned above, Ralph Hanna views the stylized script as drawing on French models. Crucially, perhaps, Butterfield notes that the *Cinkante Balades* is the earliest collection of French lyrics.[120] The individual *balades* are not only infused with the writings of Machaut, Butterfield notes, but they also participate in and partake

[117] Tim William Machan, 'The Visual Pragmatics of Code-Switching in Late Middle English Literature', in *Code-Switching in Early English*, ed Herbert Schendl and Laura Wright (Berlin: de Gruyter, 2011), 303–33, at 310.

[118] Ardis Butterfield, *The Familiar Enemy: Chaucer, Language, and Nation in the Hundred Years War* (Oxford: Oxford University Press, 2010), 241.

[119] Unpublished paper quoted by Butterfield, *The Familiar Enemy*, 244. Butterfield's own arguments about the nature of this single-author collection of poems make a similar point. Rory Critten argues that the Trentham manuscript may be an attempt to construct a lyrical Gower (Rory Critten, 'The Uses of Self-Publication in Late Medieval England' (PhD diss., University of Groningen, 2013), 17).

[120] This point may have led Yeager to suggest that Trentham may have influenced Charles d'Orléans ('John Gower's Audience', 89).

of the work of other contemporary French poets.[121] Is there a better way to celebrate Anglo-French relations and the lasting truce between England and France in a manuscript that brings together Gower's English writing and a French work that showcases the very latest cultural exchanges afforded by cross-Channel contact?

Thus, it is possible to read the entire manuscript as an attempt to balance not only English *and* French, but also England *and* France. In December 1399, Henry had still wanted to tear up the truce of Leulinghen and go to war with France, but in May 1400 he renewed the peace. Bahr has strengthened the link between the Trentham manuscript and Henry, largely on the grounds of the significance of *In Praise of Peace* and the *Cinkante Balades*: 'Given their explicit links to Henry, the fact that *In Praise of Peace* and the *Cinkante Balades* are unique to Trentham heightens the sense that this particular object, or one modelled on it, was designed for him'.[122] Bahr continues that

> we can imagine interpreting [Trentham's] multilingual codicological symmetry as an elaborate compliment to the new king: just as Trentham uses Gower's poetry to unite into a pleasing whole the multiple languages set loose upon the world by human pride at Babel, for example, so too will the manuscript's royal recipient prove able to reunite his fractious kingdom, undoing the political chaos that Gower so strongly associated with linguistic *divisioun*.[123]

Bahr stresses two significant components of the Trentham manuscript here: the appeal to Henry and the multilingual condition of this codex. Christopher Cannon, too, believes that 'the context of the *Cinkante Balades* in MS Additional 59495 could not more strongly suggest a royal connection'.[124] But since the context of *In Praise of Peace* as well as the *Cinkante Balades* lies not in England but in France or, rather, *between* England and France, I would like to argue that Gower encourages Henry to act as a peacemaker and heal the *divisioun* between the two countries. Thus, this manuscript, as so much of Gower's work,

[121] Butterfield, *The Familiar Enemy*, 246–8. See also Yeager, 'John Gower's Audience'.
[122] Bahr, 'Reading Codicological Form', 225.
[123] Bahr, 'Reading Codicological Form', 226.
[124] Christopher Cannon, 'Class Distinction and the French of England', in *Traditions and Innovations in the Study of Medieval English Literature: The Influence of Derek Brewer*, ed Charlotte Brewer and Barry Windeatt (Cambridge: D. S. Brewer, 2013), 48–59, at 59.

reveals an interest in kingship even as Henry moves into the background in the subsequent parts of Trentham.[125]

One of the most revealing insights Bahr generates is the codicological symmetry he discerns in Trentham.[126] Here, perhaps the most striking feature of Trentham's architecture is the equal length of *In Praise of Peace* and the *Traitié*, each having 385 lines, if one includes the missing material from the *Traitié* that appears in other manuscript witnesses. Discounting the brief prefatory and concluding poems in Latin, the two substantial English and French poems balance each other. This symmetry between English and French may be a structural device to convey the desire for continued peace between England and France, a theme throughout the manuscript. Hence, the poem following *In Praise of Peace*, the fifty-six-line Latin *Rex celi Deus*, reiterates Gower's desire for Henry to lead a peaceful reign (ll. 47 and 49) and establishes the collection as intended for Henry.[127] The laudatory quality of this short work serves as the formal, elevated introduction to the manuscript.

It is worthwhile remembering that Henry was not married between 1394 and 1403, whereas the peace between England and France rested on the marriage of Richard and Isabel.[128] The queen was effectively being held hostage by Henry, leaving the 'marriage' between England and France—symbolized by Richard and Isabel—in suspense. Thus, the *Traitié* (which can also mean 'treaty', 'accord') invokes two spouses, inviting comparison with England and France. This broader meaning of love and marriage—not just between lovers hoping for marriage but also as governing other parties—is reflected in the marginal notes to Balades V and VI in the *Cinkante Balades*: 'Les balades d'amont jesques enci sont fait especialement pour ceaux q'attendont lours amours par droite mariage' (The balades from the beginning up to this point are made especially for those who wait on their loves in expectation of

[125] 'In fact, the manuscript demonstrates a clear, consistent interest in kingship, including but not limited to Henry's, for the three major texts not addressed to him explicitly—"Rex celi deus", "Ecce patet tensus", and the *Traitie*—all concern royal behaviour and misbehaviour' (Bahr, 'Reading Codicological Form', 227).

[126] Bahr, 'Reading Codicological Form', 224–6.

[127] Livingston and Yeager, *The Minor Latin Works*.

[128] For the suggestion that Henry may have had marriage plans shortly after his coronation, see Linne R. Mooney, 'A Woman's Reply to Her Lover' and Four Other New Courtly Love Lyrics in Cambridge, Trinity College MS R.3.19', *Medium Aevum*, 67 (1998), 235–56.

rightful marriage). 'Les balades d'ici jesqes au fin du livere sont universeles a tout le monde, selonc les propretés et les condicions des Amantz, qui sont diversement travailez en la fortune d'amour' (the balades from here until the end of the book are universal, for everyone, according to the properties and conditions of Lovers who are diversely suffering the fortunes of Love).[129] That this universality extends beyond individuals is brought out by the envoy to the *Cinkante Balades*, exclusive to Trentham:

O gentile Engleterre, a toi j'escrits,
Pour remembrer ta joie q'est novelle,
Qe te survient du noble Roi Henri,
Par qui dieus ad redrescé ta querele:
A dieu purceo prient et cil et celle,
Q'il de sa grace au fort Roi coroné
Doignt peas, honour, joie et prosperité.

(Oh gentle England, I write for you,
For remembrance of your new joy,
Which comes to you from the noble King Henry,
By whom God has redressed your quarrel:
Let one and all therefore pray to God,
That He who with His grace crowned the King indeed
May give peace, honour, joy and prosperity.)[130]

The *Cinkante Balades* in Trentham are not addressed to Henry per se, but to an apostrophized England, which has experienced a lovers' 'querele'. It is hoped, of course, that the new king—a new lover, perhaps?—will bring 'peas' to England again.

That the lovers Gower has in mind throughout Trentham are not individuals but nations (a term used with all due caution in a premodern setting) is shown most clearly in the poem that immediately follows the *Cinkante Balades*, *Ecce pạtet tensus* (*Behold the Taut Bow*), which sources almost half its lines from Gower's *Vox Clamantis*. This short poem harks back to *In Praise of Peace*, as Bahr observes, whilst continuing the

[129] Text and translation: R. F. Yeager, ed., *John Gower: The French Balades* (Kalamazoo, MI: Medieval Institute Publications, 2011).

[130] Balade 51, ll. 25–31; text and translation from Yeager, *John Gower: The French Balades*.

amatory subject matter of the *Cinkante Balades.*[131] Written from the perspective of Cupid, it stresses the compelling force of love. But this is no simple meditation on 'omnia vincit amor' (l. 3),[132] for lines 18–20—which are not found in the *Vox Clamantis*—invoke a Cupid who targets not people but nations:

> Vulnerat omne genus, nec sibi vulnus habet.
> Non manet in terris qui prelia vincit amoris,
> Nec sibi quis firme federa pacis habet.
>
> (He wounds every nation, but receives no wound himself.
> In the wars of Love there is no victor on earth,
> Nor has anyone concluded with him a firm treaty of peace.)

Here again the main objectives of the manuscript are woven into a whole: love, nations, treaties, and peace. *Genus* in this poem may stand for 'nation' or 'people', yet it is significant that Cupid's arrows can shoot at whole nations. I believe that this poem, which draws on the *Vox Clamantis* and which emphatically repeats the blindness of Cupid, is connected to the illustrations of an old archer (believed to be Gower) found in a number of manuscripts of the *Vox Clamantis*, including British Library Cotton MS Tiberius A IV (Fig. 3). The archer is portrayed as shooting at a T-in-O map that invokes the larger scale of nations rather than that of individuals. I will return to the illustration and to this poem in the final section of this chapter, where I hope to demonstrate the active involvement of Gower in this manuscript.

Time was pressing in December 1399 and January 1399/1400. A physically modest yet internally ambitious book might have been the only way for Gower to present his appeal to the king given the rapid deterioration of relations between England and France. But if, for the sake of argument, we do not wish to accept a Gower concerned for the well-being of England and France, then we may still find that the same political circumstances may have stirred Fisher's opportunistic Gower into action: of all the known and publicly visible English poets at the time, Gower had arguably the largest stake in French culture. His career

[131] Bahr, 'Reading Codicological Form', 253.

[132] All references to and translations from this poem are from Livingston and Yeager, *The Minor Latin Works.*

FIG 3 London, British Library Cotton MS Tiberius A IV, fol. 9v. Frontispiece with Gower the Archer © The British Library Board.

peaked at and profited from Richard's truce with France. If not for the overtly political and ethical reasons of avoiding war, would the sudden prospect of the disruption of his persistent access to French cultural production not have prompted Gower to act? Asking an impetuous monarch to give way took creativity, tact, and plenty of guts. If *In Praise of Peace* tells us anything about Gower's relationship with his Lancastrian liege, then it is that sycophancy had no place in it. But events moved rapidly. Despite the seeming inevitability of renewed conflict, Henry confirmed the truce in May 1400, thereby removing the need for Gower's manuscript. This shift can be discerned in the design of Trentham itself: as Bahr has shown, even though the symmetrical design reveals prior planning, the execution progressively removes Henry from the focus of the manuscript.

Parkes's Scribe 10: Gower's Hand?

Malcolm Parkes has identified the work of two scribes in Trentham: Scribe 5, who produces the bulk of the manuscript, and Scribe 10, who adds *Ecce patet tensus* and *Henrici Quarti primus*, the final poem in the collection.[133] In addition, Scribe 10 adds a few minor revisions to the work of Scribe 5.[134] Scribe 10 is therefore the second and last hand to appear in this manuscript. Parkes adds that this scribe only worked on one other manuscript, Cotton MS Tiberius A IV, which contains a copy of the *Vox Clamantis* and some minor Latin poems. As I will show, Scribe 10 also finished Cotton MS Tiberius A IV, at a time at which Gower's gradual blindness had set in but had not yet reached its most advanced stage. In this second manuscript he adds two of the final poems, *Vnanimes esse* and *Presul ouile regis*.[135] Furthermore, these two manuscripts are believed to be the likeliest to have been supervised by Gower himself,[136] and Scribe 10 only appears in these two—each time as a concluding hand.

[133] Parkes, 'Patterns of Scribal Activity', 90–1 and 94.

[134] Parkes, 'Patterns of Scribal Activity', 94.

[135] Parkes, 'Patterns of Scribal Activity', 94.

[136] Yeager, 'Gower in Winter: Last Poems', in *The Medieval Python: The Purposive and Provocative Work of Terry Jones*, ed. R. F. Yeager and Toshiyuki Takamiya (New York: Palgrave Macmillan, 2012), 88–9, at 89.

Now that we know that Trentham most probably remained in Gower's possession until his death, the last hand to write in and make revisions to the manuscript—that of Scribe 10—must enjoy a sense of authorial approval and therefore authority. The same scribe appears to have had a similar function in the only other manuscript in which he wrote, Cotton MS Tiberius A IV. The two final poems in this manuscript, *Cultor in ecclesia* and *Dicunt scripture*, appear to have been composed some time after the manuscript had already reached its final folio, 177r. Yeager argues that *Cultor in ecclesia* may have been written between 1402 and 1408, whereas *Dicunt scripture* appears to have been composed in conjunction with Gower's will.[137] More importantly, the scribe who added these last two poems on the final folio, Parkes's Scribe 9, did so a number of years after Scribe 10 had finished the manuscript, probably even after Gower's death: 'SCRIBE 9 appears on the final leaves of three manuscripts, GC ['C' denotes 'Cotton MS Tiberius A IV'] and H. He probably belonged to a new generation, since his handwriting is characteristic of the second decade of the fifteenth century.'[138] Therefore, at the time during which Gower lost his ability to see—between 1400 and 1402—Scribe 10 was the last hand to write in and complete the only two manuscripts in which he is attested, both of which are believed to have been supervised by Gower.

The final poem of Trentham, *Henrici Quarti primus*, is of structural importance to the compilation, and Bahr has shown just how crucial the addition of *Ecce patet tensus* is for the symmetry of the collection,[139] yet his focus is not the scribe's but the design of Trentham: 'We therefore cannot prove that Gower, Scribe 5, or any other identifiable agent intended the Trentham manuscript to have the codicological form that it does'.[140] But what if Scribe 10, who corrected the work of Scribe 5, was the last to work on Trentham *and* the manuscript stayed with Gower? After all, Parkes argues that 'the scribes . . . who were most likely to have had the opportunity to work with Gower are, perhaps, 4 and 5'.[141] Scribe 10 adds some of the most significant features to

137 Livingston and Yeager, *The Minor Latin Works*, introduction.
138 Parkes, 'Patterns of Scribal Activity', 94.
139 Bahr, 'Reading Codicological Form', 261.
140 Bahr, 'Reading Codicological Form', 223.
141 Parkes, 'Patterns of Scribal Activity', 95.

Trentham, yet the connections shared by *Ecce patet tensus* and *Henrici Quarti primus* have not been noticed.

Henrici Quarti primus, the final poem in the Trentham manuscript, is the first of three versions of the same lyric about Gower's failing eyesight:

Henrici quarti primus regni fuit annus
  Quo michi defecit visus ad acta mea.
Omnia tempus habent; finem natura ministrat,
  Quem virtute sua frangere nemo potest.
    Ultra posse nichil, quamvis michi velle remansit;
  Amplius ut *scribam* non michi posse manet.
Dum potui *scripsi*, set nunc quia curua senectus
  Turbavit sensus, *scripta* relinquo scolis.
Scribat qui veniet post me discrecior alter,
    Ammodo namque manus et mea penna silent.
Hoc tamen, in fine verborum queso meorum,
  Prospera quod statuat regna futura Deus. Amen.

(It was in the first year of the reign of King Henry IV
  When my sight failed for my deeds.
All things have their time; nature applies a limit,
  Which no man can break by his own power.
I can do nothing beyond what is possible, though my will has remained;
  My ability to *write* more has not stayed.
While I was able I *wrote*, but now because stooped old age
  Has troubled my senses, I leave *writing* to the schools.
Let someone else more discreet who comes after me *write*,
  For from this time forth my hand and pen will be silent.
Nevertheless I ask this one final thing, the last of my words:
  That God make our kingdoms prosperous in the future. Amen.)

(My emphasis)[142]

The second version of this poem makes only small changes, mainly by giving not the first (1399–1400) but the second (1400–1) regnal year in the first line. But the second version also changes the second line of the poem, adding a finality to Gower's blindness: whereas the Trentham recension has 'when my sight failed for my deeds', the second version

[142] For the text and translation of all three versions, see Livingston and Yeager, *The Minor Latin Works.*

gives 'when I stopped writing, because I am blind'. The three versions are usually interpreted as indications that Gower was progressively losing his eyesight,[143] yet he only seems to have stopped writing after Trentham had been produced. This means that he could have performed some physical writing in the winter of 1399–1400 and thereafter. But what exactly does Gower mean by 'writing'? It is generally assumed that his use of the verb *scribere* denotes writing in a looser sense, that is, writing as composing, the work done by an author. Yet when medieval authors speak of composing, they use words for editorial tasks, such as 'compile' or 'edit'. In fact, Gower himself uses such a phrase in the explicit to *In Praise of Peace*, when he appears as Henry IV's orator: 'suus humilis orator Iohannes Gower composuit'.[144] I believe that *scribere* in this poem carries an indexical meaning and denotes physical writing, not composing. In the third and longest version of the poem Gower differentiates between 'writing' and 'composing':

> Quamuis exterius scribendi deficit actus,
> Mens tamen interius scribit et ornat opus.
> Sic quia de manibus nichil amodo scribo valoris,
> Scribam de precibus que nequit illa manus
>
> (Although the act of writing externally now fails me,
> Still my mind writes within me and adorns the work.
> Thus because I can write nothing further with my hands,
> I will write with my prayers what my hand cannot.)[145]

Jonathan Hsy explains that Gower offers here 'the most expanded discussion of his compositional practice as a blind poet, carefully distinguishing a physical capacity to write from an ability to compose in the mind'.[146] Hence, the four-fold use of *scribere* in the Trentham version refers to the physical ability to write and not to composing. In addition, in line 10 he adds that 'from this time forth' he will stop writing with his hand. This poem, however, he appears to have *written* himself. If *scribere* stands for the physical capacity to write by hand,

[143] On Gower's self-identification as a progressively blind writer, see Jonathan Hsy, 'Blind Advocacy: Blind Readers, Disability Theory, and Accessing John Gower', *Accessus*, 1 (2013), article 2, 1–38, and Yeager, 'Gower in Winter'.

[144] See my discussion of the explicit to *In Praise of Peace* above.

[145] Lines 11–14, Livingston and Yeager, *The Minor Latin Works*.

[146] Hsy, 'Blind Advocacy', 14.

and Gower tells us here that from this point on he will no longer *write*, then in all probability Scribe 10 could be Gower himself. *Henrici Quarti primus* is a typically indexical poem, as is Trentham itself, written and overseen by Gower and to be read by an audience familiar with the poet.

The second version of the poem tells us that his blindness only prevented him from writing in the second year of Henry's reign; it follows, therefore, that Gower still possessed some ability to write in 1399–1400, when Scribe 10 entered *Henrici Quarti primus* in Trentham. It is often overlooked that the Trentham version of *Henrici Quarti primus* actually does not say that he is blind. The word Gower uses to describe his blindness in the two later versions of the poem is *cecus* (blind), employed twice in each poem.[147] The identification of Scribe 10 with Gower gains support when considering that this same authorizing hand made the final revisions to Trentham and Cotton MS Tiberius A IV and across two manuscripts only wrote four short Latin poems, the longest of which, *Ecce patet tensus*, covers only one page.[148]

All four poems in the two manuscripts in which Scribe 10 writes are short enough to be manageable for someone coping with impaired sight. It is difficult to determine on the basis of Trentham alone whether Scribe 10 suffered from a loss of vision, but his stints in Trentham and Cotton MS Tiberius A IV reveal one feature common in writers who have difficulty seeing. Most scribes use the bottom of the x-height as a reference point, so that shaft strokes move to the left or right in anticipation of reaching the ruled line. Scribes can judge when their shaft is 1–2mm above the ruled line, at which point they produce the foot. But Scribe 10 draws each shaft all the way to the ruled line (Figs 4 and 5). Although not uncommon for scribes, in disability studies this is called baseline writing, and it is usually indicative of

[147] Livingston and Yeager, *The Minor Latin Works*. The term 'cecus' also appears in the Latin poem *De lucis scrutinio*, which Yeager dates to ca. 1392–95 (*The Minor Latin Works*, introduction). However, the meanings of 'cecus' and 'scribere' become much more nuanced and sharper after winter 1399–1400.

[148] A hand in the margin clarifies the word 'laudis' next to line 22 (fol. 33v), but it is difficult to ascertain whether this is Scribe 10 correcting himself or perhaps a later addition, possibly made by a monk at St Mary Overeys. One cannot be certain that the poem is complete as it stands, though there is no reason to posit that it is unfinished: Yeager describes the last line as 'open-ended but nonetheless credible' (*The Minor Latin Works*, introduction).

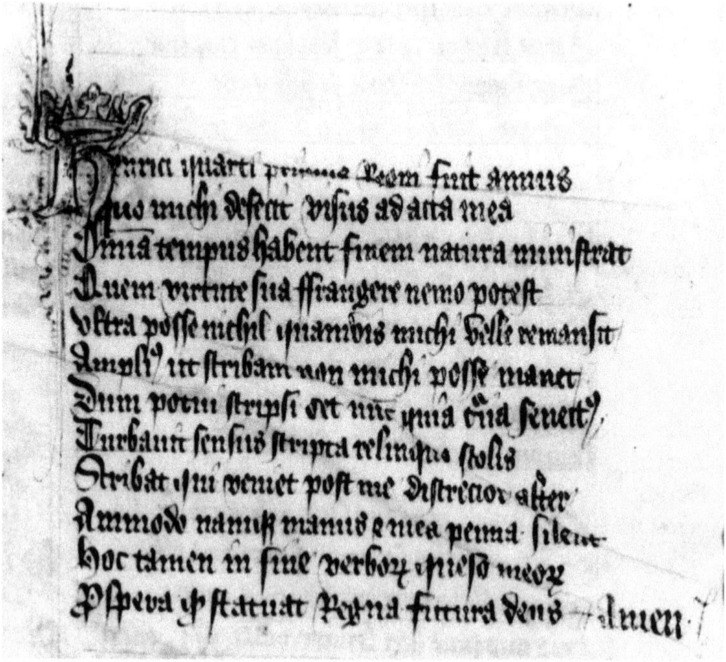

FIG 4 British Library Add. MS 59495, fol. 39v.
Scribe 10; *Henrici quarti primus* © The British Library Board.

the use of a writing aid such as a ruler, grid, or thread.[149] Even if Gower could still partially see, perhaps as a result of debilitating cataracts—the most common cause of blindness—the ruled bottom line of the x-height could have given him additional security. Neither the other scribe in Trentham, Scribe 5, nor the scribes in Cotton MS Tiberius A IV employ this practice.

149 Roy A. Huber and A. M. Headrick, *Handwriting Identification: Facts and Fundamentals* (London: Taylor and Francis, 1999), 193–4. Huber and Headrick add that baseline or straightedge writing is also referred to as 'blind-man's writing' (194). I am not referring to special-education assessments of 'baseline writing' in the context of scholarship on cognitive or developmental disabilities; instead I am concerned with physical motor and visual impairments.

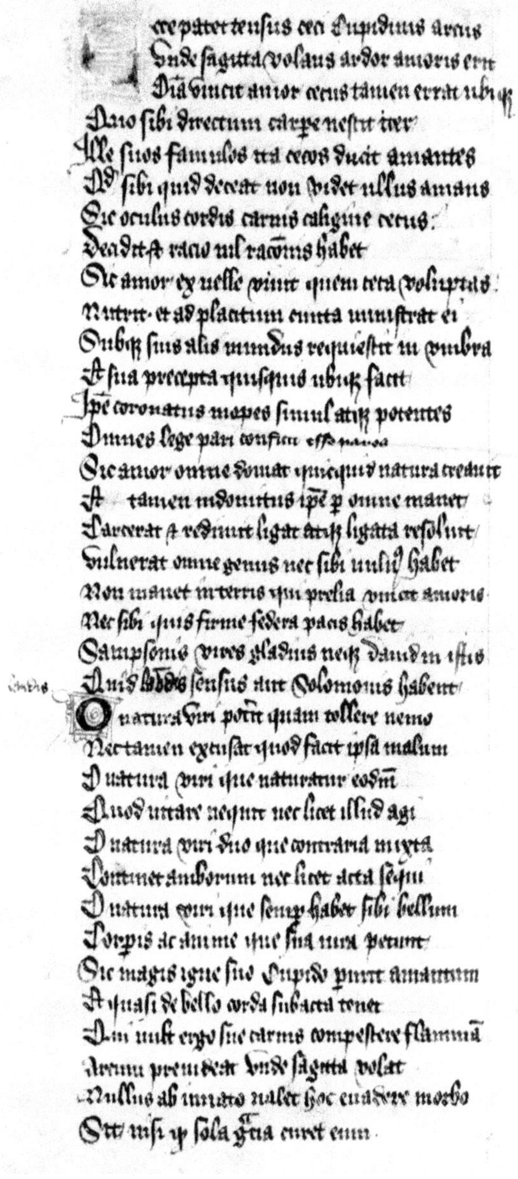
Ecce patet tensus ceci Cupidinis arcus
Unde sagitta volans ardor amoris erit
Qua vincit amor cecus tamen errat ubique
Quo sibi directum carpere nescit iter
Ille suos famulos ita cecos ducit amantes
Ut sibi quid deceat non videt ullus amans
Sic oculus cordis carnis caligine cecus:
Deviat et racio nil racionis habet
Sic amor ex velle venit quem ceca voluptas
Nutrit et ad placitum cuncta ministrat ei
Undique suis alis mundus requiescit in umbra
Et sua precepta quisquis ubique facit
Ipse coronatus inopes simul atque potentes
Omnes lege pari cogit esse pares
Sic amor omne domat quicquid natura creavit
Et tamen indomitus ipse per omne manet
Carcerat et redimit ligat atque ligata resolvit
Vulnerat omne genus nec sibi vulnus habet
Non manet in terris qui prelia vincat amoris
Nec sibi qui firme federa pacis habet
Sampsonis vires gladius neque David in istis
Quis sensus aut Salomonis habent
O natura viri potuit quam tollere nemo
Nec tamen excusat quod facit ipsa malum
O natura viri que naturatur eodem
Quod vitare nequit nec licet illud agi
O natura viri duo que contraria mixta
Continet amborum nec licet acta sequi
O natura viri que semper habet sibi bellum
Corporis ac anime que sua iura petunt
Sic magis igne suo Cupido punit amantum
Et quasi de bello corda subacta tenet
Cum nisi ergo sine carnis compescere flammam
Armum prevideat unde sagitta volat
Nullus ab innato valet hoc evadere morbo
Cui nisi ex sola gratia curet eum

FIG 5 British Library Add. MS 59495, fol. 33v.
Scribe 10; *Ecce patet tensus* © The British Library Board.

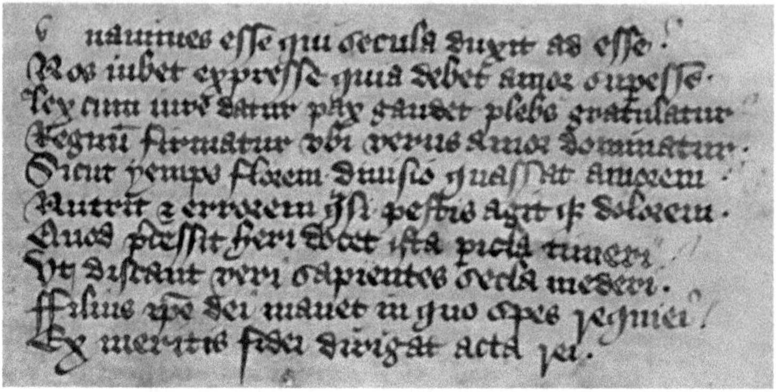

FIG 6 British Library Cotton MS Tiberius A IV, fol. 176v.
Scribe 10; *Vnanimes esse* © The British Library Board.

In or after 1402, when Scribe 10 entered *Vnanimes esse* and *Presul ouile regis* in Cotton MS Tiberius A IV, Gower's eyesight had deteriorated, and the scribe indeed makes a remarkable mistake in the first of these two poems. In line 7 of *Vnanimes esse*, starting in the middle of the line at 'docet', the hand veers from the writing line and gradually slumps below the bottom of the x-height (Fig. 6). The degree to which line 7 departs from the ruled border is so considerable that the final two letters of the last word, 'timeri', are located almost entirely below the x-height.[150] However, the ruled line marking the bottom of the x-height remains clearly visible. In addition, the script in lines 6–8 is much bigger than in the remaining lines.[151] It would be an eccentric choice to employ a scribe who has difficulties executing his hand in a manuscript most likely overseen by the poet, unless this scribe was Gower himself. At the very least one would have to explain why in two manuscripts that were so closely supervised by Gower (and one of which Gower almost certainly retained until his death) an insecure hand that appears nowhere else in the poet's considerable body of material texts was

[150] The final word of l. 7, 'timeri', and the final word of the following line, 'mederi', which has been affected by 'timeri' above, have been corrected in the same hand. Their position relative to the x-height has not been modified.

[151] I am grateful to Linne Mooney for adding this observation.

permitted to provide only the finishing touches, consisting of two very short and personal poems. In theory it is possible that Gower employed as his amanuensis an unreliable scribe, perhaps an older monk at St Mary Overeys, but it is altogether more probable that these additions were made by Gower himself. In addition, the two poems written by Scribe 10 in Cotton MS Tiberius A IV amount to only seventeen lines in total and, taken together, are therefore much shorter than his contributions to Trentham two years earlier. These observations correspond to the rate at which Gower's condition deteriorated between 1400 and 1402, as the three versions of his poem about the onset of blindness document.

The significance of blindness and the shooting of arrows by Cupid in *Ecce patet tensus*, the other poem in Trentham written by Scribe 10, has only been once connected with illustrations of what is believed to be Gower as an archer in copies of the *Vox Clamantis*.[152] In particular, the image in Cotton MS Tiberius A IV stands out (Fig. 3). Scribe 5, the main scribe of Trentham, also worked on Cotton MS Tiberius A IV, as did Scribe 10. In fact, the Cotton manuscript may contain Gower's drawing hand. Jeremy Griffiths has traced a controlling hand over the outlines of the illuminations of the figure of the archer, including in the version in Cotton MS Tiberius A. IV, and R. F. Yeager believes this tracing hand to be Gower's:

> If Gower's involvement with the copying of his works is as extensive as we believe—and I for one agree that it must have been, especially over a handful of early manuscripts including BL Cotton Tiberius A.iv—then to one degree or another [the tracing hand] was most likely Gower's.[153]

In *Ecce patet tensus—Behold the Taut Bow*—the blind archer Cupid sends out his arrows into the hearts of nations, much as the Gower figure aims at the Isidorean globe in Cotton MS Tiberius A IV. Throughout, the poem speaks of Cupid as blind, *cecus*, a word that is used five times in the poem and which Gower uses twice in the later

[152] To my mind, only Candace Barrington has made the comparison, although she sees the blind Cupid of 'Ecce patet tensus' as capturing a different sense of blindness from that portrayed by illustrations of the old archer in manuscripts of the *Vox Clamantis* ('The Trentham Manuscript as Broken Prosthesis', 18–19).

[153] Yeager, 'Gower in Winter', 89.

version of *Henrici Quarti primus* to describe his own condition.[154] The connection with Gower's other blind archer, the illustration of the old man in copies of the *Vox Clamantis*, is further made by the fact that *Ecce patet tensus* borrows almost half its lines from *Vox Clamantis*. These lines, however, appear in rearranged order, which is indicative perhaps of Scribe 10 writing the lines from *Vox Clamantis* in *Ecce patet tensus* from memory; after all, writing a short piece from memory might be less taxing than locating lines in a copy of a long poem and copying them, complete with the perils of eye-skip and concomitant problems. The depiction of Gower with the bow in Cotton MS Tiberius A IV is accompanied by a short poem, written by one of the manuscript's many scribes:

> Ad mundum mitto mea iacula, dumque sagitto;
> At vbi iustus erit, nulla sagitta ferit.
> Sed male viuentes hos vulnero transgredientes;
> Conscius ergo sibi se speculetur ibi.
>
> (I send my darts at the world and simultaneously shoot arrows;
> But mind you, wherever there is a just man, no one will receive arrows.
> I badly wound those living in transgression, however;
> Therefore, let the thoughtful man look out for himself.)[155]

This is moral Gower, then, as he wanted to be seen in his last years; an old man with failing eyesight, who meant to reach out to kings and nations, stirring them to love and peace. Even as the poet is withdrawing his manuscript from circulation and, hence, himself from public life at a crucial moment in English history, he reinserts himself through his deictic persona in the Trentham manuscript into the wider political universe as a moral force. That Gower cared about his textual persona and saw his writing as indexical resonates throughout his work, and many scribes and illustrators attempted to preserve his presences. As Sonja Drimmer points out, one manuscript of the *Confessio Amantis* has been particularly conscientious in registering the author's presence: in Cambridge, University Library MS Mm.2.2 the scribe has left the

[154] Livingston and Yeager, *The Minor Latin Works*.
[155] Livingston and Yeager, *The Minor Latin Works*, introduction.

following instruction for the limner: 'hic fiat Gowere' (make here Gower).[156]

Candace Barrington has shown that uniquely among Gower's work the Trentham manuscript is permeated by traces of impairment and disability, to the extent that this collection behaves as a prosthesis, 'demonstrating the inherent fantasy in wholeness, completion, wellness, and perfection'.[157] But this could be equally expressed as an indexical manuscript that summons and is built around Gower's authorial and authorizing presence. Trentham, then, was begun to encourage Henry to confirm the truce with France but was completed as an early draft of Gower's very own *ars moriendi*, his way of learning to die privately as well as publicly, anticipating Hoccleve's *Series* in its indexical use of the deictic self as withdrawing from the world. Gower's exercise in the art of dying is perfected in his trilingual funereal monument in St Mary Overeys, now a part of Southwark Cathedral. Unsurprisingly, Trentham shares this concern for Gower's memory with Cotton MS Tiberius A IV. A few years after Scribe 10/Gower had finished the manuscript by entering *Presul ouile regis* in the final folio, Scribe 9 inserted the last two Latin poems in the remaining space on the same folio. The last of these two poems, *Dicunt scripture*, dated by Yeager to the time of Gower's will,[158] reinforces the indulgenced plea 'orate pro anima Johannis Gowr' found on fol. 174v, and Jennifer Summit therefore observes that *Dicunt scripture* conflates 'the poet's manuscript with his tomb'.[159] But this conflation is indexical: the Trentham manuscript is Gower's tomb, and it is only completed by the author's presence, just as his presence completes this 'prosthetic' manuscript. Gower's careful planning of his tomb finds an echo in the poet's hand closing and therefore authorizing these two manuscripts, one of which we now know for certain to have remained with him until his death.

[156] Drimmer, *The Art of Allusion*, 99.

[157] Barrington, 'The Trentham Manuscript as Broken Prosthesis', 29.

[158] Livingston and Yeager, *The Minor Latin Works*, introduction.

[159] Jennifer Summit, *Memory's Library: Medieval Books in Early Modern England* (Chicago, IL: University of Chicago Press, 2008), 190. See also Siân Echard, 'Last Words: Latin at the End of the *Confessio Amantis*', in *Interstices: Studies in Late Middle English and Anglo-Latin Texts in Honour of A. G. Rigg*, ed. Richard Firth Green and Linne Mooney (Toronto: University of Toronto Press, 2004), 99–121 (in particular, 99–100).

At the time at which Scribe 10/Gower completed Trentham and Cotton MS Tiberius A IV—and on that reasoning Gower may also have owned the latter manuscript—Gower could still write, albeit increasingly poorly and slowly. It could be added here that *Henrici Quarti primus* is the most personal of Gower's works or, at the least, the earliest version of his most personal poem. It is also a poem in which he tells us through his deictic self that he can still write but will no longer do so. Read closely, Trentham contains not only his most personal but also one of the last poems Gower may very well have physically *written*—is it not understandable, then, that he would have wished to hold on to this manuscript?

2

The *Series*

Thomas Hoccleve's Year of Mourning

Thomas Hoccleve's final years are marked by a burst of literary and professional activity. The *Series*, some of his shorter poems, and the Formulary all fall into this last stage of his long career as a scribe and writer. This chapter will introduce an important but hitherto unknown life record for Hoccleve that demonstrates his ties to the Bedfordshire village of Hockliffe and shows that he owned property there in the 1420s. The new document, a will by Hoccleve's fellow Privy Seal clerk John Bailey, provides a revised context for the *Series*, which I read as the poet's attempt to mourn the death of a friend and contemplate his own mortality. I adjust the dating of the *Series* to November 1420 to Spring 1421, and consider this cycle of poems as an attempt to fulfil Hoccleve's indexical self spiritually and socially, through his textual alter ego Thomas, and in preparation of his own death. The structural emphasis on *Learning to Die* in the *Series* is crucial for understanding the spiritual aspiration of the porous self to achieve a harmonious balance with its surrounding metaphysical reality.

John Bailey of St Clement Danes

In his facetious petitionary *Balade to Somer*, written between 1408 and 1410, Hoccleve prompts Henry Somer, the then under-treasurer of the

Last Words: The Public Self and the Social Author in Late Medieval England.
Sebastian Sobecki, Oxford University Press (2019). © Sebastian Sobecki.
DOI: 10.1093/oso/9780198790778.001.0001

Exchequer, to pay arrears owing to Hoccleve and three fellow Privy Seal clerks:

> We, your seruantes, Hoccleue & Baillay,
> Hethe & Offorde, yow beseeche & preye,
> 'Haasteth our heruest / as soone as yee may!'
> For fere of stormes / our wit is aweye;
> Were our seed Inned / wel we mighten pleye,'
> And vs desporte / & synge / & make game,
> And yit this rowndel shul we synge & seye
> In trust of yow / & honour of your name.[1]
>
> (25–32)

The three named individuals have previously been identified with ease as Hoccleve's colleagues at the Privy Seal: John Bailey, John Hethe, and John Offord. All three frequently appear in records in combination with Hoccleve, and their careers overlapped for the most part with that of the poet.[2] None of them rose to a higher position in the Privy Seal office. The regularity of their presence in the archive strongly suggests that these four men—Hoccleve, Bailey, Hethe, and Offord—formed the nucleus of the active scribes at the Privy Seal from the second half of Henry IV's reign until the death of Henry V. As with Hoccleve, documents written and signed by Hethe and Offord have survived.[3]

[1] All references to Hoccleve's shorter poems outside of the *Series* are to *Hoccleve's Works: The Minor Works*, ed. Frederick J. Furnivall and others, EETS ES 61, 73, 2 vols (Oxford: EETS, 1970).

[2] On each of these clerks see in turn: 1. Offord: J. H. Kern, 'Der Schreiber Offorde', *Anglia*, 1916/40 (1916), 374; J. Otway-Ruthven, *The King's Secretary and the Signet Office in the XV Century* (Cambridge: Cambridge University Press, 1939), 180–1; A. L. Brown, 'The Privy Seal Clerks in the Early Fifteenth Century', in *The Study of Medieval Records: Essays in Honor of Kathleen Major*, ed. D. A. Bullough and R. L. Storey (Oxford: Clarendon Press, 1971), 262 note 2, 267 note 2, 274; Malcolm Richardson, 'Hoccleve in His Social Context', *Chaucer Review*, 20/4 (1986), 318–19, 321; J. A. Burrow, *Thomas Hoccleve* (Aldershot: Variorum, 1994), iv, 7 note 24, 12 note 46; 2. Hethe: Brown, 'The Privy Seal Clerks', 262 note 2, 267 note 2, 268; Richardson, 'Hoccleve in His Social Context', 318; Burrow, *Thomas Hoccleve*, iv, 3, 7 note 24, 9, 11; and 3. Bailey: Brown, 'The Privy Seal Clerks', 262 note 2, 267 note 2, 268; Richardson, 'Hoccleve in His Social Context', 31 (mistakenly given as 'Lawrence Bailay'); Burrow, *Thomas Hoccleve*, iv, 7 note 24, 11 note 43, 12 note 46.

[3] There are three known letters signed by Offord, two of which are personal: a French letter to the Privy Seal and council clerk Robert Frye, preserved in the cache of Frye letters in TNA E 28/29, probably written by Offord (it is signed 'J. O.'), printed in Brown, 'The Privy Seal Clerks', 274; and an English letter from Sens in France, dated 6 June 1420, no

Both are also connected to writing produced outside of the Privy Seal office. Offord appears to be referenced as 'offord' in the margin on fol. 49r in the sole complete holograph manuscript of the *Series*, Durham, MS Cosin V. iii. 9, whereas Hethe received 66s. on 22 February 1422 for having acquired an impressive sixty-six quires of calf skins to write a bible for Henry V.[4] That Hethe was chosen to copy a bible is not surprising because he was an accomplished Latin clerk who wrote the elegant copy of the extensive Treaty of Troyes for Henry's chancellor in Normandy, John Kemp, now at the Archives nationales in Paris (AE III 254, *olim* J 646 15), dated 21 May 1420.[5] I will return to Hethe and Offord later, but there are good reasons to remain with Bailey for the time being. Although he may be the least known of these three clerks, Bailey emerges as the most significant person for clarifying Hoccleve's circumstances in the last years of his life.

John Bailey's will has survived in TNA PROB 11/2B/363, but has gone unnoticed, probably because his name is very common, and nothing in the opening section of the will connects him with the Privy Seal. The will of John Bailey of St Clement Danes is dated 6

longer surviving in the badly damaged BL Cotton MS Caligula D V, printed by Thomas Rymer in *Foedera*, ed. George Holmes, 3rd edn (The Hague: J. Neaulme, 1743), 8.1–ii, 3:177. A further document from France, signed at Bois de Vincennes under the Privy Seal on 27 August 1422, also survives in Offord's hand (TNA C 81/669/1204). A number of letters signed by Hethe are extant. He produced the significant Treaty of Troyes document in Paris, Archives nationales, AE III 254 (*olim* J 646 15), and a privy seal warrant on 19 December 1419 at Rouen (TNA C 81/557/910) (see Pierre Chaplais, *English Medieval Diplomatic Practice: Part I, Documents and Interpretation* (London: H. M. Stationery Office, 1982), i, 2:636, note 331). There are also two letters, both dated 8 October 1420, from Melun: these are TNA C 81/1365/24 and C 81/1543/21. They have been calendared in John Lavan Kirby, *Calendar of Signet Letters of Henry IV and Henry V (1399–1422)* (London: H. M. Stationery Office, 1978), 184, and printed by John H. Fisher, Malcolm Richardson, and Jane L. Fisher, *An Anthology of Chancery English* (Knoxville, TN: University of Tennessee Press, 1984), 131–2.

[4] The reference to Offord has been discussed by J. A. Burrow and A. I. Doyle, eds, *Thomas Hoccleve: A Facsimile of the Autograph Verse Manuscripts*, EETS SS 19 (Oxford: Oxford University Press for EETS, 2002), xxxi; H. K. S. Killick, 'Thomas Hoccleve as Poet and Clerk' (unpublished PhD, University of York, 2010), 180; and Rory Critten, *Author, Scribe, and Book in Late Medieval English Literature* (Cambridge: D. S. Brewer, 2018), 63–5. For the payment to Hethe, see Frederick Devon, ed., *Issues of the Exchequer* (London: Murray, 1837), 372.

[5] The document is printed in Chaplais, *English Medieval Diplomatic Practice*, i, 2:629–36.

November 1420 and was proved five days later, on 11 November. In this will Bailey makes significant bequests to Hoccleve and his wife. But before I discuss this new information, I shall adduce evidence that correctly identifies this John Bailey as Hoccleve's colleague at the Privy Seal. Bailey's Westminster parish was St Clement Danes, and the parish church itself was located exactly opposite Chester Inn, where Hoccleve and numerous Privy Seal clerks lived at the time.[6] Furthermore, the first bequest in Bailey's will is made to the rector of Middleton Cheney, in the diocese of Lincoln. On 28 October 1399, Bailey was presented by privy seal to the parish church of Middleton Cheney as his benefice.[7] Crucially, though, his eventual burial site confirms the identification of Bailey of St Clement Danes with the Privy Seal clerk John Bailey.

In his will, Bailey expresses the wish to be buried in the Carmelite Priory on Fleet Street before the image of the Salutation of the Blessed Virgin: 'In p*ri*mis lego an*im*am mea*m* deo o*mni*potenti et b*ea*te Marie et omnib*us* s*anc*tis eius et corpus meu*m* ad sepeliend*um* [burial] cora*m* [before] ymagine salutac*ion*is b*ea*te Marie in eccl*es*ia f*ratr*um Carme-lit*arum* in Fletestrete londoniarum'[8] (First, I bequeath my soul to omnipotent God and blessed Mary and all His saints and my body to be buried before the image of the Salutation of Blessed Mary in the Carmelite Priory in London's Fleet Street). However, this wish is conditional on Bailey's executors being able to secure his preferred burial site for 'a reasonable' amount of money, 6s 8d: 'si executor*es* mei cu*m* fori*bus* ibi*de*m concordar*i* pot*er*int per co*m*pete*n*te*m* s*u*mma p*er* s*e*cura sepulcri mei et p*er* sex solid*os* et octo denar*ios* *per* fractur*a* t*er*re ib*ide*m et si hoc adquirere' (if my executors are able to secure this burial site for my tomb for a reasonable sum and obtain a portion of the ground for 6s 8d). If the executors fail to secure his preferred burial site for this sum ('no*n* pot*er*int p*er* s*u*mma p*re*dic*t*a'), then he wishes that his body be laid to rest 'near the altar called Hatton Altar in the church of the Franciscan Priory in Newgate, London': 't*u*nc volo q*uo*d corp*us*

[6] 'At Chestres In, right faste by the Stronde, / As I lay in my bed upon a nyght', Thomas Hoccleve, *The Regiment of Princes*, ed. Charles Ramsay Blyth (Kalamazoo, MI: Medieval Institute Publications, 1999), ll. 5–6.

[7] *Calendar of the Patent Rolls: Henry IV, 1399–1401* (London: H. M. Stationery Office, 1903), 24.

[8] TNA PROB 11/2B/363. All translations from the will are my own.

meu*m* sepeliatur cora*m* altari vocat*o* Hatton aweter in eccl*es*ia fratru*m* Minor*um* infra newgate Londoni*arum*'.

It turns out that Bailey's executors did not succeed in persuading the Carmelite friars, and he was indeed buried in his second choice of final resting place, the Franciscan Priory in Newgate. The surviving records of the priory show that Bailey was buried 'in the seventh bay in S. Francis' Chapel, i.e., near the west end of the Chapel'.[9] The altar was endowed by Brother Thomas Hatton, 'who did much good in the priory' ('qui multa bona fecit in conventu'). Hatton died a year before Bailey, on 20 November 1419, and was buried in the fifth bay in the chapel.[10] The Register of the Grey Friars of London confirms that the John Bailey interred in the seventh bay of the chapel of St Francis was indeed the Privy Seal clerk John Bailey: 'Et ad sinistram eorum jacet sub lapide Johannes Bayly, quondam vnus clericorum de priuato Sigillo domini Regis Henrici 5ti: qui obiit in festo sancti Leonardi Ao Regni eiusdem Regis octauo'[11] (And to his left under the stone lies John Bailey, a former clerk of the Privy Seal of the Lord King Henry V, who died on the feast of St Leonard in the eighth year of this king [6 November 1420]).[12] Having established the identity of John Bailey of St Clement Danes as Hoccleve's fellow clerk at the Privy Seal, it is now worth examining the poet's role in Bailey's will.

The will itself is unusually long for someone of Bailey's social status, and the majority of the document amounts to a list of mostly minor bequests to his relatives. Many of these gifts are necklaces and other jewellery, though a few more substantial items, such as a two-horse cart, are also included. The list begins with a small bequest of vestments to the rector of Middleton Cheney, Bailey's Lincolnshire benefice: 'It*em* do et lego R*e*ctori de Middilton Chenduyt et p*a*rochi*us* ib*ide*m et successor*es* suis inp*er*p*etu*um vn*um* vestimentu*m* cu*m* les Orfreours eiusd*e*m h*ab*ent sig*n*um vel fane*m* et Ihc de auro' (Next I bequeath and

[9] C. L. Kingsford, 'Additional Material for the History of the Grey Friars, London', in *Collectanea Franciscana II*, ed. C. L. Kingsford (Manchester: Manchester University Press, 1922), 90.

[10] Kingsford, 'Additional Material', 90.

[11] C. L. Kingsford, *The Grey Friars of London: Their History with the Register of Their Convent and an Appendix of Documents* (Manchester: Manchester University Press, 1915), 99.

[12] The translation is mine.

leave in perpetuity to the rector and parish priest of Middleton Cheney and his successors a vestment with orphrey[13] [detailed embroidery] featuring a sign or emblem and IHC in gold). A gift of money to the same rector follows. The nature and sequence of bequests to the rector of Middleton Cheney conforms to a characteristic pattern in similarly beneficed clerics. Leaving vestments and money to one's benefice belongs to the formal, fixed opening sequence of a clerical will. The ensuing list of beneficiaries mainly consists of relatives from Bailey's Lancashire family—the Clitheroes and Shirburnes—and other regional families from his home parish in Mitton (now Great Mitton in the Ribble Valley in Lancashire). However, the beneficiary who spearheads Bailey's list and who is by far the most generously treated individual in this will is Thomas Hoccleve.

Immediately after completing the fixed sequence of bequests that ends with the rector of Middleton Cheney, Bailey turns to Hoccleve (Fig. 7): 'Item do et lego Thome Occlyf vnu*m* standy*nge* Byker*e* de argento cu*m* coop*er*tor*is* eiusd*em*' (Next I bequeath and leave Thomas Hoccleve a standing beaker cup of silver with a cover of the same). This is obviously a personal gift, singling out Hoccleve above Bailey's family members. Its placing may suggest that Bailey too was a member of the Temple dining club, the 'Court of Good Company'.[14] If this is correct, then there perhaps may also be embedded references to the Court of Good Company in Hoccleve's 1408–10 *Balade to Henry Sommer*. In the

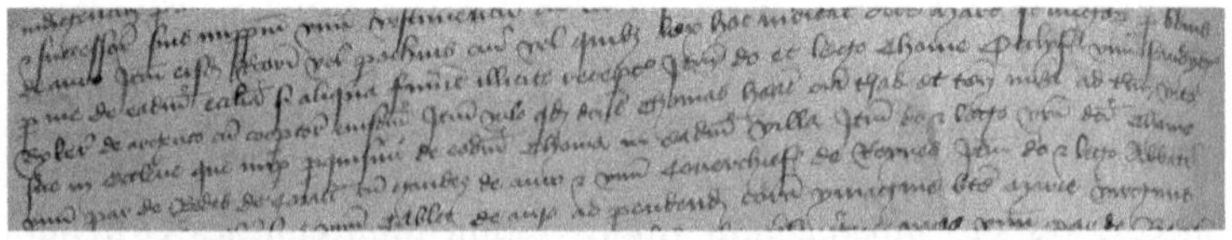

FIG 7 London, TNA PROB 11/2B/363. The will of John Bailey of St Clement Danes, 6 November 1420.

[13] William St John Hope and E. G. Cuthbert, *English Liturgical Colors* (London: SPCK, 1918), 265; for other examples of vestments with orphrey, see *passim*.

[14] For Hoccleve's membership, and that of Henry Somer, see Burrow, *Thomas Hoccleve*, iv, 28–9.

next line Bailey appears to secure Hoccleve's income for the remainder of his life: 'Item volo *quod dicte* Thomas *habeat omnia terras* et tene*menta* ad *termin*um vite sue in Occleue que nup*er* p*er*quisiui de eadem Thoma in eadem villa' (I will that the said Thomas will have until the end of his life all my lands and houses in Hockliffe which I had lately bought from the same Thomas in the same village). This remarkable and unique bequest is followed by another personal gesture to the Hoccleves: 'Item do et lego vxor*is* d*icte* Thome vnu*m* par de Bedes de Corall cu*m* gaudez de auro et vnu*m* couerchieff de Reynes' (Next I bequeath and leave the wife of the said Thomas a pair of coral rosary beads with large ornamental beads of gold and a kerchief of Rennes cloth). Rennes cloth was a finely woven fabric considered a luxury item at the time. Again, the combination of the kerchief and the exquisite rosary left to Hoccleve's wife overshadows the list of gifts left to the members of Bailey's family in the remainder of the will: those who are bequeathed jewellery receive at most only a rosary. The testament then moves on to the Abbot of Sawley and Bailey's relatives, none of whom receives any land or property.

It is hard to overstate the bespoke character, sheer magnitude, and privileged place in Bailey's testamentary order of the three bequests to the Hoccleve household. First, the gifts to Hoccleve's wife exceed those made to other women in Bailey's testament; second, the initial position of Hoccleve in this will and the extent of the bequests made to him and his wife point to a close relationship with the testator; and, finally, this will identifies Hoccleve as having owned, sold, and owned again property in Hockliffe, the Bedfordshire village from which his name is thought to have been derived. He may thus have been born there or had inherited the land from his parents. This does not, of course, preclude the possibility that he is the same Thomas Hoccleve, son of William Hoccleve, who is mentioned in a 1408 London transaction discovered by Linne Mooney and Estelle Stubbs.[15] But Bailey's will shows that Hoccleve did have ties to and certainly owned property in Hockliffe. His name, therefore, follows the same pattern as John Bailey, who, as I have been able subsequently to establish, came from Bailey, a hamlet near Mitton parish in Lancashire, and who appears to have

[15] Estelle Stubbs and Linne Mooney, 'A Record Identifying Thomas Hoccleve's Father', *Journal of the Early Book Society*, 14 (2011), 233–7.

been related to the Clitheroe and Shirburne families of Stonyhurst (Bailey may have been a brother of Richard de Bailey, later Richard de Shirburne).[16] Other families from the Craven area of Yorkshire, which was administratively a part of Lancashire, are also mentioned: Whalley, de Lenesay, and Knolles. As for Hoccleve, whose surname should now perhaps be pronounced 'Hockliffe', the land and buildings he receives in the testament seem to have been an attempt to make him financially secure in his final years, particularly as the fact that he had only recently sold these lands to Bailey may suggest that he had needed to raise cash at the time. Hoccleve's sale of this land cannot have taken place more than a few years before 1420 ('nup*er* p*er*quisiui') and could therefore be taken as an indication of his continued financial difficulties.[17] Being granted his old land and properties again is particularly generous, especially as Bailey does not leave land or houses to any other individual. He did, however, own a certain amount of property: in addition to Hockliffe, his will speaks of possessions in London, Lancashire, and Kent.

In this context, Bailey's earlier purchase of Hoccleve's holdings in Hockliffe stands out as an unusual acquisition that disrupts the ownership pattern of his other land and tenements. That Bailey had goods and property in London is obvious given his residence and place of work there. The Lancashire holdings have family ties and may very well have been his inheritance. The lands in Kent are tied to agricultural items, and servants are mentioned in connection with them; all this points to a farm or farms held as an investment. But buying the land in

[16] On Richard de Shirburne (d. 1441) (formerly de Bailey) see Charles Davies Sherborn, *A History of the Family of Sherborn* (London: Mitchell and Hughes, 1901), 12–17. The Agnes de Shirborne in Bailey's will may be Richard's wife Agnes (d. 1444), whose will is printed in Sherborn, *A History of the Family of Sherborn*, 15–16; and *Testamenta Eboracensia* (London: J. B. Nichols, 1836), 2:75–6 and 105–6. See also C. A. Newdigate, 'The Chantry of St John Baptist at Bailey', *Transactions of the Historic Society of Lancashire and Cheshire*, 68 (1916), 121, 135–6 and Thomas Dunham Whitaker, *The History and Antiquities of the Deanery of Craven, in the County of York*, 2nd edn (London: Nichols, 1812), 20. John Bailey could also have been the son of John de Bailey (John Brownbill and William Farrer, *A History of the County of Lancaster* (London: Constable, 1912), vii, 4).

[17] Hoccleve regularly deploys his supposed penury as an effective literary device (Robert J. Meyer-Lee, 'Hoccleve and the Apprehension of Money', *Exemplaria*, 13/1 (2001), 173–214).

Hockliffe—a sole village in Bedfordshire—seems likely to have been a gesture for a friend. A later passage in Bailey's will perhaps holds a part of the answer to why Hoccleve sold his Hockliffe property to Bailey in the first place: 'It*e*m volo q*uo*d iiii libre de ill*a* vii l*ibr*i in Occleue michi debit*ur* debitoribu*s* p*ar*donent*ur* et q*uo*d sexaginta s*olidos* residu*os* de*mitt*it*ur* ad inueniend*um* quend*a*m cap*ellanum* apud Londoni*um* celebratur p*ro* an*im*a mea et an*im*abu*s* sup*ra* d*icti*s quond*a*m ill*a* lv s*olidos* durabu*ntur*' (Next I will that £4 of the £7 owed to me in Hockliffe by my debtors be written off and that the remaining 60s [£3] be made over to find a chaplain in London to celebrate [masses] for my soul and the souls of those mentioned above for as long as these 60s will last). The collective debt amounting to £7 from Bailey's tenants in Hockliffe is not insignificant. If some or all of this outstanding amount dated from the period of Hoccleve's ownership of these properties, then his sale to Bailey may have been a means to ease his own cash flow. Now that the will returns the lands in Hockliffe to their former owner, this passage can only have been meant as instruction for Hoccleve himself, since Bailey's Bedfordshire debtors can hardly have been expected to make arrangements for funeral masses to be celebrated in London. Besides, these debtors have now become Hoccleve's tenants again.

There is one further reference in the will to the terms on which Hoccleve was to hold the lands in Hockliffe. The bequest itself states that Hoccleve may enjoy these lands and properties as a leasehold 'ad t*ermin*um vite sue' (until the end of his life), and later in the will Bailey specifies that all his land be sold except for that which is located in Hockliffe: 'It*e*m volo q*uo*d o*mn*ia t*erre* et ten*ementa* mea infra regum anglie p*er* omnes executore*es* meos vendant*ur* ac Rem*is*sio dict*e* tene*menta* de Occleue ad quend*am* cap*tum* p*er*petuum in dict*e* eccl*e*sia de Mitton' (Next I will that all my land and properties throughout the kingdom of England be sold by my executors except for the said houses in Hockliffe which are to be seized from a certain person [Hoccleve] in perpetuity by the said church of Mitton). Here Bailey ensures that after Hoccleve's death the land in Hockliffe will revert to his home parish in Mitton in Lancashire, expressly protecting Hoccleve's enjoyment of these possessions for the remainder of his life by exempting them from his blanket instructions to his executors to sell all the land he owns 'throughout the kingdom of England'.

Dating the *Series*

Bailey's extraordinarily preferential treatment of Hoccleve strongly suggests a close friendship between the two men. The nature and extent of the testamentary bequests to the poet and his wife are remarkable, while the unusual character of Hockliffe in Bailey's property portfolio indicates that this acquisition was to ease his friend's financial situation.

With Bailey's death in November 1420, Hoccleve lost a close friend or, at the very least, an old colleague with whom he had worked closely over more than two decades and to whom he had every reason to be grateful for the remainder of his life. Thus, the occasion and setting of the *Series*, which is believed to have been composed at this time, calls for reassessment. In what follows, I will suggest that although the *Series* may be Hoccleve's attempt to justify his own social reintegration following an illness that had already passed five years earlier, it is also a sequence of poems prompted by grief for a friend and structured by a year-long cycle of mourning.

John Burrow, following Johan Kern, pushed back to November 1419 the date at which Hoccleve is thought to have composed the *Series*.[18] Burrow did so based on the internal reference in the *Dialogue* that the Hoccleve persona, whom I shall call 'Thomas' to comply with James Simpson's distinction between writer and narrator,[19] put quill to parchment as soon as he heard that Duke Humphrey of Gloucester had returned from France:

> Yee sikir, freend, ful treewe is your deemynge;
> For him it is þat I this book shal make.
> As blyue as þat I herde of his comynge
> Fro France, I penne and ynke gan to take,

[18] J. A. Burrow, ed., *Thomas Hoccleve's Complaint and Dialogue*, EETS OS 313 (Oxford: Oxford University Press, 1999), lvii–lviii. As early as 1916, Kern first proposed setting the *Complaint* and *Series* in 1419 (J. H. Kern, 'Die Datierung von Hoccleve's *Dialog*', *Anglia*, 1916/40 (1916), 370–3).

[19] James Simpson, 'Madness and Texts: Hoccleve's *Series*', in *Chaucer and Fifteenth-Century Poetry*, ed. Julia Boffey and Janet Cowen (London: King's College London, Centre for Late Antique and Medieval Studies, 1991), 17. This is also the convention established in the study of Margery Kempe following the lead of Lynn Staley, 'Margery Kempe: Social Critic', *Journal of Medieval and Renaissance Studies*, 22 (1992), 159–84; and *Margery Kempe's Dissenting Fictions* (University Park, PA: Penn State Press, 1994).

And my spirit I made to awake,
Þat longe lurkid hath in ydilnesse
For any swich labour or bisynesse.
(II. 540–6)[20]

Burrow draws attention to the accompanying line in the margin of fol. 19v in the Durham manuscript ('Scilicet de secundo reditu suo de Francia' (That is [concerning] his second return from France)), noting that this passage refers to Duke Humphrey's second return from France in late 1419 and that the fictionalized conversation is therefore taking place during Humphrey's first regency, since Humphrey is said to be regent at the time ('Vnto my lord þat now is lieutenant, / My lord of Gloucestre? Is it nat so?', II. 533–4).[21] The duke governed on Henry V's behalf during the king's absence in France, that is, from 30 December 1419 to early February 1421.[22] A little later, the friend reveals that 'now the holy seson is of Lente' (II. 662), which Burrow finds to be chronologically inconsistent, given Hoccleve's reference in the *Complaint* to late November and the last All Saints' Day on 1 November (I. 17 and 55).[23] This inconsistency, however, is actually explained in the opening lines of the *Dialogue*:

Opne thy dore! Me thynkith ful yore
Syn I thee sy. What, man, for Goddes ore
Come out, for this quarter I nat thee sy.
(II. 3–7)

The friend explicitly states that he has not seen Thomas for a quarter, that is, a quarter of a year. It is surprising that this reference has received so little critical attention, especially because the *Series* is a sequence of poems that insist on their temporal reality and that embed themselves in a consistently progressing annual chronology—All Saints' Day, late November, Lent, and Easter, with references to the preceding September and other shorter durations. The chronological

[20] All quotations from the *Complaint* and *Dialogue* are taken from Burrow, *Hoccleve's Complaint and Dialogue*. I have added punctuation where Burrow has a forward slash to mark mid-line caesurae. I also follow the practice of consecutively numbering the five parts of the *Series* using roman numerals.

[21] Burrow, *Hoccleve's Complaint and Dialogue*, lvii–lviii.

[22] Burrow, *Hoccleve's Complaint and Dialogue*, lvii–lviii.

[23] Burrow, *Hoccleve's Complaint and Dialogue*, lviii.

inconsistency Burrow speaks of is resolved by this very passage: Thomas was in his rooms, dwelling on the *Complaint* for a quarter, that is, a full three months. This duration directly bears on the rationale behind the *Series*, and I will return to this point below.

Almost every commentator on the opening stanza of the *Complaint* has noted its deep seasonal setting:

> Aftir þat heruest inned had his sheeues,
> And þat the broun sesoun of Mighelmesse
> Was come and gan, the trees robbe of hir leeues
> Þat greene had been and in lusty fresshnesse,
> And hem into colour of yelownesse
> Had died and doun throwen vndir foote,
> Þat chaunge sank into myn herte roote.
>
> (I. 1–7)

This is a *vanitas*-laden autumn opening. One common observation is that it presents a disquieting alternative to the bouncy April lines in Chaucer's *Canterbury Tales.*[24] It seems to me that Hoccleve's rhyme royal opening, with its darker colours, invocation of decay and mortality, and restless run-on lines with heavy initial stress, clearly prefigures the dystopian nature opening in T. S. Eliot's *Wasteland*, which is equally fitted into seven lines:

> April is the cruellest month, breeding
> Lilacs out of the dead land, mixing
> Memory and desire, stirring
> Dull roots with spring rain.
> Winter kept us warm, covering
> Earth in forgetful snow, feeding
> A little life with dried tubers.
>
> (1–7)

Surely Eliot borrowed the design for these lines from his fellow London clerk-poet Hoccleve, rather than just from Chaucer. But the analogy with Eliot's stanza teases out the underlying motif in Hoccleve's opening—Eliot's doomed spring is held back in its promise by mortality or, rather, by the memory of mortality: the 'dead land' was covered

[24] For instance, Burrow, *Hoccleve's Complaint and Dialogue*, 73, notes to ll. 1–14.

in 'forgetful snow'. But there is no snow to spread over the memory of the dead in the *Complaint*. Cruel autumn goes unchecked, felling the good in their prime: 'the trees robbe of hir leeues / Þat greene had been and in lusty fresshnesse'—the trees were robbed of their leaves when they least expected it—cruelly, 'leeues' bitterly puns on 'lives'. The second stanza of the *Complaint* no longer veils its preoccupation with mortality: 'Deeth vndir foote shal him thriste adoun, / Þat is euery wightes conclusioun' (I. 13–14). As in the *Wasteland* opening, death arrives lexically in the first stanza, though in a pun on 'dyed' as the leaves are flattened and pounded by the elemental violence of Michaelmas season: 'And hem into colour of yelownesse / Had died and doun throwen vndir foote'. Michaelmas, or to be precise, 'thende of Nouembre' (I. 17), suddenly seizes life, colours it with its sickly hue, only to end it. This very realization makes Thomas so pensive: 'Þat chaunge sank into myn herte roote'. 'Þat' is not a demonstrative pronoun here; it is a causal, emphatic *Þat* explained by the crushing presence of sudden, wasteful death.

The Michaelmas season invoked here, I believe, is not 1419 but 1420, and Thomas's thoughts about death would then be triggered by the passing of his friend John Bailey on 11 November of that year. Bailey's death was sudden and unexpected, at least in June 1420. On 6 June, their fellow Privy Seal clerk John Offord, who was then based in France in the Norman section of the Privy Seal office, sent a letter from the siege of Sens. Offord was one of the four clerks in Hoccleve's petitionary poem to Henry Somer, quoted above. He ends this letter with greetings to his Westminster friends: 'Comande me to Abel Hoet, and Bayly, and to Sir J. Brokholes, and to grete weel Richard Priour (whom the fayr Town of Vernon on Seene Gretith Weel also) and Will. Albtoo Lark, and all the Meyne, and Kyng Barbour and hys Wyf'.[25] 'Abel Hoet' is the Privy Seal clerk Abel Hessill; 'Will. Albtoo' is William Alberton, another Privy Seal clerk, and 'Bayly' must be John Bailey. The other people can be identified, too, except for 'Lark' and 'Kyng Barbour and hys Wyf'. 'Lark' may be a surname or a nickname (perhaps for an early riser?), and it would be droll to think that 'Kyng Barbour and hys Wyf'

[25] Rymer, *Foedera*, 8.1–ii, vol. 9, consulted online at https://www.british-history.ac.uk/rymer-foedera/vol9/pp910-921. The letter was once contained in the now severely damaged BL Cotton MS Caligula D V.

could be Hoccleve and his wife, since the king's barber was with Offord in France, but Hoccleve could also be included in 'all the Meyne'—the 'gang'. But the point here is that Bailey is simply greeted by Offord without any reference to his condition. Bailey, then, it seems was taken by Michaelmas 'in lusty fresshnesse'.

In a self-referential, indexical gesture that would have been recognized by Hoccleve's familiar Westminster audience, the autumn opening of the *Complaint* wistfully echoes the stanza in the *Balade to Somer* with which I opened this chapter and which playfully teases the under-treasurer's name:

> We, your seruantes, Hoccleue & Baillay,
> Hethe & Offorde, yow beseeche & preye,
> 'Haasteth our heruest as soone as yee may!'
> For fere of stormes our wit is aweye;
> Were our seed Inned wel we mighten pleye,'
> And vs desporte & synge & make game,
> And yit this rowndel shul we synge & seye
> In trust of yow & honour of your name.[26]
>
> (25–32)

To my knowledge, only David Watt, one of Hoccleve's most perceptive readers, has noticed this link between the *Balade* and the *Complaint*.[27] 'Heruest' appears in both stanzas, as does the gathering of the harvest, 'inned'. While in the *Balade* 'heruest' stands for the Privy Seal clerks' income—the fruits of their scribal labour—in the *Complaint* 'heruest' is a memory, cast aside by the savage onset of Michaelmas. Watt astutely infers that 'the similarities in diction between this poem and the *Complaint* arise in part because both imply they are meant to circulate among those at work in the Privy Seal and elsewhere in Westminster Hall'.[28] It is hard to imagine anything but a confidential audience for this work. However, the link between the *Balade* and the *Complaint* is even more intimate, and the intended audience therefore even smaller, limited to those who knew Bailey. The *Balade* stanza captures the single

[26] All references to Hoccleve's shorter poems outside of the *Series* are to *Hoccleve's Works: The Minor Works*.

[27] David Watt, *The Making of Thomas Hoccleve's Series* (Liverpool: Liverpool University Press, 2013), 30–1.

[28] Watt, *The Making of Thomas Hoccleve's Series*, 31.

instance in which Hoccleve names Bailey in his surviving oeuvre, and he does so right next to his own name in a stanza that now appears to foreshadow and lexically anticipate the opening lines of the *Complaint*. Even more telling is the exclamation in l. 28 that 'for fere of stormes our wit is aweye'. This metaphor of severing himself from his wit resembles Hoccleve's pathologising idiom in the *Complaint*, where it is the stinging storms of Michaelmas following 'heruest' that motivate Thomas to revisit his illness, which he repeatedly articulates as his wit leaving and returning to him, just as 'our wit is aweye' in the *Balade*: 'My wit and I han been of swich accord' (I. 59), 'my wit were hoom come ageyn' (I. 64), 'my wit is goon' (I. 207), 'Debat is now noon twixt me and my wit, / Althogh þat ther were a disseuerance / As for a tyme betwixt me and it' (I. 247–9), etc. His 'wit' leaving him is a central conceit of the *Complaint*—the ultimate fear of fracturing the self as felt by sociocentric persons—and it would appear that the Bailey stanza in the *Balade* already contains in miniature all central elements of the *Complaint*.

The November stanzas at the start of the *Complaint* are not an instance of run-of-the-mill *memento mori* but appear to amount to a string of precise chronological and lexical references to the death of a friend, framed in the premodern figurative language of transience, the only set of apposite expressions available to a fifteenth-century poet. Bailey died on 11 November, so the setting of Hoccleve's opening bouts at 'thende of Nouembre' (I. 17) is entirely appropriate. What is more, the 'quarter' during which Thomas was locked in his chamber in the *Complaint* and during which his friend did not see him supports the Bailey setting of the *Complaint*. In 1421, Easter was early, on 23 March, so Lent began much earlier than in other years, namely on 9 February. Hence, in this year, exactly ninety days separated 11 November, Bailey's death, from the beginning of Lent on 9 February. In other words, when the friend says at the beginning of the *Dialogue* that he had not seen Thomas for a quarter and that it is now Lent, this reference works perfectly for a setting of the *Complaint* in late November 1420 and the *Dialogue* in February 1421. Measured from the beginning of Lent, the *Complaint* and *Dialogue* are separated by much more than a quarter in 1419, but they are separated by *exactly* one quarter in 1420. During the *Complaint*, Thomas may have been in the first phase of mourning, and precisely a quarter after Bailey's death his friend visits him, just as the liturgical year enters a new phase.

I am of course not advocating a one-dimensional form of biographical or autobiographical criticism here. Simpson has convincingly argued for Hoccleve's narrator—Thomas—to be read as a literary construct devised to reconcile that which Hoccleve could not reconcile in his own life.[29] Reading Thomas in a similar vein, Ethan Knapp has Hoccleve's persona compensate for the bureaucratic anonymity in Westminster,[30] but this argument needs to be weighed against the practice of adding scribal signatures in the course of the fifteenth century. As a deictic persona Thomas springs from Hoccleve and remains umbilically tied to his originator not because Hoccleve wishes for his audience to conflate his narrative and biological selves, but precisely because, in a characteristically premodern feint, Hoccleve has his literary self accomplish what he as a person has repeatedly failed to achieve:

> Hoccleve's problem as an author is that his voice is publicly regarded as being unstable after his madness. What he tries to do in the *Dialogue* especially is to convince his public, in the person of the friend, that his voice is, in the most essential respects, stable. He does not want his madness to become the subject of his poetry; instead he wants his position as teller regarded as stable, at least as regards his sanity.[31]

But this strategy relies on similarity not difference: for Hoccleve's narrative device to work, Thomas must be recognizable as Hoccleve; his struggles, fears, and situatedness in fifteenth-century reality must correspond 'in the most essential respects' to those of the writer. Hence, Thomas is not Hoccleve's literary alter ego as such, but his literary indexical self, an instrument to process experience, at once rooted in reality yet not a part of it. In other words, Thomas, as so many named medieval narrator-selves, is a synecdoche that represents and is *in* the writer, but does not form a simple holographic avatar. Thus, the relationship between such medieval narrator-selves and their writers is equivalent to that between a physical manuscript and the text it conveys: a physical instance of a writer's text varies from and does

[29] Simpson, 'Madness and Texts', 15–29.

[30] Ethan Knapp, *The Bureaucratic Muse: Thomas Hoccleve and the Literature of Late Medieval England* (Philadelphia, PA: Pennsylvania State University Press, 1997), 36.

[31] Simpson, 'Madness and Texts', 22.

not fully capture its original idea, and each manuscript—being ambigraphic, in Sonja Drimmer's words—is somehow pressed into service to perform a task or achieve an aim to which the text it carries cannot always be reduced.[32] Thomas is therefore a functional, recognizable, yet fictionalized incarnation of Hoccleve. It follows then that the mechanism behind Thomas as explained by Simpson must rely on a small, familiar audience with access to Hoccleve himself. After all, how does one experience or 'taaste and assaye' (I. 210) the literary Thomas if not by engaging the biological Hoccleve in a conversation? This principle is borne out by Watt's study of the material aspects of the *Series*: 'he can circulate his "Complaint" as a deed which others can 'taaste'.[33] Hoccleve's texts, personae, and holographs complement him; they are prostheses (in the sense in which Candace Barrington applies to his term to Gower's Trentham manuscript),[34] built around his person and meant to be completed by his presence.

By moving the composition date for this part of the *Series* from 1419–21 to 1420–1, there emerge two questions, both in connection with references to Duke Humphrey. My proposed dating still falls into the period after Humphrey's second return from France, and just toward the end of his first regency. Burrow reads ll. 541–3 of the *Dialogue* as occurring immediately after the Duke's return from France in 'late November or December 1419':[35]

> For him it is þat I this book shal make.
> As blyue as þat I herde of his comynge
> Fro France, I penne and ynke gan to take.

Perhaps 'blyue' indeed means 'soon', 'quickly', but it could equally denote 'readily', 'gladly', suggesting that Hoccleve thought of making this book, the *Series*, with the same gladness and delight that he had felt on hearing of the duke's return from the campaign in France. However, Hoccleve could not have started the *Complaint* immediately on Duke Humphrey's return from France because the poem is set in late

[32] On 'ambigraphic', see Drimmer, 'The Manuscript as an Ambigraphic Medium'. See also my discussion of Drimmer's term in the Introduction.

[33] Watt, *The Making of Thomas Hoccleve's Series*, 34.

[34] Barrington, 'The Trentham Manuscript as Broken Prosthesis'.

[35] Burrow, *Hoccleve's Complaint and Dialogue*, 100, note to ll. 542–3.

November whereas the joint instructions to the Duke of Bedford to raise an army and cross into France while Humphrey was asked to return to England were only issued on 21 November 1419.[36] Humphrey was certainly appointed regent on 30 December, but he could not have returned to London before the end of November. In other words, the *Complaint* is not set in November 1419, which preceded Humphrey's second return from France, but in November 1420. Furthermore, the friend remembers that Thomas had promised to write a book for Humphrey last September ('in the monthe of Septembre / Now last, or nat fer from', II. 528–9), but if the duke's return from France only prompted him to do so, then this would be the first genuinely problematic chronological inconsistency in the *Series*. Therefore, the September meant here was surely September 1420, *after* Duke Humphrey's return from France and appointment as regent in December 1419, but *before* the November in which Hoccleve sets the *Complaint*.

Humphrey's regency ended with Henry's return to England on 2 February 1421, but at the start of Lent, 9 February 1421, Humphrey could still have been seen by the friend and Thomas as acting out the final days of the regency ('Vnto my lord þat now is lieutenant, / My lord of Gloucestre? Is it nat so?', II. 533–4). No Privy Council minutes have survived from the period November 1420 to May 1421, but it was actually not until the middle of February 1421 that Henry reached the capital. Although Henry and Catherine of Valois, his queen, landed on 2 February in Dover, she only entered London on 21 February.[37] From Dover Henry instead decided first to visit Canterbury,[38] and he made his formal entry into London as late as 14 February,[39] so until that time it would be perfectly natural for Hoccleve and his friend to speak of Duke Humphrey as acting regent.

[36] The document is TNA C64/11, m. 4d. See Jonathan Sumption, *The Hundred Years War, Volume 4: Cursed Kings* (London: Faber and Faber, 2017), 834, note 30.

[37] William Marx, ed., *An English Chronicle, 1377–1461: Edited from Aberystwyth, National Library of Wales MS 21068 and Oxford, Bodleian Library MS Lyell 34* (Woodbridge: Boydell Press, 2003), 135.

[38] Alfred Leslie Rowse, *Bosworth Field, from Medieval to Tudor England* (Garden City, NY: Doubleday, 1966), 81.

[39] Sumption, *The Hundred Years War IV*, 717.

At any rate, Thomas could not have made any progress following the duke's return in October 1419 since sickness, among other reasons, made him delay the taking up of his work for quite some time:

> He sholde han had it many a day ago;
> But seeknesse and vnlust and othir mo
> Han be the causes of impediment.
> (II. 536–8)

'Many a day ago' can hardly refer to a three-month period, since Thomas would have had to have composed his work before giving it to Humphrey ('han had'), so this line makes much more sense if more time had elapsed between Humphrey's return in late 1419 and Thomas's admission to his friend in Lent that the duke should have received his book 'many a day ago'. A period of over a year, then, to account for composing and the time that would have elapsed following the missed opportunities to present the book make for a much better fit. Finally, there is one more aspect of the dating that merits consideration: if the *Dialogue* is indeed set in early February 1421 and if Thomas can be trusted as a narrator when he says that 'Of age am I fifty wyntir and three' (II. 246), then Hoccleve was born in 1368.

A further implication of moving the composition date for the *Complaint* and the *Series* to the year between the dates proposed by M. C. Seymour (1421–2) and those by Kern and Burrow (1419–20) is the timing of Hoccleve's illness. Since Thomas states that he was cured of his condition five years ago on All Saints, Burrow logically settles for 1414, while Seymour, also following his preferred composition date of 1421, counts back five years to 1416.[40] Linne Mooney prefers a middle way: while agreeing with Burrow's early composition dates, she nevertheless concurs with Seymour's dating of the illness to 1416 partly because Hoccleve's annuity payment was collected by his clerk John Welde on one occasion in 1416.[41] The resulting discrepancy between only three years separating 1416 from 1419, instead of the five given by Hoccleve, argues Mooney, may be an instance of Hoccleve forgetting to update the correct number after he had finished writing the *Complaint*:

[40] *Selections From Hoccleve*, ed. M. C. Seymour (Oxford: Clarendon Press, 1981), xiii.

[41] Linne R. Mooney, 'Some New Light on Thomas Hoccleve', *Studies in the Age of Chaucer*, 29 (2007), 303–4.

> we cannot know whether the single word 'five' [I. 56, where Thomas backdates his recovery] might not also have been changed to update the poem at the time it was presented to the duke. Thus the 1419 start-date for *The Series* cannot be taken as conclusive evidence of a 1414 illness.[42]

But why would he have written 'five' in the first place?

The attractiveness of Mooney's case for 1416 as the year in which Hoccleve overcame his illness persuasively rests on a lacuna in the production of Privy Seal documents written in his hand between August 1415 and late 1416, a much longer span of inactivity than a previous gap in 1414. A potential counterargument is the possibility that Hoccleve may have been in France during these months. August 1415 happened to be the moment at which Henry V crossed for the first time with his invading force into France. Although Hoccleve describes his *Remonstrance against Sir John Oldcastle* as having been written when Henry was in Southampton preparing for the crossing,[43] suggesting that he may have joined the king in France, there is a document in Hoccleve's hand that dates from September of that year and gives the place as Westminster. Also, it seems to me that placing the composition of the *Remonstrance* in Southampton during Henry's delayed embarkation would have been associated at the time with the ad hoc treason trial there of Baron Henry Scrope of Masham and his co-conspirators. After all, the *Remonstrance* is a warning to traitors.

Mooney's 1415–16 gap is supported by Helen Killick's research into Privy Seal records.[44] Killick has found a further 900 records written by Hoccleve in addition to the 100 or so identified by Mooney.[45] Killick's findings confirm the lacuna. Mooney also astutely suggests that Hoccleve's condition may have been caused by overwork, given the high levels of output by the Privy Seal office in the months and weeks in

42 Mooney, 'Some New Light on Thomas Hoccleve', 304.

43 The heading in the holograph manuscript San Marino, Huntington Library MS HM 111, reads on folio 1r: "Ceste feust faicteau temps que le Roy Henri le Vth (que Dieu pardoint) feust a Hampton sur son primer passage vers Harflete'.

44 Killick, 'Thomas Hoccleve as Poet and Clerk'.

45 Killick and Mooney list the Hoccleve records at the end of their respective studies (Killick, 'Thomas Hoccleve as Poet and Clerk'; Mooney, 'Some New Light on Thomas Hoccleve', 293–340).

the run-up to Henry's ambitious first French campaign.[46] To my mind, there are two strong reasons to support this hypothesis. First, Thomas's condition as described by him in the *Complaint* shows signs of many of the symptoms commonly associated with extreme exhaustion and burnout syndrome.[47] Second, if Hoccleve did suffer from burnout—which medieval clerks often labelled as *acedia*, 'sloth'[48]—then it would explain why his friend is so concerned that Thomas take not on too much writing:

> But thy werk hard is to parfourme, I dreede.
> Thy brayn parcas therto nat wole assente.
> (II. 296–7)

And a little later it becomes evident that the friend is less worried about the nature of Thomas's work than its volume:

> I am seur þat thy disposicioun
> Is swich þat thow maist more take on hoonde
> Than I first wende in myn oppinioun,
> By many fold / thankid be Goddes soonde.
> (II. 519–22)

But any modern diagnosis of Hoccleve as refracted through Thomas is fraught with the underlying risk of misinterpreting the porous, indexical premodern self. The clinical psychiatrist Atwood Gaines alerts practitioners to the dangers of understanding the sociocentric indexical self though contemporary assumptions:

> the self is perceived as constituted or 'indexed' by the contextual features of social interaction in diverse situations. As a result, the indexical self does not retain lasting, trans-situational characteristics,

[46] Mooney, 'Some New Light on Thomas Hoccleve', 308. For another understanding of Hoccleve's condition, see Matthew Boyd Goldie, 'Psychosomatic Illness and Identity in London, 1416–1421: Hoccleve's *Complaint* and *Dialogue* with a Friend', *Exemplaria*, 11/1 (1999), 23–52.

[47] For an excellent overview of clerical burnout syndrome in the Middle Ages, see Rainer E. Jehl, '*Acedia* and Burn-Out Syndrome: From an Occupational Vice of the Early Monks to a Psychological Concept in Secularized Professional Life', in *In the Garden of Evil: The Vices and Culture in the Middle Ages*, ed. Richard Newhauser (Toronto: Pontifical Institute of Medieval Studies, 2005), 455–76.

[48] As the vice *acedia*, burnout syndrome had a distinguished history among medieval writers. Jehl, 'Acedia and Burn-Out Syndrome', 455–76. See also Anna K. Schaffner, *Exhaustion: A History* (New York: Columbia University Press, 2016).

> traits, wishes, or needs of its own separate from its relationships and contexts. From a Western psychological perspective this version of the self may be misinterpreted as resistant to treatment. Similarly, the inability to reflect on the self as separate from others could be misunderstood as lack of 'insight'. A sociocentric client who appears to describe him/herself in contradictory ways may also be misconstrued as having borderline personality organization, a manifestation of 'splitting' or compartmentalizing, as in the western defined symptom of paranoia.[49]

It is not difficult to recognize modern misreadings of Hoccleve's illness in these remarks, where we may understand his condition as residing in himself and not in his environment, thus running the risk of interpreting what may have been an episode of burnout as a personality disorder.

Whether it was burnout or a psychological condition, it is entirely possible that he experienced his collapse in the summer of 1415 and took a forced hiatus, and that by 1 November 1415 he was better. The following nine to ten months would then have been dedicated to his continued recovery and staying away from work. 'Recovery' can mean different things to different people, and the information shared by Thomas in the *Series* is autodiagnostic. In the minds of his fellow Privy Seal clerks this would explain why their impression of the magnitude of Hoccleve's illness was enhanced by his prolonged absence. If the *Complaint* is set in late November 1420, following Bailey's death, then Hoccleve would have been cured on 1 November 1415, taking a period of leave from the Privy Seal.

A recovery date of 1 November 1415 almost certainly rules out the speculation that Hoccleve had meant for the date of his recovery to coincide with the opening of the Council of Constance on 1 November 1414, as Vincent Gillespie argues.[50] That said, Gillespie may be correct in suspecting that Hoccleve 'had an eye on the events unfolding in Konstanz':[51] the John Forester or Forster who wrote to Henry V from Constance on 2 February 1417 with a report on the council may have

[49] Gaines, 'Cultural Definitions, Behavior and the Person in American Psychiatry', 182.

[50] Vincent Gillespie, 'Chichele's Church: Vernacular Theology in England after Thomas Arundel', in *After Arundel: Religious Writing in Fifteenth-Century England*, ed. Vincent Gillespie and Kantik Ghosh (Turnhout: Brepols, 2011), 39–40.

[51] Gillespie, 'Chichele's Church', 39.

been the same John Forester who is named as one of the three executors in Bailey's will.[52]

'For hem þat hens shuln wel departe': Grief and Remembrance

The reasons Thomas provides for delaying his work on the *Series* point to the practice of mourning. The narrator gives his reasons as 'seeknesse and vnlust and othir mo' (II. 537). The word 'vnlust' can mean 'idleness' or 'weariness', but under meaning 2 the *MED* gives 'sorrow' or 'grief', as in the fitting and equally Lenten sentence 'I had lenyd me long al a Lentyn tyme / In vnlust of my lyf and lost al my joye' (12–13) from the late fourteenth-century poem *A Bird in the Bishopswood* in the Guildhall MS 25125/32.[53] In fact, Ruth Kennedy, who discovered this poem, notes its similarity to Hoccleve's writing, and although she is thinking of *Le Male Regle*, her observation is equally suited to the *Complaint*: 'especially, perhaps, Hoccleve, as here we find echoes of that poet's recounting of psychological detail, something of the genre of complaint, and a London setting'.[54]

If grief is indeed the trigger for the *Complaint*, then the three months of mourning, that is, the exact quarter that has elapsed between the beginning of the *Complaint* and the start of the *Dialogue*, is not an unusual mourning period for a close relative or a friend, though the most commonly prescribed duration was one year, as the bereaved passed through various stages of grief. Bailey's will specifies the common trental of masses to be celebrated in his memory; a trental amounted to thirty masses over a period of at least thirty days.[55]

52 On the Forester letter, see Gillespie, 'Chichele's Church', 6; and C. M. D. Crowder, 'Correspondence between England and the Council of Constance, 1414–1481', *Studies in Church History*, 1 (1964), 203. A second letter from Forester is listed in Crowder, 'Correspondence', 202.

53 Ruth Kennedy, '"A Bird in Bishopswood": Some Newly-Discovered Lines of Alliterative Verse from the Late Fourteenth Century', in *Medieval Literature and Antiquities: Studies in Honour of Basil Cottle*, ed. Myra Stokes and T. L. Burton (Woodbridge: D. S. Brewer, 1987), 83.

54 Kennedy, '"A Bird in Bishopswood"', 81.

55 Christopher Daniell, *Death and Burial in Medieval England, 1066–1550* (London: Routledge, 1997), 46 and 185.

Then there were also the 60s, or £3, from Bailey's Hockliffe tenants that were to be used for masses in London 'for as long as these 60s will last' (quondam illa lv solidos durabuntur). Bailey envisaged that the 6s 8d he set aside for his tomb would also cover the trental of masses 'throughout the city and environs of London' (Ciuitate londoniensis et in suburbiis eiusdem), but the 60s from Hockliffe should then stretch the additional masses in his memory over the better part of the year. By comparison, the going rate for a trental in early sixteenth-century York was 10s.[56] If 60s would have bought 180 masses a hundred years later, then, even without accounting for inflation, there would be masses sung in Bailey's memory in London for much if not most of 1421. Since Bailey's Hockliffe debtors were now Hoccleve's tenants, Hoccleve would thus have been occupied with making his friend's mourning and remembrance arrangements for that year, particularly because this instruction in Bailey's will places an indirect financial obligation on Hoccleve to commemorate Bailey in addition to an obvious expectation to do so, given Hoccleve's privileged position in Bailey's testament. The Chaucer portrait in the *Regement* may perform a similar function: Drimmer argues that the portrait should be understood as a 'codicological chantry' instead of a more vague act of homage.[57] Hoccleve, it would appear, is accustomed to invoking a very specific part of medieval religious, memorial culture.

Fittingly, the *Complaint* belongs to that widely used late medieval form of the complaint, itself ultimately descended from and rooted in the *planctus*, the dirge or mourning poem.[58] There are many embedded references to mourning and loss in the poem and the *Series* as a whole, starting with Hoccleve's very aptly chosen 'remembraunce':

> For fresshly broghte it to my remembrance
> Þat stablenesse in this world is ther noon.
> (I. 8–9)

[56] Daniell, *Death and Burial*, 46.

[57] Drimmer *The Art of Allusion: Illuminators and the Making of English Literature*, 76–7.

[58] On elegiac and commemorative aspects of Hoccleve's poetry, see Jennifer E. Bryan, 'Hoccleve, the Virgin, and the Politics of Complaint', *PMLA*, 117/5 (2002), 1172–87; and *Looking Inward: Devotional Reading and the Private Self in Late Medieval England* (Philadelphia, PA: University of Pennsylvania Press, 2013), 187–203.

'Remembrance' is not just 'reflection' or 'thought'; it can also denote 'keepsake', 'memento', 'commemoration', 'remembering' (*MED*). It is repeatedly in this sense of remembering and mourning that this poem imagines itself. And to be in mourning at this late stage of life is prudent and part of the *Series*' overall investment in the *ars moriendi*:

> Lond, rente, catel, gold, honour, richesse,
> Þat for a tyme lent been to been ouris,
> Forgo we shole sonner than we gesse.
> (II. 281–3)

These lines, while conveying the transient nature of material possessions, echo some of the bequests received by Hoccleve from Bailey's estate.

But why would a series of poems motivated by grief and by coping with loss begin with a poem preoccupied with the narrator's own sickness and recovery? An answer is again provided by the chronology of the liturgical year that structures the *Series*. One crucial date that pervades this list of poems and binds the *Complaint* to *Learning to Die*, which Christina von Nolcken in my view correctly identifies as lying at the heart of the *Series*,[59] is All Saints' Day, 1 November. In the *Complaint* Hoccleve says that he was cured of his condition on All Saints:

> Made it for to retourne into the place
> Whens it cam which was at Alle Halwemesse,
> Was fiue yeer, neither more ne lesse.
> (I. 54–6)

Starting with the eve before the feast, All Saints marked the sombre celebration of two paired holidays, All Saints on 1 November and All Souls on 2 November, the Day of the Dead, as it was also known.[60]

[59] Christina von Nolcken, '"O, why ne had Y lerned for to die?": *Lerne for to Dye* and the Author's Death in Thomas Hoccleve's *Series*', *Essays in Medieval Studies*, 10 (1993), 27–51. For readings of the *Series* that also prioritize *Learning to Die*, see Hisashi Sugito, 'The Limits of Language and Experience', *Journal of Medieval Religious Cultures*, 39/1 (2013), 43–59, and Amy Appleford, *Learning to Die in London, 1380–1540* (Philadelphia, PA: University of Pennsylvania Press, 2015), 106, 127–36. A penitential reading of the *Series* is offered by Robyn Malo, 'Penitential Discourse in Hoccleve's *Series*', *Studies in the Age of Chaucer*, 34 (2012), 277–305.

[60] Jean-Claude Schmitt, *Ghosts in the Middle Ages: The Living and the Dead in Medieval Society* (Chicago, IL: University of Chicago Press, 1998), 173.

This is certainly how Hoccleve understood this holiday in the centrepiece of the *Series*, *Learning to Die*. In closing his translation from Henry Suso's *Horologium Sapientiae*, Hoccleve comments on the ninth lesson for All Saints, which formed a unity with All Souls:

But as the ixe lesson which is rad
In holy chirche vpon a[ll] halwen day
Witnessith, syn it ioieful is and glad
For hem þat hens shuln wel departe away
And to the blisse go þat lastith ay,
Translate wole Y, nat in rym but prose,
For so it best is, as þat Y suppose.
(IV. 925–31)

If All Souls is the day on which to pray for the souls of the departed, then All Saints is the day on which to pray for those who will ('shuln') depart or who have died and are about to ascend to Heaven.

The joint treatment of these two holidays was common in medieval England, just as it remains so in many Catholic traditions today. The contemporary manuscript Oxford, Bodleian Library MS Ashmole 61, an interlaced miscellany of romances and religious verse, includes a piece on the creation of the feast of All Saints, also known as *The Feasts of All Saints and All Souls*. Following the pattern of including All Souls in the foundation legend of All Saints as described in Jacobus Voragine's *Golden Legend*,[61] the 600-line Middle English poem describes the creation and nature of this joint feast in sequence. Starting with All Saints ('Festum Omnium Sanctorum', l. 1),[62] the text defines this holiday as initiating a 'dubull' or duplex feast:

All Halow Dey that men call,
A dubull fest and ever schall be
Thorowout all Chrystyanté.
(20–2)

In its liturgical significance, All Saints is outranked by its twin, All Souls, which counts as a solemnity, but the author of *The Feast of*

[61] George Shuffelton, ed., *Codex Ashmole 61: A Compilation of Popular Middle English Verse* (Kalamazoo, MI: Medieval Institute Publications, 2008), introduction.

[62] All references to *The Feaṣt of All Saints and All Souls* are taken from the edition by Shuffelton, *Codex Ashmole 61*.

All Saints and All Souls understood 'double' to mean the twinning of All Saints with All Souls:

> The Pope anon, be all asent,
> Ordeynd be hys comandment
> Thorowoute all Crystyanté
> All Halow Dey to halowyd be.
> Double fest to be ever more
> The fyrst dey of November,
> Men for to hallow fro all werkys
> To here servys of prestys and clerkys.
> All Salle Dey be onne the morow
> Fro peynes of purgatory them borow,
> And ever more among mankyndscilic
> To praye for them and have in mynd.
> (567–78)

'Double' here clearly means that All Saints follows the next day ('onne the morow'). The analogous nature of the two feasts is expressed in their combined salvific potential, so that the penitential prayer work of these two days is welded into a single process:

> As all seyntys be halowyd ryght
> To pray for us to God allmyght,
> So all saules in ther maner
> Be relesyd throw prayers here,
> And com to joy of paradys clere.
> (579–83)

In other words, while All Saints offers the devout the possibility to pray to all the saints to intercede on behalf of the departed, so All Souls encourages direct prayers for the departed. Hence, the double feast of All Saints and All Souls was commonly understood, and is still treated, as offering prayers for the departed, first indirectly, then directly. In *Learning to Die*, Thomas, as Amy Appleford has shown, attempts to prepare himself in an individualistic and bespoke way so that the passage of his own soul will not have to rely on others' prayers: 'focusing on shaping the soul to be less reliant on the potentially mechanistic economy of purgatorial prayers, with their attendant social forms of chantries and indulgences, and on the voicing of a poetic version of ascetic identity this reformulated religiosity makes possible'.[63] Perhaps Hoccleve's experience of the countless masses and prayers that were offered for Bailey during the writing of the *Series* prompted him to revise the strategy for his own death.

Therefore, the lesson at the end of *Learning to Die* only appears to make sense if the *Series* has indeed reached the feast of All Saints, that is, 1 November 1421. Why else would Hoccleve break the chronological sequence which is maintained throughout this cycle of poems? Indeed, *Learning to Die* is set later in the year because at the beginning of the next and final part of the *Series*, the *Tale of Jonathas*, the friend refers to Easter as lying in the past:

> 'Thomas,' he seide, 'at Estren þat was last,
> I redde a tale, which Y am agast
> To preye thee, for the laboures sake
> That thow haast had, for to translate and make'.
> (V. 4–7)

Hoccleve's year of mourning has come full circle, after Thomas reaches All Saints' Day with *Learning to Die*, having completed the remembrance that started with Bailey's death in November 1420, just as All Souls marks the end of the mourning year in the liturgical calendar: 'In the later Middle Ages, All Souls Day provided a climax for activities that went on continually through the year, the Office for the Dead and memorial Masses'.[64] This would explain why the last tale appears to be a hindsight, an afterthought to the *Series*: 'Hic additur alia fabula ad instanciam amici mei predilecti assiduam' (Here is added another tale at the earnest request of my dear friend). The word 'additur' (is added) in the heading does not suggest that this last poem formed part of the original plan for the *Series*. 'Additur' could also be understood as additional to or exceeding the chronological scope of the *Series* so far, which stretches from November 1420 to All Saints' Day 1421, thus completing a year of mourning and the liturgical cycle of commemoration. In a sense, this liturgical cycle has been anticipated by von Nolcken, but more fully articulated by Watt.[65] But it is Bailey's commemoration

63 Appleford, *Learning to Die*, 136.
64 Shuffelton, *Codex Ashmole 61*, introduction.
65 von Nolcken, '"O, why ne had Y lerned for to die?"', 41; Watt, *The Making of Thomas Hoccleve's Series*, 81.

that furnishes this cycle with its initial rationale. And it is actually only to an outside audience that the year in the *Series* would appear as liturgical: save for All Saints' day, Hoccleve's annual chronology is actually that of the Exchequer year and the four terms of Westminster's legal courts. All Saints, of course, marks the personal, setting itself off from the bureaucratic chronology of the remainder of this group of poems in an arrangement that echoes Knapp's remark on Hoccleve's narrative persona: 'Hoccleve's interest in the self as its own end is thus generated only in opposition to bureaucratic anonymity'.[66]

Although many readers have viewed the *Series* as inconsistent and confused, it is held together by a consistent framework narrative. I am therefore not persuaded that the multivalence of the *Series* is indicative of its author's confusion. To my mind, these five poems are reminiscent of an abandoned story cycle held together by a master narrative—this is Hoccleve's *Westminster Tales*, perhaps left unfinished, just as those of his literary idol and predecessor, Chaucer. If consistency is a measure of a writer's mental health, then it is certainly hard to extract a single unifying view on anything from *The Canterbury Tales*. But what disconcerts modern readers about the *Series* is that tendency to prize the self above its environment, to recognize the posited value of the individual, and thus buffer it. Thus, to us the *Series* is a cycle about Hoccleve. To a sociocentric self and perhaps to Hoccleve the *Series* may have been an indexical piece of *méta-écriture* about the text *qua* text, the production of texts, and the telling of tales as a measure to cope with grief and accept one's own mortality.

That Thomas indeed intended to end the *Series* after *Learning to Die* ('This book thus to han ended had Y thoght', V. 1–8) gains even more support when viewed through Watt's persuasive analysis of the principle of booklet production undergirding the *Series*.[67] Watt argues that *Learning to Die* may have existed as a separated booklet available to Hoccleve's Westminster audience or that they may have imagined that it did exist.[68] I would go a step further still: building on Watt's booklet argument, I believe that the first four poems of the *Series*, though perhaps also *Jonathas*, were serialized by Hoccleve and circulated

[66] Knapp, *The Bureaucratic Muse*, 36.
[67] Watt, *The Making of Thomas Hoccleve's Series*, 76–82.
[68] Watt, *The Making of Thomas Hoccleve's Series*, 81.

consecutively at the appropriate moment in the Exchequer calendar that governed their Privy Seal lives.

Hoccleve's interlocutor throughout the *Series*, the friend, has attracted considerable attention in recent years.[69] While Hoccleve clearly wished for him to remain anonymous, it is not impossible that his presence is not only literary, given the number of analogous interlocutors in medieval literature, but also ghostly and thus reflecting his deceased friend, John Bailey. Mourning was, after all, the time during which the dead were thought to visit the living as ghosts. Jean-Claude Schmitt notes that such apparitions are tied to the liturgical year, and that they appear during the period of grieving, usually on anniversaries or at various cut-off points in the calendar:

> Starting from the date of the death, the liturgical time of prayers and masses for the dead person was celebrated for three, seven, or thirty days (the trental) and at the 'head of the year' (on the anniversary of the death), resulting in a number of apparitions... The dead returned at a different times after the prayers and masses from which they benefited directly, in order to attest to the efficacy of those suffrages, to ask the living for an additional effort, and to thank them for their help before disappearing forever.[70]

Each deceased person had their own bespoke calendar of the dead: 'This time frame, which was unique to the dead person and which depended completely on the date of the death, intersected with the collective time of the living, that of the calendar and feast days, the days of the week, and the division between daytime and nighttime activities'.[71] This calendar, Schmitt continues, ends with All Souls. Since Bailey died after All Souls 1420, his mourning calendar would run for almost the entire year. If the friend is a ghostly apparition modelled on Bailey, then this begs the question why the friend has a fifteen-year-old son, for

[69] Tim W. Machan, 'Textual Authority and the Works of Hoccleve, Lydgate and Henryson', *Viator*, 23 (1992), 281–99; Lee Patterson, '"What Is Me?": Self and Society in the Poetry of Thomas Hoccleve', *Studies in the Age of Chaucer*, 23/1 (2001), 437–70; Sebastian James Langdell, '"What World Is This? How Vndirstande Am I?": A Reappraisal of Poetic Authority in Thomas Hoccleve's *Series*', *Medium Aevum*, 78/2 (2009), 282–99; and Jane Griffiths, '"In Bookes Thus Writen I Fynde": Hoccleve's Self-Glossing in the *Regiment of Princes* and the *Series*', *Medium Aevum*, 86/1 (2017), 91–107.

[70] Schmitt, *Ghosts in the Middle Ages*, 173.

[71] Schmitt, *Ghosts in the Middle Ages*, 173.

whom he requests the final poem in the *Series* (V. 23). Since Bailey was a priest, a son would be illegitimate, and the friend could be viewed as an instrument to grant him anonymity.[72] On the other hand, since the last poem is an addition, it might further fictionalize the character of the friend and introduce the detail of the son to remove him from the historical Bailey.

If grief and its commemoration stand behind the *Series*, then this further strengthens the potential dedication of the Durham holograph manuscript to Joan Beaufort, Countess of Westmoreland. Burrow and Doyle date this manuscript to Hoccleve's final years, 1422–6,[73] and hence a few years after the completion of the *Series*, the last revision of which must have taken place after March or April 1422.[74] Rory Critten points out that the production of the Durham manuscript 'coincided with an important turning point in its dedicatee's career', the death of her husband, Ralph Neville, in 1425.[75] This would have made a fitting tribute, given the origin of the *Series* in Hoccleve's attempt to come to terms with the loss of his friend John Bailey, were it not for the anti-feminism of the final tale that complicates a dedication to Joan, as Rory Critten observes.[76] Lee Patterson offers an ingenious solution in Hoccleve's alleged bitterness, suggesting that the poet attacked

[72] One individual, a Robert Cliderowe, receives some attention in Bailey's will, and his relationship to the testator is not specified, although a Margaret Cliderowe is called Bailey's 'consanguinee' (relation). The Church's main opposition to illegitimate children of the clergy was of course the fear that Church property could be alienated. See R. H. Helmholz, 'Bastardy Litigation in Medieval England', *American Journal of Legal History*, 13/4 (1969), 360–83; Laura Wertheimer, 'Illegitimate Birth and the English Clergy, 1198–1348', *Journal of Medieval History*, 31/2 (2005), 211–29; Laura Wertheimer, 'Children of Disorder: Clerical Parentage, Illegitimacy, and Reform in the Middle Ages', *Journal of the History of Sexuality*, 15/3 (2006), 382–407; Janelle Werner, 'Just as the Priests Have Their Wives": Priests and Concubines in England, 1375–1549' (unpublished PhD, University of North Carolina at Chapel Hill, 2009); and 'Living in Suspicion: Priests and Female Servants in Late Medieval England', *Journal of British Studies*, 55/4 (2016), 658–79.

[73] Burrow and Doyle, *Facsimile*, xi, xx–xxi.

[74] This date is marked Duke Humphrey's third return to France, so that the marginal note on fol. 19v of the Durham manuscript clarifies that the text refers to his second return (Burrow, *Hoccleve's Complaint and Dialogue*, lvii).

[75] Critten, *Author, Scribe, and Book*, 57–8.

[76] Critten, *Author, Scribe, and Book*, 58.

the countess through his dedication.[77] But Critten's solution for the Durham manuscript as never truly meant for the countess strikes me as more convincing: 'the collection's ultimate anti-feminism can also be understood as a nod to the all-male clerical readership that accompanied Hoccleve throughout his poetic and bureaucratic careers'.[78] Furthermore, if, as Critten and Watt have argued,[79] the *Series* was destined for Hoccleve's Westminster circle (as I think it is), then the dedication may even be a joke at the expense of the countess intended for Hoccleve's colleagues' eyes only.

Critten finds support for this observation in the marginal note 'offord' on fol. 49r, which is placed next to one of the final stanzas of *Jereslaus' Wife*:

> O, many a wrecche is in this lond, Y weene,
> Þat thogh his wyf lenger had been him fro,
> No kus, but if it had been of the spleene
> Shee sholde han had, and forthermore also
> Fyndynge of hir had been to him but wo,
> For him wolde han thoght þat swich a fyndynge
> To los sholde han him torned, and harmynge.
> (III. 939–45)

The word 'offord' occurs next to line 942, 'Shee sholde han had, and forthermore also', and has been interpreted by Burrow and Doyle as 'a characteristic semi-jocose (or, if posthumous, nostalgic?) reference by Hoccleve to the subject of the stanza, a wretch whose wife's return would be less welcome than that of the Empress just described'.[80] That this remark is posthumous can be excluded because Offord died shortly before 19 October 1442, when the fellow Privy Seal clerk Henry Benet was granted Offord's annuity from the Exchequer.[81] I believe that this is

[77] Patterson, '"What Is Me?"', 450. Carol Meale also considers the Durham manuscripts as dedicated to the countess, '". . . Alle the Bokes That I Haue of Latyn, Englisch, and Frensch": Laywomen and Their Books in Late Medieval England', in *Women and Literature in Britain, 1150–1500*, ed. Carol M. Meale (Cambridge: Cambridge University Press, 1993), 144–5.

[78] Critten, *Author, Scribe, and Book*, 58.

[79] Watt speaks of an 'initial audience' and maintains that the Durham manuscript was meant for Countess Joan (Watt, *The Making of Thomas Hoccleve's Series*, 33–9, 54–9).

[80] Burrow and Doyle, *Facsimile*, xxxi.

[81] Otway-Ruthven, *The King's Secretary*, 181.

indeed a jocose reference to Offord as someone in no hurry to be reunited with his wife, should he have been married. Although David Watt notes we do not have evidence that Offord was married,[82] a closer look at his career and circumstances supports Burrow and Doyle's suggestion. When the Privy Seal office was divided, between 1417 and 1422, with one half being based in France,[83] Hoccleve's fellow clerks Hethe and Offord went abroad.[84] As mentioned above, we have surviving documents written by them in France. Yet in the case of Offord the period of service in France appears to have been longer and lasted throughout the entire composition of the *Series*: in addition to the June 1420 letter from Sens in which he informally greets his Westminster friends, Offord also wrote a letter signed at Bois de Vincennes under the Privy Seal on 27 August 1422 (TNA C 81/1544/1, *olim* C 81/669/1204).[85] Since Offord was part of the section of the Privy Seal that was based in France while Hoccleve wrote the *Series*, he would have been separated from his wife (if, indeed, he had one),[86] so that the joke assumed by Burrow and Doyle would be entirely plausible. J. Otway-Ruthven surmised that Offord did not receive any ecclesiastical preferment because he was illegitimate,[87] but another reason for his lack of

[82] Watt, *The Making of Thomas Hoccleve's Series*, 58.

[83] Brown, 'The Privy Seal Clerks', 262 and 265.

[84] On 5 February 1420, 'John Offorde and John Hethe, clerks of the privy seal office, who are said to be with the king in Normandy on his service', were permitted by the customers of the port of London to victual their France-bound ship (CCR 1419–22, 72). There are also letters of attorney made on 8 January 1420 for one John Offord in connection with joining the campaign in France (TNA C 76/102, m. 5, found on www.medievalsoldier.org). Hethe was already in France in 1417 with the Signet office (Richardson, 'Hoccleve in His Social Context', 318).

[85] The letter is printed in Eugène Déprez, *Études de diplomatique Anglaise: de l'avènement d'Édouard 1erà celui de Henri VII (1272–1485)* (Paris: H. Champion, 1908), i, 37–8.

[86] On married Privy Seal clerks at the time, see Janice Gordon-Kelter, 'The Lay Presence: Chancery and Privy Seal Personnel in the Bureaucracy of Henry VI', *Medieval Prosopography*, 10/1 (1989), 53–74.

[87] Otway-Ruthven, *The King's Secretary*, 181. Offord was indeed illegitimate, but he was not the son of Laurence Pabenham of Offord in Bedfordshire as has been hitherto assumed. Given the grant of land in Cambridgeshire in connection with being identified with his father's name (Otway-Ruthven, *The King's Secretary*, 181) he may have been the son of Laurence de Pabenham of Cambridgeshire, whose mother was Alice de Ufford (Douglas Richardson, *Royal Ancestry* (Salt Lake City, UT: Author, 2013), 4:29). The clerk Offord therefore used his more prestigious paternal grandmother's name, in all likelihood because he was related to John Offord, the mid-fourteenth-century keeper of the Privy Seal.

benefices could simply be that, like Hoccleve, he was married. Offord was indeed born out of wedlock, and the grants he received were either secular or, in the case of one ecclesiastical pension, passed on: in 1409, Offord received a grant of two shops in London, and in November 1410 he surrendered a pension payable by the monastery of Reading (for which he had been nominated by the king only in August 1409) to his clerk John Auncell.[88] If Offord did have a wife, it is likely that he married her between August 1409 and November 1410.

Prompted by Bailey's death, the *Series*, then, may very well be Hoccleve's final and most personal farewell in which sets out, through his deictic self, on his own process of learning to die at the age of fifty-three. Neither the short poems he wrote in 1421–2 nor the Formulary, assembled between 1422 and 1424, have a similar ambition. To my mind, the Formulary is not much more than a handover document prepared after William Alnwick, the new keeper of the Privy Seal, was appointed in 1422. With one half of the four trusted senior clerks in France—Hethe and Offord—and, of the other half, one deceased (Bailey), while the other one (Hoccleve) was getting on in age, Hoccleve was simply the only Privy Seal clerk present in Westminster capable of executing the task. The Formulary (British Library Add. MS 24062) may have been overseen and was certainly owned by Henry Benet, the same clerk who received Offord's annuity in 1442. His name appears on top of fol. 1v, which is written in his own hand. Based on the surviving records signed by him that I have examined,[89] he wrote fols 1v, 3v, 31r, 102v, and 124r, in addition to marginal notes on 48v, 50r, 68v, and 101v. Benet was certainly closer to keeper Alnwick than Hoccleve had been to the incumbents of this office during his career: in his will Benet bequeaths to his relative John Gygour a copy of pseudo-Augustine's *Meditations* which he had

[88] Otway-Ruthven, *The King's Secretary*, 181.

[89] These are the following Privy Seal documents, listed here by language: (English) TNA C 81/729/5913, C 81/729/5915, C 81/729/5919, C 81/729/5922, C 81/729/5955, C 81/729/5927, C 81/729/5969A, C 81/729/5970; (French) C 81/729/5959, C 81/729/5964; and (Latin) C81/729/5907B, C 81/729/5916, C 81/729/5920, C 81/729/5925B, C 81/729/5956, C 81/729/5963, C 81/729/5969B. For a tentative indication of the sections possibly written by Benet, see Burrow and Doyle, *Facsimile*, xxxvi note 1.

earlier received from Alnwick: 'my boke of meditacions that was Alnewykes Busshope of Lincoln'.[90]

Everything about the *Series* is configured for an intimate, private audience that was 'in the know' and familiar with Hoccleve's life and immediate situation—familiar enough, that is, to appreciate his situation and effect a change. The *Series* is thus a quintessential indexical cycle of poems. In this sense, the degree to which the Exchequer calendar—Michaelmas, Lent, Easter—and not the *sanctorale* structures the *Series* mirrors what Ethan Knapp and David Watt have so thoroughly examined about Hoccleve's use of Privy Seal forms and material aspects, respectively.[91] Hoccleve's ingrained institutionalized writing even extends to his deictic 'I', Thomas, who is not limited to being an attempt at rehabilitating Hoccleve, but amounts to 'creative use of "documentary poetics"'—'creative' in the sense that it is indexical and requires a bureaucratic Westminster audience personally familiar with Hoccleve.[92] Just as it is unlikely that the Durham manuscript was presented to Countess Joan, I think it highly improbable that the *Series* was ever intended to reach Duke Humphrey. Much of this sequence of poems is self-absorbed, while the *Dialogue* is a discussion about suitable topics for Duke Humphrey and, at the same time, via Thomas, a test of Hoccleve's mental robustness for the task at hand. This is not material for Humphrey's eyes. If anything, the *Dialogue*—even more than the *Complaint*—aims solely at Hoccleve's inner circle as a work in which the poet-narrator admits that he failed in his task to write for the duke. This very intimacy of Hoccleve's poetry also extends to his other verse beyond the *Regement of Princes*. Even Hoccleve's poems for Henry V and the *Remonstrance* could be considered anti-occasional, as Jenni Nuttall maintains, and aimed at the poet's Westminster circle.[93] This intimacy is nowhere more present than in his autograph manuscripts, which Hoccleve understood as indexical, and hence, as conveying his presence and authority: '[Hoccleve] felt that a book written in his

[90] Benet's will was proved in 1468, TNA PROB 11/6/37. He also donates a glossed psalter to the Guildhall.

[91] Knapp, *The Bureaucratic Muse*; and Watt, *The Making of Thomas Hoccleve's Series*.

[92] Matthew Clifton Brown, '"Lo, Heer the Fourme": Hoccleve's *Series*, Formulary, and Bureaucratic Textuality', *Exemplaria*, 23/1 (2011), 28.

[93] Jenni Nuttall, 'Thomas Hoccleve's Poems for Henry V', in *Oxford Handbooks Online* (Oxford: Oxford University Press, 2015).

own hand would have some of the prestige that autograph manuscripts now enjoy'.[94]

In the *Series*, a cycle of poems probably prompted by the death of Hoccleve's friend, Thomas passes through a year of mourning, moving from grief to an acceptance of his own mortality in a poetic sequence built around *Learning to Die*, a poem that, as Appleford shows, was meant to seek ascetic withdrawal from the physical world that surrounded Hoccleve in anticipation of his own death: 'Crucially, *Lerne to Dye* is at once the poem the narrator announces will end his writing career ("I nevere þinke / More in Englissh after be occupied") and the poem that the friend would prefer him not to write at all'.[95] *Learning to Die* and, by extension, the *Series*, is to Hoccleve what the Trentham version of *Henrici Quarti primus* was to Gower and what *The Testament* was to Lydgate: this group of poems is not a return to public life but a departure from this world. The *Series* is Hoccleve's most personal and final literary testament, his last words.

[94] Watt, *The Making of Thomas Hoccleve's Series*, 48.
[95] Appleford, *Learning to Die*, 129.

3

Parting Shots

Richard Caudray's Libelle of Englyshe Polycye

When England's military fortunes in France first began to wane, then rapidly plummet, in the 1430s and 1440s, criticism was primarily aimed at Henry VI's divided administration. The pivotal event during the final stages of the Hundred Years' War came in 1435, when Burgundy withdrew from its strategic alliance with England following the Congress of Arras, Europe's first large-scale international peace conference. The Anglo-Burgundian league had successfully held France's military might in check, whereas the powerful duchy's subsequent rapprochement with France irreparably damaged England's position in the conflict.[1] The Congress of Arras caught England's feuding ruling council off guard: Henry VI would not emerge from his minority until the following year, while Cardinal Beaufort and Duke Humphrey of Gloucester, the king's uncle, pursued opposing strategies in the war with France.

The years immediately following the Congress of Arras gave rise to a new generation of English political poems, and no work was as knowledgeable and far-seeing in questioning law, governance, and decision

[1] Joycelyne Gledhill Dickinson, *The Congress of Arras, 1435: A Study in Medieval Diplomacy* (Oxford: Clarendon Press, 1955), vii–x.

Last Words: The Public Self and the Social Author in Late Medieval England.
Sebastian Sobecki, Oxford University Press (2019).
DOI: 10.1093/oso/9780198790778.001.0001

making in the corridors of power as the *Libelle of Englyshe Polycye* (henceforth: *Libelle*).[2] The *Libelle* takes as its starting point the situation following the Congress. To a large extent, the poem was written in direct response to the fallout from the collapse of the crucial Anglo-Burgundian alliance. In a first demonstration of Burgundy's new strategic partnership with France, Philip the Good laid siege to English-held Calais in 1436. Duke Humphrey promptly responded with a relief force, subsequently raiding Flanders. This relief effort coincided with the preparations for Henry VI's coming of age, and a savvy publicity campaign was launched to shape a political persona for the young king by associating him personally with the defence of Calais.[3] The author behind the *Libelle* seized this opportunity to formulate an alternative set of policies for England in a precisely situated effort to build consensus around a resolute mercantilist agenda advanced by a strong admiralty.[4] There is no doubt that the *Libelle* offers a devastating critique of current Lancastrian policy, and yet—much as Thomas Hoccleve's *Regement of Princes*—its criticism is not directed against the Lancastrian government *qua* Lancastrian. Instead, it praises the leadership of the late king, Henry V.

The first of the *Libelle*'s two recensions was composed in the aftermath of Burgundy's failed siege of Calais in the summer of 1436, though not later than December 1437, shortly after the death of

[2] All quotations in this chapter will be taken from the edition in Anthony Bale and Sebastian Sobecki, eds, *Medieval English Travel: A Critical Anthology* (Oxford: Oxford University Press, 2019). The poem has been previously edited by Thomas Wright, *Political Poems and Songs Relating to English History*, Vol. 2 (London: Longman, Green, Longman, and Roberts, 1861); Wilhelm Adolf Boguslaw Hertzberg and Reinhold Pauli, eds, *The Libell of Englishe Policye, 1436: Text und metrische Übersetzung* (Leipzig: Hirzel, 1878); and George Frederic Warner, ed., *The Libelle of Englyshe Polycye: A Poem on the Use of Sea-Power, 1436* (Oxford: Clarendon Press, 1926).

[3] Sebastian Sobecki, 'Bureaucratic Verse: William Lyndwood, the Privy Seal, and the Form of *The Libelle of Englyshe Polycye*', *New Medieval Literatures*, 12/1 (2011), 268–82; David Wallace, *Premodern Places: Calais to Surinam, Chaucer to Aphra Behn* (Oxford: Blackwell, 2006), 117; James A. Doig, 'Propaganda, Public Opinion and the Siege of Calais in 1436', in *Crown, Government and People in the Fifteenth Century*, ed. Rowena Archer (Stroud: Sutton, 1995), 79–106; James A. Doig, 'A New Source for the Siege of Calais in 1436', *English Historical Review*, 110/436 (1995), 413–14; and James A. Doig, 'Political Propaganda and Royal Proclamations in Late Medieval England', *Historical Research*, 71/176 (1998), 271–5.

[4] Sobecki, 'Bureaucratic Verse', 251–88.

Emperor Sigismund.[5] A second recension with a modified envoy circulated before June 1441; this recension was subsequently revised.[6] The *Libelle* has reached us in twenty medieval and early modern manuscripts, and we know of the existence of at least a handful of now lost copies.[7] Despite being an acute political work that situates itself in the specific political circumstances of the collapse of the Anglo-Burgundian alliance, the 1,100-line poem enjoyed an illustrious readership over the next two centuries. It is remarkable how the deep legal implications of the *Libelle* are reflected in the list of its known later owners—among its famous readers are chief justices and archbishops. John Paston, who trained in the law, owned a copy in the fifteenth century. William Cecil, Elizabeth's secretary of state, was another reader, while Richard Hakluyt, who owned two copies of the poem, closes his list of medieval precedents for English naval rule in the second edition of his *Principal Navigations* (1598–1600) with the *Libelle*, where it replaces Mandeville's *Travels*. Chief justice Matthew Hale also owned the poem, and the influential lawyer John Selden drew on it for *Mare clausum*, his advocacy for the concept of territorial waters, a work written to challenge Hugo Grotius's *Mare liberum*, a comprehensive defence of open seas and one of the pivotal treatises in the early history of international law. Finally, Samuel Pepys, clerk of the Acts to the Navy Board, owned both the *Libelle* and Selden's *Mare clausum*.[8] The *Libelle* holds the key to understanding not only late medieval foreign policy but also the budding imperial ambitions of Elizabethan and Jacobean England.

[5] See note 64.

[6] On the composition history of the poem, see Warner, *The Libelle of Englyshe Polycye*, introduction.

[7] Frank Taylor, 'Some Manuscripts of the "Libelle of Englyshe Polycye"', *Bulletin of the John Rylands Library*, 24/2 (1940), 376–418; Carol M. Meale, '*The Libelle of Englyshe Polycye* and Mercantile Culture in Late-Medieval London', in *London and Europe in the Later Middle Ages*, ed. Julia Boffey and Pamela King (London: Centre for Medieval and Renaissance Studies, Queen Mary and Westfield College, 1995), 181–228; and A. S. G. Edwards, 'A New Manuscript of *The Libelle of English Policy*', *Notes and Queries*, 46/244 (1999), 444–5.

[8] The list of owners is derived from Warner, *The Libelle of Englyshe Polycye*, xiv–xv; Taylor, 'Some Manuscripts', 376–418; G. A. Lester, 'The Books of a Fifteenth-Century English Gentleman: Sir John Paston', *Neuphilologische Mitteilungen*, 88 (1987), 205; Meale, '*The Libelle of Englyshe Polycye*', 219–21; and Wallace, *Premodern Places*, 138 n 121.

The Authorship of the Poem

I believe that Sir George Warner (1845–1936), the editor of the standard edition of the poem, came very close to identifying the author of the *Libelle.* Warner, keeper of manuscripts at the British Museum, was a competent librarian and judicious textual editor. His 1926 text of the *Libelle* remains serviceable almost a century after its publication, while his *Catalogue of Western Manuscripts in the Old Royal and King's Collections* (1921), completed by his successor Julius Gilson, still provides the basis for most descriptions of manuscripts from the Royal collection in the online catalogue of the British Library.[9] The careful scrutiny which Warner lavished on the *Libelle* led him to close in on the proposed identity of the writer behind the poem. By understanding the bureaucratic context from which this unusual poem sprang, Warner posited that the author of the *Libelle* was Adam Moleyns (d. 1450), clerk of the ruling council and later bishop of Chichester.[10] He first suggested Moleyns as the poem's author in an 1878 review of a previous edition of the *Libelle*, noting that much of the information provided in the poem had its source in the work of the ruling council, the meetings of which were minuted by the clerk of the council.[11] The poem's interest in Ireland, Warner adds later in his edition, 'would have naturally come under [Moleyns'] notice as clerk of the Council in London'.[12]

Similarly, the terms in which the poem frames the historical and strategic importance of Calais 'agree curiously with those used in the

[9] Warner, *The Libelle of Englyshe Polycye*; and George F. Warner and J. P. Gilson, *Catalogue of Western Manuscripts in the Old Royal and King's Collections* (London: Trustees of the British Museum, 1921).

[10] Bill Smith, 'Moleyns, Adam (d. 1450)', *ODNB* (Oxford: Oxford University Press, 2004), <https://doi-org.proxy-ub.rug.nl/10.1093/ref:odnb/18918>.

[11] G. Warner, 'Wilhelm Hertzberg, ed., *The Libell of Englishe Policye , 1436: Text und metrische Uebersetzung von W. Hertzberg* (Leipzig, 1878)', *Academy*, 14 (1878), 492.

[12] Warner, *The Libelle of Englyshe Polycye*, xxxiii. The Ireland passage, in particular, has generated attempts to identify the poem's author. The most recently proposed name in this context is an Irishman, Nicholas Lacy, suggested by Michael Bennett, ' *The Libelle of English Policy*: The Matter of Ireland', in *The Fifteenth Century XV*, ed. Linda Clark (Woodbridge: Boydell Press, 2017), 11–21. But although Lacy wrote on Ireland elsewhere, Bennett exaggerates the importance of Ireland in the *Libelle*, and what little is known of Lacy's career does not at all correspond to the remainder of the poem. As Warner has shown, what the poem has to say about Ireland is contained in council correspondence, including a 1435 letter from Thomas Stanley ('Wilhelm Hertzberg, Ed., *The Libell of Englishe Policye*', 492).

instructions from the Council to the commissioners for raising a loan for its defence earlier in 1436'.[13] Warner is certainly correct in seeing council discussions (and their minutes) as offering striking parallels for the poem's remarks about Calais, but the suggestion that Moleyns 'may himself have drafted them' needs qualifying because Moleyns was only appointed clerk of the council on 16 May 1438, and the first document he is known to have signed in this capacity is dated 28 May 1438.[14] Warner adds that '[f]rom what [the narrator] says in conclusion, it seems that he intended to write further on Calais elsewhere, and he also mentions warnings he had previously given of the impending loss of Harfleur in 1435, which had passed unheeded'.[15] Warner continues:

> among other qualifications for his task he had . . . sound political judgement and an extensive knowledge of trade, and . . . his ideas on the subject of sea-power were in advance of his time. His translation from an early chronicle shows that he was a Latin scholar and had studied English history, and the theological tone of his peroration makes it probable that he was an ecclesiastic . . . [H]e was brought into personal relations with men of rank and eminence in public affairs and at court, and apparently had free access to proceedings in Parliament, confidential state-papers, and other official documents, it may fairly be inferred that he held a position of consequence and responsibility.[16]

As Warner details here, Moleyns's biography appears to qualify him eminently for this position.

Most importantly, many of Warner's arguments centre on Moleyns's role as clerk of the council, albeit his appointment probably postdates the *Libelle*:

> While [Moleyns's] office as clerk of the Council gave him unequalled opportunities for becoming acquainted with public men and affairs, he seems to have been particularly employed in commissions relating to trade, ranging in importance from negotiations for commercial

[13] Warner, *The Libelle of Englyshe Polycye*, xxxiv.

[14] Warner makes this assertion on p. xxxiv of his introduction (*The Libelle of Englyshe Polycye*). For Moleyns's likely tenure on the council, see Alfred L. Brown, *The Early History of the Clerkship of the Council* (Glasgow: University of Glasgow, 1969), 29–32.

[15] Warner, *The Libelle of Englyshe Polycye*, xxxiv.

[16] Warner, *The Libelle of Englyshe Polycye*, xxxix.

> treaties to inquiries into the legality of the seizure of ships. Evidently his position in the Council among the great nobles, prelates, and State officials, of whom it was mainly composed, was that of a trained man of business, whose talents were freely employed in any matter that required expert knowledge and diplomatic ability.[17]

Furthermore, certain aspects of Moleyns's career align him with a personal interest in Ireland (given one of his hoped-for preferments to an Irish see), his involvement in the wool trade, and his participation in peace negotiations in subsequent years.[18]

Warner's identification continued to be accepted until, in 1961, George Holmes rejected it on political grounds.[19] Holmes points out that Moleyns was a leading supporter of Cardinal Beaufort's faction on the council, while the author behind the *Libelle* is firmly in the camp of Duke Humphrey: 'It is unthinkable that a leading supporter of the Beaufort faction should have written a pamphlet so entirely critical of its policy from beginning to end. Whoever wrote it was on the opposite side in politics.'[20] This assessment effectively ended Moleyns's association with this poem. Subsequent discussions of the *Libelle* have therefore situated the poem in mercantile circles.[21]

In two studies, published in 2008 and 2011, I drew attention to the legal and bureaucratic aspects of this poem.[22] The *Libelle*'s deeply bureaucratic nature and its author's ready access to members of the king's intimate household extend to a detailed knowledge of Henry V's

[17] Warner, *The Libelle of Englyshe Polycye*, xliii.

[18] Warner, *The Libelle of Englyshe Polycye*, xli–xliv.

[19] G. A. Holmes, 'The Libel of English Policy', *English Historical Review*, 76/299 (1961), 193–216.

[20] Holmes, 'The "Libel of English Policy"', 212. This remains the consensus among historians and literary historians. The only noteworthy exception is Volker Henn, who argues that Gloucester's interest would also have been damaged by implementing the policies proposed in this poem ('"The Libelle of Englyshe Polycye": Politik und Wirtschaft in England in den 30er Jahren des 15. Jahrhunderts', *Hansische Geschichtsblätter*, 101 (1983), 43–65). But Henn's argument assumes comprehensive fluency in complex economic relationships that does not readily appear in this poem.

[21] The most significant of these are Meale, '*The Libelle of Englyshe Polycye*', 181–228; and John Scattergood, '*The Libelle of Englyshe Polycye*: The Nation and Its Place', in *Nation, Court and Culture: New Essays on Fifteenth-Century English Poetry*, ed. Helen Cooney (Dublin: Four Courts Press, 2001), 28–49.

[22] Sebastian Sobecki, *The Sea and Medieval English Literature* (Cambridge: D. S. Brewer, 2008), v, 140–60; and Sobecki, 'Bureaucratic Verse', 251–88.

will and the secret codicils to that will, in addition to the Great Seal, which was kept in the Chancery.[23] At the time, I linked the poem with William Lyndwood, keeper of the Privy Seal, and he may well have influenced the author, but on reassessing the *Libelle* in its documentary setting I have come to the conclusion that, while Moleyns cannot have been the poem's author for the political reasons detailed by Holmes, the criteria for authorship advanced by Warner in connection with Moleyns remain robust and compelling. Given the legal and administrative aspects to which I have previously drawn attention, there is one person who optimally fits Warner's description and whose professional roles and biography, in addition to his specific legal knowledge, meet all the criteria for the poem's authorship: Moleyns's direct predecessor, Richard Caudray, clerk of the council from 1421 to 1435.

Caudray was an exceptionally adept administrator and legal mind, and his career saw him closely associated with the central persons mentioned in the *Libelle*. Having graduated from Cambridge, Caudray came to the attention of Henry Chichele, then bishop of St David's.[24] On Chichele's election to the see of Canterbury in 1414, Caudray became scribe and notary public in the archbishop's court of audience. Chichele is actually one of the three dedicatees of the second recension of the poem, as identified in one of the poem's manuscripts, Manchester, John Rylands Library MS English 955.[25] In fact, he is the only dedicatee named in any of the surviving copies of the second recension.

Between 1418 and 1421, Caudray spent much of his time abroad in royal service in France writing for the chancery in Rouen. By late 1418, he was acting as scribe and notary for negotiations with the French,

[23] Sobecki, 'Bureaucratic Verse', 270–7.

[24] The biographical details on Caudray follow A. B. Emden, *A Biographical Register of the University of Cambridge to 1500* (Cambridge: Cambridge University Press, 1963), 126–7; Brown, *The Early History of the Clerkship*, 20–1; Shannon McSheffrey, *Seeking Sanctuary: Crime, Mercy, and Politics in English Courts, 1400–1550* (Oxford: Oxford University Press, 2017), 65; and Shannon McSheffrey, 'Richard Caudray (c. 1390–1458): Fifteenth-Century Churchman, Academic, and Ruthless Politician', *Medieval Prosopography*, 33 (2018), 167–79. I would like to thank Shannon McSheffrey for granting me access to her forthcoming article.

[25] Taylor, 'Some Manuscripts', 377. The same manuscript has a seventeenth-century note on the last folio, stating this copy was presented by John Lydgate to Chichele in 1436 (Taylor, 'Some Manuscripts', 377). On the *Libelle*'s broad agreement with Chichele's views, see Sobecki, 'Bureaucratic Verse', *passim*.

while the following year saw him described as clerk of the council in Normandy.[26] In 1419 and 1420, Caudray is recorded as the king's secretary, and he served on diplomatic missions of the utmost political sensitivity: in April 1420, he was among those sent to receive the oaths of the king and queen of France to the terms of the Treaty of Troyes.[27] From 1421 to 1435, Caudray was clerk of the council, before that role passed to Moleyns. He was also notary-apostolic and secondary of the Privy Seal office,[28] the office responsible for issuing letters for the use of the Great Seal, the obverse and reverse of which are discussed in detail in the poem. As the king's secretary and clerk of the council he would have been closest to the drafting of Henry V's will and secret codicils, both of which were known to the author of the *Libelle* though not necessarily to some of England's most powerful magnates. Henry's will was prepared in June 1421, before his departure for France, while the codicils were written on 26 August 1422, five days before the king's death at Bois de Vincennes.[29] In June 1420, Caudray was still the king's secretary, and by 1421 he had taken on the role of clerk of the council.

Everything Warner had to say about Moleyns qualified him to be the poem's author, except for Moleyns's political allegiance, which, as has been subsequently shown, rules him out. Caudray, however, meets all of Warner's criteria for Moleyns, and he possessed the correct political affiliation of having belonged to Gloucester's camp. In addition, Caudray's association with Chichele and his role as the king's secretary, with probable access to (and perhaps even involvement in) Henry V's will and codicils, point to his role in composing the *Libelle*. At least one royal signet letter bears Caudray's signature.[30]

[26] Brown, *The Early History of the Clerkship*, 20–1; McSheffrey, 'Richard Caudray', 167–79.

[27] Otway-Ruthven, *The King's Secretary and the Signet Office in the XV Century*, 154; Brown, *The Early History of the Clerkship*, 20–1; and McSheffrey, 'Richard Caudray', 167–79.

[28] Arnold Judd, *The Life of Thomas Bekynton, Secretary to King Henry VI and Bishop of Bath and Wells 1443–1465* (Chichester: Moore and Tillyer for the Regnum Press, 1961), 42.

[29] P. Strong and F. Strong, 'The Last Will and Codicils of Henry V', *English Historical Review*, 96/378 (1981), 80.

[30] This is TNA C 81/1365/7, dated 23 June 1419. Kirby, *Calendar of Signet Letters of Henry IV and Henry V*, 177, item 868. The letter has been printed in Fisher et al., *An Anthology of Chancery English*, 116–17, item 63.

We know from internal evidence that the earliest version of the poem was composed after the siege of Calais in August 1436 but before the end of 1437. This recension was clearly written in response to the Treaty of Arras. Caudray was an experienced negotiator with the French. He produced an account of the negotiations with the dauphin in 1413,[31] and he crafted the long account of the proceedings at the Anglo-French peace conference at Alençon in November 1418.[32] In 1420, he was part of the crucial delegation during the Treaty of Troyes.[33] Most significantly, Caudray was involved in preparing the English embassy to Arras.[34] His work for the council stops exactly at the beginning of the Congress: the last council endorsements written by him date to July 1435—almost right up to the Congress, which began on 5 August.[35] Caudray left his post as clerk of the council after having served in this role for fourteen years—two under Henry V and the remainder during Henry VI's minority. He was thus at liberty to write with greater independence and experience of foreign policy than Moleyns ever could have at this point in his life. And Caudray was free to write on policy in which he was no longer involved.

John Holland, Admiral of England, and *The Black Book of the Admiralty*

What gave Caudray this liberty to write on English foreign policy were the two posts he took up in 1435. Almost immediately after stepping down from the council, he became dean of St-Martin-le-Grand in London, in addition to remaining warden of King's Hall, Cambridge

[31] Judd, *The Life of Thomas Bekynton*, 42.

[32] Chaplais, *English Medieval Diplomatic Practice*, 207–23.

[33] Otway-Ruthven, *The King's Secretary*, 154; Brown, *The Early History of the Clerkship*, 20–1; and McSheffrey, 'Richard Caudray', 167–79.

[34] His name also appears as the executing clerk under some correspondence in the run-up to the Congress; see for instance Dickinson, *The Congress of Arras*, 214–16.

[35] Brown, *The Early History of the Clerkship*, 27. While Moleyns was appointed in May 1438, Henry Benet, a Privy Seal clerk and Caudray's assistant, was paid in February 1438 for two and a half years of interim work for the council, confirming the date of Caudray's retirement from the clerkship as August 1435 (Brown, *The Early History of the Clerkship*, 28–9). For Benet's tenure at the Privy Seal, see Brown, 'The Privy Seal Clerks in the Early Fifteenth Century', 262n2.

(a post he had held since 1431), and chancellor of the university until 1435.[36] Crucially, at the same time, Caudray became secretary to John Holland, earl of Huntingdon, and admiral of England. Holland and Caudray had overlapped on the council in Rouen and when Holland was in England, certainly from 1432.[37] Holland attended council 'assiduously during the first months of 1433'.[38] He also represented Gloucester's point of view at the Congress of Arras in 1435, where he provided 'counter to Beaufort's influence and views'.[39] The earl was also attending council in November 1435, after his return from France, and occasionally during the early months of 1436.[40] Caudray and Holland had clearly spent much time together on the council in England and France, even before Caudray joined the earl's service in 1435. R. A. Griffiths notes that 'After Henry VI came of age (1436–7), Huntingdon [i.e. Holland], like Gloucester, was eased out of the king's counsels'.[41] Holland was appointed admiral of England on 2 October 1435,[42] and this would certainly explain why Caudray had to surrender his post as clerk of the council.

Caudray would become Holland's right-hand man until his patron's death some fifteen years later. This turned out to be a defining role for Caudray: '[his appointment] began a bond with the Holland family that was to endure for the rest of Caudray's life'.[43] Holland was married to Beatrice of Portugal in 1433, illegitimate daughter of the king of Portugal.[44] Sole among the many nations under attack in the *Libelle*, the poem makes an exception for the Portuguese: 'Portugalers with us have trouth in hand: / Whose Marchandy commeth much into England / They ben our friends' (ll. 128–30).

Holland was firmly linked to Chichele and to Gloucester's camp.[45] Perhaps most importantly, he was associated with Lord Hungerford, with whom he had served under the Duke of Bedford in France.[46]

[36] McSheffrey, 'Richard Caudray', 170.

[37] Michael Stansfield, 'The Holland Family, Dukes of Exeter, Earls of Kent and Huntingdon, 1352–1475' (unpublished DPhil., University of Oxford, 1987), 206.

[38] Stansfield, 'The Holland Family', 207.

[39] Stansfield, 'The Holland Family', 208.

[40] Stansfield, 'The Holland Family', 208.

[41] R. A. Griffiths, 'Holland, John, First Duke of Exeter (1395–1447)', *ODNB* (Oxford: Oxford University Press, 2006).

[42] Stansfield, 'The Holland Family', 208.

[43] McSheffrey, 'Richard Caudray', 171.

[44] Stansfield, 'The Holland Family', 206–7.

[45] Griffiths, 'Holland, John'; and Stansfield, 'The Holland Family', 208.

[46] Stansfield, 'The Holland Family', 181.

Hungerford, who had been an admiral at a naval victory off Harfleur during the campaign of 1415,[47] is after all invoked in the poem as having read, vetted, and undersigned its contents:

> That seth it is soth in verray fayth,
> That the wise Lord Baron of Hungerford
> Hath thee overseene, and verely he saith
> That thou art true, and thus hee doeth record,
> Next the Gospel: God wotte it was his worde,
> When hee thee redde all over in a night.
> Goe forth trew booke, and Christ defend thy right.
> (ll. 1150–6)

Hungerford's approval and his status as the last living executor of Henry V's will are central to the *Libelle*.[48] Holland and Hungerford, both distinguished military leaders in France, continued to be associated with similar sentiments for centuries: contemporary chroniclers, giving their account of the Battle of Agincourt in 1415, offer either Holland or Hungerford as the source for Westmoreland's celebrated sentence that triggered the king to utter his St Crispin's Day speech in Shakespeare's *Henry V*: 'O that we now had here / But one ten thousand of those men in England / that do not work today' (4.3.17–19).[49]

As admiral of the fleet, Holland was keenly aware of the need to police and 'keep the sea'—a core demand of the *Libelle*. He was certainly qualified for this post, having already served in 1416 as 'commander of the fleet to relieve Harfleur and patrol the seas'.[50] It may have been during Holland's tenure as admiral of England that *The Black Book of the Admiralty* (now TNA HCA 12)—the oldest set of

[47] Charles Kightly, 'Hungerford, Walter, First Baron Hungerford (1378–1449)', *ODNB* (Oxford: Oxford University Press, 2006).

[48] Sobecki, 'Bureaucratic Verse', 263, 268–77.

[49] William Shakespeare, *King Henry V*, ed. Andrew Gurr (Cambridge: Cambridge University Press, 1992), 166. For the historical claims to Holland and Hungerford, see *Shakespeare's History of King Henry the Fifth*, ed. Samuel Neil (Glasgow and London: Collins, 1878), 152; *King Henry V*, 287; Alison K. McHardy, 'Religion, Court Culture and Propaganda: The Chapel Royal in the Reign of Henry V', in *Henry V: New Interpretations*, ed. Gwilym Dodd (Woodbridge: Boydell, 2013), 156; and Craig Taylor, 'Henry V, Flower of Chivalry', in *Henry V: New Interpretations*, ed. Gwilym Dodd (Woodbridge: Boydell Press, 2013), 228. The anonymous *Gesta Henrici Quinti* attributes these lines to Hungerford (Frank Taylor and John S. Roskell, eds, *Gesta Henrici Quinti, Deeds of Henry the Fifth* (Oxford: Clarendon Press, 1975), 78).

[50] Griffiths, 'Holland, John'.

sea laws in England—was written.[51] Holland had every reason to assert the role of the court of the admiralty and maritime laws. While he was 'little called upon to carry out any military duties' (with the notable exception of the relief of Calais in 1346), he indeed took measures to look after admiralty legislation: 'the enforcement of the admiralty's jurisdiction was a more active aspect of his tenure of the post'.[52] Holland's Court of the Admiralty was busy, with regional officers being deployed all over England and cases were adjudged on 'all aspects of maritime activity'.[53] Much of this activity is gathered in *The Black Book of the Admiralty*.[54] I have previously demonstrated the *Libelle*'s familiarity with the civilian legal concept of territorial waters and the writings of the jurist Bartolus of Sassoferrato on maritime law, noting a number of curious similarities with the *Black Book of the Admiralty*.[55]

As Admiral Holland's secretary and right-hand man, besides being a trained civilian, Caudray intimately understood the civilian legal process—there are many documented instances of petitions and legal interventions written by Caudray on behalf of St Martin-le-Grand.[56] This is particularly relevant since *libellus* is the technical term for the bill of complaint submitted in civil law jurisdictions, including ecclesiastical courts and the Court of Admiralty.[57] The *Libelle*, invoking the category of the 'bill-poem' and styling itself as clamour writing,[58] is based on a petitionary *libellus* used in civil law courts, such as the Court of Admiralty and certain mercantile jurisdictions: 'A *libellus* is a writing in which are contained the suit which is sued, the case for the suit, and the name of the disputant and the action'.[59] Thus, the *oblatio libelli* or

[51] Travers Twiss, ed., *The Black Book of the Admiralty*, Monumenta Juridica, 4 vols (London: Longman and Trübner, 1871), 1:xii.

[52] Stansfield, 'The Holland Family', 209.

[53] Stansfield, 'The Holland Family', 209.

[54] Twiss, *The Black Book of the Admiralty*, 1:xxvii, xxxvii; and Stansfield, 'The Holland Family', 209–10.

[55] Sobecki, *The Sea and Medieval English Literature*, v, 140–60.

[56] On this, see McSheffrey, *Seeking Sanctuary*, 58–82.

[57] Sobecki, 'Bureaucratic Verse', 251–88.

[58] For 'bill-poems', see Matthew Giancarlo, *Parliament and Literature in Late Medieval England* (Cambridge: Cambridge University Press, 2007), 144–5. Clamour writing is the subject of Wendy Scase, *Literature and Complaint in England, 1272–1553* (Oxford: Oxford University Press, 2007).

[59] William Craddock Bolland, *Select Bills in Eyre, AD 1292–1333* (London: Quaritch, 1914), xiii–xiv. The translation is from Scase, *Literature and Complaint in England*, 61.

presentation of the bill of complaint', open the *processus ordinarii*, or legal suit. These are the terms which the *Libelle* uses to classify itself at the beginning of the poem: '[t]he true processe of English policie', followed by 'the processe of the Libel of English policie'.[60] There is even evidence that medieval readers considered the poem to be evoking a *libellus* or bill of complaint: one of the surviving manuscripts belonging to the second recension replaces the word 'libelle' (l. 1,142) in the envoy with 'little bylle'—a bill of complaint as used in the common law.[61]

The word 'libelle' in the poem's title can carry two meanings, then: the first is 'small book' or 'booklet', while the second, more specifically legal, understanding of the term is a *libellus*, a bill presented in a civil law court, such as the Court of Admiralty or an ecclesiastical court. Internally, the *Libelle* offers two significant legal dimensions, one reveals the author's fluency in international law and negotiations, the other shows just how familiar he was with civilian courts and its legal procedures. The first aspect stands behind the poem's progressive use of the concept of territorial waters, a notion that had not yet been formulated, and the *Libelle* is one of the first texts, certainly in England, to have done so. Significantly, the writer was intimately familiar with the complex legal arguments underlying territorial waters.[62] This is borne out by the work's ingenious reservoir of justifications for 'keeping the sea': from using imperial *regalia* following Emperor Sigismund's visit, over calling on the precedents of Edgar, Edward III, and Henry V, and invoking the spectre of piracy, to an insistence on demonstrating that land and sea can both be considered territory. Caudray was a seasoned negotiator with a detailed knowledge of international law, as participation in negotiations demonstrates.

Many commentators have noted the degree to which the *Libelle* is concerned with Calais—its value, strategic importance, and the paramount nature of its defence. At the very beginning of the poem, the *Libelle* dedicates a considerable amount of space to Calais, and the first fifty or so lines linger on the defence of the town. It was Holland, as admiral of England, who helped defend Calais in August 1436, shortly

[60] See the incipit as well as ll. 1, 1049, 1078, and the English explicit.
[61] Sobecki, 'Bureaucratic Verse', 251–88.
[62] Sobecki, *The Sea and Medieval English Literature*, 145–60.

before the poem was composed.[63] Tellingly, in the first stanza the preservation of the office of the admiral is front and centre: 'Cherish Marchandise, keepe the admiraltie' (l. 6). No one would have profited from this poem more than the new admiral, whose right-hand man, Richard Caudray, met all the criteria for the poem's authorship as initially listed by Warner.

The poem's opening bouts are dedicated to sea keeping, the admiralty, and Calais, which is now left at the mercy of the Burgundians. Betraying its bitterness at Burgundy's defection, the *Libelle* thus compensates for the loss of its ally with a personal, and affective, opening passage that invokes Emperor Sigismund's visit to England in 1416 (ll. 8–21). Although nominally the purpose of this passage is for Sigismund to confirm the strategic significance of Calais for England's defence, the emperor prefaces his observations to his host Henry V with the affectionate address 'my brother' (l. 15). Sigismund's spectral presence is summoned here, much like the ghost of Hamlet, Sr., to speak to the conscience of a people and to offer consolation after Arras: England may have lost the friendship of the Duchy of Burgundy, but it still enjoys the love of the Holy Roman Empire.[64] The source for the author's knowledge of Sigismund's visit, Warner suggests, may have been Hungerford, who was attached to the emperor's service during the latter's visit.[65] Yet Hungerford need not have been the (only) source for the emperor's thoughts on Calais: Holland was ordered back to London by 16 April 1416 to receive the emperor.[66] More importantly, the inventory of Holland's goods, prepared by Caudray after his patron's death in 1447, includes a piece bearing the arms of the emperor, presumably a gift that 'may have been presented by Sigismund in 1416'.[67]

Furthermore, when Holland was lieutenant general to the Duke of Bedford, himself admiral between 1426 and 1435, Holland's seal mirrored the English noble described at a number of places in the *Libelle*,

[63] Griffiths, 'Holland, John'.

[64] The words following Sigismund's first appearance in the text, 'Wich yet reigneth' (l. 8), reveal the *terminus ante quem* of December 1437 (the date of Sigismund's death) for the first recension of the *Libelle*. The ghost of the late Sigismund in the second recension of the poem is hence even more effective in offering his minatory message.

[65] Warner, *The Libelle of Englyshe Polycye*, 59–60, note to l. 8.

[66] Taylor and Roskell, *Gesta Henrici Quinti, Deeds of Henry the Fifth*, 131 n2.

[67] Stansfield, 'The Holland Family', 301.

FIG 8 'Appendix', *Archaeologia*, 18 (1817), 434–5. The seal of John Holland, admiral of England.
With permission from the Bavarian State Library.

showing a ship with England's flag. (Warner, in fact, printed Holland's seal as Plate VI in his edition of the *Libelle* to illustrate this very point).[68] During his tenure as admiral of England, Holland's seal carried his family's arms on the sail of the ship—the *Libelle* thus describes not only the noble and the Great Seal of England but also the admiral's seal, especially since Holland's seal (Fig. 8) differed profoundly from that of his predecessor.[69]

[68] Warner, *The Libelle of Englyshe Polycye*, plate VI.
[69] 'Appendix', *Archaeologia*, 18 (1817), 434–5.

Not only did Holland succeed Bedford as admiral, but Holland's policies, at least on sea, were a direct continuation of those of the duke. During Gloucester's effort to relieve Calais, it was Holland who with Gloucester, Stafford, and Warwick razed Poperinge and Bailleul,[70] an event distinguished in the *Libelle*:

> In the Townes of Poperinge and of Bell;
> Which my Lord of Glocester with ire
> For her falshed set upon a fire.
> And yet they of Bell and Poperinge
> Could never drape her wooll for any thing,
> But if they had English woll withall.
>
> (ll. 251–6)

Caudray's *Book of the Council*

But the most significant evidence for Caudray's probable authorship of the *Libelle* is of a material nature, itself deeply rooted in the poem's self-referential invocation of bureaucratic forms and formats. As I have shown elsewhere, the *Libelle* understands itself as a policy document and, as such, embeds itself among numerous other administrative document types:

> The poem refers to itself variously as 'libelle', 'libellus', 'tretyse', 'processe'/'processus', and 'bo(o)ke'. Then there are likely allusions to royal wills as well as a number of other forms of written documents: the writer calls for an 'ordinaunce' to be made (ll. 643–44), seals and nobles are invoked (ll. 34–35, 43–44, 416, and 586–97), the 'auctorite' of a 'cronique' corroborates a historical passage (ll. 944–45, chronicles are also summoned in ll. 865, 920, and 951), letters are cited (ll. 415, 851), and the writer receives a 'scrowe' from a good squire (l. 180; a scroll is mentioned also at l. 835).[71]

At line 851 the deictic writer behind the *Libelle* refers to the poem as a 'letter': 'My soule discharge I by this presente lettere'. Shortly before

[70] G. L. Harriss and M. A. Harriss, 'III: John Benet's Chronicle for the Years 1400 to 1462', *Camden Fourth Series*, 9 (1972), 185.
[71] Sobecki, 'Bureaucratic Verse', 263.

that, he speaks of scrolls he has written frequently ('by and bye') on other aspects of England's policy:

> And if ye woll more of Caleise here and knowe,
> I caste to writte wythine a litell scrowe,
> Lyke as I have done byforene by and bye
> In othir parties of oure pollicie.
>
> (ll. 834–7)

Scrolls are a quintessentially diplomatic format, used for convenient filing in boxes and for easy expansion by sewing extensions to them. They are not suitable for circulation, which requires for the purposes of transport the durability and economy of flattened formats such as quires, booklets, or bound books. The author of these lines, and of the poem as a whole, is thus a high-ranking government official who frequently writes scrolls on English policy rather than produces tracts for a wider audience. Yet 'litell scrowe' and 'as I have done byforene by and bye' are not indexical references to Caudray's council minutes, which would have been kept as strips of parchment. Instead, these lines point to Caudray's most remarkable administrative achievement, the so-called *Book of the Council.*

During his tenure as clerk, Caudray assembled *The Book of the Council*, an unprecedented digest of council minutes now spread over two manuscripts, London, British Library Cotton MSS Cleopatra F III and F IV.[72] This collection of material, covering mostly the early reign of Henry VI up to the end of Caudray's tenure in 1435, remains unusual in early English administrative history. *The Book of the Council* is actually a misnomer because it was originally not a book but a set of short scrolls—'litell scrowe[s]'—originally sewn together to make rolls; their delivery in 1449 to the Treasury for safe keeping lists them as four separate rolls.[73] Subsequently, 'the rolls were . . . cut up, the edges were severely trimmed, and pasted back-to-back for binding into books, probably for Sir Robert Cotton', as Alfred Brown explains.[74] The materials in *The Book* are a thorough selection of council minutes

[72] On the *Book of the Council*, see Brown, *The Early History of the Clerkship*, 21–7.
[73] Brown, *The Early History of the Clerkship*, 21.
[74] Brown, *The Early History of the Clerkship*, 21.

and policy documents, most of them copies but some are originals. Caudray exercised judgement in making the selection which is itself evidence of his understanding of and interest in foreign policy. The two manuscripts now referred to as *The Book of the Council* still show the format of the original scrolls—policy digests, abstracts, and highlights cut and pared with stitching marks. Having examined the sole surviving letter known to have been signed by Caudray, TNA C 81/1365/7, dated at Mantes 23 June 1419, the secretary hand in Caudrey's letter matches in appearance, aspect, and letter forms the majority of those sections of *The Book of Council* that contains entries written during his tenure as clerk. These occupy the bulk of BL Cotton MS Cleopatra F IV. The entries in the earlier part of *The Book*, BL Cotton MS Cleopatra F III, are almost all in the hand of Robert Frye, clerk of the council and Privy Seal clerk, and they match his hand in his Formulary (Edinburgh University Library MS 183) and examples of documents and private letters signed by him.[75] My identification is further corroborated by inspecting another letter I discovered that was sent by Caudray during his tenure as the king's secretary (London, British Library Cotton MS Caligula D V, fol. 85). This badly damaged personal letter to Henry V, in which Caudray impresses on the king the food shortage among the Parisians and arranges to pass on a copy of Ptolemy to Henry (with the words 'that I Caudray wrote to you of'), is dated at Paris, 17 June 1420, and has been written in the same hand as the signed 1419 letter.

Caudray was clearly drawn to producing ambitious digests and collections. Not long after 1440, during his tenure as dean of St Martin-le-Grand, he assembled the *Register of the College of St Martin le Grand*, a gathering of judgements, petitions, and letters related to the liberties of his institution, now preserved among the Westminster Abbey Muniments as WAM 5.[76] And if two such registers were not enough: it was during his time as Holland's secretary that *The Black Book of the Admiralty* was expanded, evidently for Holland.

[75] For a private letter signed by Frye, see Pierre Chaplais, *English Royal Documents: King John—Henry VI, 1199–1461* (Oxford: Clarendon Press, 1971), plate 19b.

[76] McSheffrey, *Seeking Sanctuary*, 66; and 'Richard Caudray', 174.

On looking closely at *The Book of the Council*, most of the topics touched on by the *Libelle* have their counterparts in *The Book*: 'the patient and zealous investigator of the annals not only of this country, but of France, Germany, Spain, Holland, and other nations, will find some of the most valuable and authentic sources of historical information', as the text's nineteenth-century editor advertises.[77] Furthermore, specific topics and locations mentioned in the poem—Dartmouth, Calais, piracy, Brittany, war preparations, Scandinavian trade—feature in *The Book*, too. These appear to be the 'litell scrowe[s]' the author of the *Libelle* claims to 'have done by forene by and bye / In othir parties of oure pollicie' (ll. 835–6).

In particular, there are a number of specific connections between the *Libelle* and *The Book of the Council* that deserve attention. At one stage, the poem's narrator identifies a 'good Squire' who provided him with an account of Edward III:

> Here bring I in a storie to mee lent,
> That a good Squire in time of Parliament
> Tooke unto mee well written in a scrowe.
> (ll. 178–80)

In the second recension of the poem 'a good Squire' is replaced with 'Hampton squyere', identified by Warner as John Hampton (a. 1391–1472), usher to the Chamber and squire to the Body of Henry VI.[78] 'In time of Parliament' probably refers to the Parliament of May 1432, the only one at which John Hampton's presence was attested.[79] Caudray, too, was present during this Parliament. And the two men certainly knew each other. Both were among the seven

[77] Harris Nicolas, ed., *Proceedings and Ordinances of the Privy Council of England 4* (London: Record Commission, 1835), cxx. The contents of the two manuscripts have been edited in the 1830s by Harris Nicolas in Volumes 3 and 4 of his *Proceedings and Ordinances of the Privy Council of England.*

[78] Warner, *The Libelle of Englyshe Polycye*, 69, note to l. 179; David Starkey, *The English Court: From the Wars of the Roses to the Civil War* (London: Longman, 1987), 30; and Sobecki, 'Bureaucratic Verse', 266.

[79] During the May 1432 Parliament, Hampton was among the household signatories of a petition ('Pro officiariis computantibus hospitii domini regis') to pay the arrears dating to Henry V's death (Chris Given-Wilson, *The Parliament Rolls of Medieval England, 1275–1504* (Woodbridge: Boydell Press and TNA, 2005)).

witnesses in a quitclaim of 1433 to Henry Benet, Caudray's clerk at the time:

> William Gygur to Henry Benet, his heirs and assigns. Quitclaim with warranty of all the lands, rents and services in Lodewelle, Fawlore, Dunstewe and 'Liteltewe' which the said Henry, Thomas Slyman and Agnes his wife recovered against William Gygur and an assize of novel disseisin. Witnesses: Richard Caudray clerk, John Broughton, John Hampton, William Rasshe esquires, John Swyft of Wodestoke, John Lavyngton of Redyng, Simon Somerton. Dated 29 January 11 Henry VI. Memorandum of acknowledgement, 3 February.[80]

The Henry Benet mentioned here must the same individual as the Privy Seal clerk who received John Offord's annuity on the latter's death and whose hand appears in Hoccleve's Formulary, which he may have owned.[81] This identification is further supported by the name 'William Gygur' who seems to be linked to Benet's relative John Gygour, fellow of All Souls College Oxford and the recipient of William Alnwick's former copy of pseudo-Augustine's *Meditations* in Benet's will of 1468.[82]

More important still in connection with Hampton is Warner's argument, used in favour of Moleyns's proposed authorship in light of his role on the council, that the author of the *Libelle* (as mediated through his deictic 'I') 'intended to write further on Calais elsewhere, and he also mentions warnings he had previously given of the impending loss of Harfleur in 1435, which had passed unheeded'.[83] Warner refers to a passage in the poem in which the narrator laments the fall of Harfleur in 1435 to the French:

> Howe was Harflew cried upon, and Rone,
> That they were likely for shought to be gone;
> Howe was it warned and cried on in England,
> I make record with this pen in my hand.
> It was warned plainely in Normandie,
> And in England, and I thereon did crie.
>
> (ll. 842–7)

[80] Quitclaim with warrant from A. E. Stamp, ed., *Calendar of the Close Rolls, Henry VI: Vol. 2, 1429–1435* (London: H. M. Stationery Office, 1933), 233.

[81] See Chapter 2, p. C2.P101.

[82] See Chapter 2, p. C2.P102.

[83] Warner, *The Libelle of Englyshe Polycye*, xxxiv.

The poet adds in a nonchalantly bureaucratic manner that he made 'record with this pen in my hand' (l. 845) of the warning given at the time. The verb 'record' occupies a number of formal senses in Middle English, all of which confer 'witnessed authority' or veracity (*MED* senses 1–7), yet here 'record' is not a verb but a noun; the verb is 'make'. To 'make record' is to produce a document in senses 5 and 6 for the noun 'record' in the *MED*: 'an official document of a government department or municipal office, a written account of parliamentary proceedings'.[84] These senses also include accounts of legal proceedings kept as conclusive evidence, the condition of having been officially recorded, an official record or document, an affidavit, and so on. Clearly, the speaker is referring to council minutes, not least because Warner's account of this passage needs to be corrected: the warnings of the 'impending loss of Harfleur' were not given by the textual 'I'; lines 844 and 846 precisely state in the third person neuter that 'it was warned' and 'howe was it warned', while the intervening line, 845, has the speaker express his agency, in the first person, only in producing a record of these warnings, not in issuing these warnings. These lines, then, by accurately rehearsing how a repeated opinion was committed to official document by the author, capture the minuting of council discussions, all of which were presided over and recorded by Caudray at the time.

This passage is part of the sequence discussed earlier about writing 'litell scrowe[s]' on English policy—the small scrolls produced by Caudray from his council minutes and records that are now in *The Book of the Council*. Yet the subject matter—the state of Harfleur—holds more clues. The *Libelle*'s lament for Harfleur's fall in the year in which Caudray surrendered his duties on the Council forms a resounding 'I told you so', couched in the affected complaint of the poem performed by the author's deictic self. Unsurprisingly, Harfleur appears frequently in the council minutes, but the person perhaps best informed about the exact state of Harfleur's defences at the time was John Hampton—the 'Hampton squire' who provided the author behind the *Libelle* with scrolls. Hampton was not only Henry's

[84] Hans Kurath, Sherman M. Kuhn, and R. E. Lewis, eds, *The Middle English Dictionary*, 19 vols (Ann Arbor, MI: University of Michigan Press, 1952).

household usher and squire, but he had also been master of the king's ordnance.[85] An important council record preserved in Caudray's *Book of the Council* demonstrates the extent of Hampton's familiarity with the state of Harfleur's defences. On 16 April 1430, when the council met at Canterbury, it was decided that,

> William Minors, Captain of Harfleur, and Richard Bokeland, Treasurer of Calais, were to be commanded to deliver to John Hampton, Master of the King's ordnance, the great and small guns, 'bombardos', stones for guns, sulphur, saltpetre, gunpowder, leaden mallets, pavises, 'vangas', shovels, picktoises, baletts, lances, gables, great hawsers and other small ropes, and artillery, and other instruments of war, offensive and defensive, being in their custody, retaining, however, what might be necessary for the defence of the said towns; £2,212 17 lid. to be paid to the Master of the Ordnance for the provision of ordnance for the use of the King in his wars—£1,000 to be paid to Cardinal Beaufort, who was going into France to be of the King's Council there, but a reduction was to be made therefrom in case he should return into England within a quarter of a year without the King's express command—£ 200 to be delivered to John Merston, the Keeper of the King's Jewels, for the private expenses of the King's Chamber, as well in France as in England.[86]

Harfleur and Calais were being stripped for parts, and no one knew this better than Hampton, who received the two towns' artillery and ammunition stocks, leaving them only with 'what might be necessary for the defence of the said towns'. This entry, selected and preserved in Caudray's book (and written in his hand, as I will show later), demonstrates that Hampton possessed an actuarial knowledge of the nature, condition, and precise stock of Harfleur's arms and defences. As master of the ordnance he could form the most accurate view of the town's ability to withstand and assault. It is furthermore telling that the first mention of Harfleur occurs in the same sequence as the appearance of the (Hampton) squire in the poem. But Hampton was also heavily

[85] Oliver Frederick Gillilan Hogg, *English Artillery, 1326–1716: Being the History of Artillery in This Country Prior to the Formation of the Royal Regiment of Artillery* (London: Royal Artillery Institution, 1963), 99.

[86] Nicolas, *Proceedings and Ordinances*, v–vi, for the record in French, see pp. 33–4. The original document in Caudray's Book of the Council is in BL Cotton MS Cleopatra F IV, on fol. 49v.

invested in the war himself, having participated in various campaigns, including Henry's coronation in Paris.[87] Finally, Hampton himself appears to have taken it on himself to compile a formulary for the royal household and chamber office, the *Ryalle Book*.[88] As such, he mirrors Caudray's efforts to codify the council in his *Book* and, later, when dean of St Martin-le-Grand, the *Register*. There is also the equally innovative *Black Book of the Admiralty*, which may date from Holland's tenure, when Caudray was his secretary and chief bureaucrat. It seems that pioneering digests, formularies, and registers follow the path of Caudray's administrative career.

Dean of St-Martin-le-Grand

When discussing Irish gold, the *Libelle* invokes a London jeweller ('As in London saith a Juellere', 692) who testifies to the superior quality of gold from Ireland: 'as they touch, no better could be seene' (695). Caudray, in his capacity as dean of St Martin-le-Grand, a position he assumed immediately on leaving the council in 1435, had frequent documented dealings with London goldsmiths at the time.[89] Much of this contact arose from the circumstance that the collegiate church enjoyed the liberties of sanctuary.[90] As such, many goldsmiths and jewellers outside of London's guild structure set up their shops within the sanctuary perimeter of Caudray's institution.[91] Egged on by the guilds, the city authorities consistently tried to accuse the goldsmiths and jewellers of St Martin-le-Grand of counterfeiting.[92] This accusation became so common that St Martin-le-Grand became a byword for

[87] Juliet Barker, *Conquest* (Cambridge, MA: Harvard University Press, 2012), 145.

[88] Gwilym Dodd and Sophie Petit-Renaud, 'Grace and Favour: The Petition and Its Mechanisms', in *Government and Political Life in England and France, c. 1300–c. 1500*, ed. Christopher Fletcher, Jean-Philippe Genet, and John Watts (Cambridge: Cambridge University Press, 2015), 242.

[89] Stansfield, 'The Holland Family', 299n4; and Alfred J. Kempe, *Historical Notices of the Collegiate Church or Royal Free Chapel and Sanctuary of St. Martin-Le-Grand, London* (London: Longman, 1825), 133–5.

[90] McSheffrey, *Seeking Sanctuary*, 58–82.

[91] I am indebted to Shannon McSheffrey for clarifying the role of St Martin-le-Grand in connection with goldsmiths.

[92] Kempe, *Historical Notices*, 133–5.

counterfeit products, well into the seventeenth century, allowing Samuel Butler to rail against them in *Hudibras*: 'those false St Martin's beads, / Which on our lips you place for reds'.[93] In 1447, Caudray had to strike a compromise between the complaints of London goldsmiths and the many goldsmiths and jewellers who had set up shop in the precinct of St Martin's.[94] The king wrote directly on this matter to Caudray, ordering that his former clerk permit a search of the sanctuary since there were 'divers persons dwelling within our Seinctuarie of St Martin's that forge and sell laton and coper, some gilt and some sylved, for gold and silver, unto the grete deceipt and injurie of our lege people'.[95] This correspondence led to one of Caudray's surviving petitions, TNA SC 8/270/13497 (written in 1440).[96] As executor of John Holland's will, Caudray stored all of his former patron's London possessions in St Martin-le-Grand, having them valued by London goldsmiths. The valuation was carried out by Caudray on 12 November 1450.[97]

As the 1440 petition and the 1419 signet letter show, Caudray wrote not only in Latin and French, but also in English, the language of the *Libelle*, which contains marginal annotation in Latin. He also used English for a number of documents in the *Register* of St Martin-le-Grand and for the inventory he prepared after Holland's death (WAM 6643). The original dialect of the *Libelle*, represented in the best and earliest manuscript (Oxford, Bodleian Library MS Laud 704), is identical to Caudray's and matches the *LALME* profiles for the London and Windsor area. Significantly, spelling and turns of phrase are consistent across the Holland inventory and the *Libelle*, as the following instances document: 'yeve/yeven' (give), 'hede' (heed, head), 'pees' (peace), 'alle maner', 'castell', 'kyng', 'Fraunce', 'emperour', 'eche' (each), 'citee', and lexical choices that are not common 'trusse/trussying' (packed up, bound together).[98] Caudray's 1440 petition to the king (TNA SC 8/270/13497, a copy with six minor differences but in the same hand is preserved in the *Register*, WAM 5, fol. 42r–v), and the only known

93 Kempe, *Historical Notices*, 133.
94 Kempe, *Historical Notices*, 134.
95 Kempe, *Historical Notices*, 135.
96 On this event, see McSheffrey, *Seeking Sanctuary*, 65–82.
97 Stansfield, 'The Holland Family', 303.
98 For the instances in the inventory, see Stansfield, 'The Holland Family', 301, 317–18.

document in Caudray's hand, the signet letter of 1419 (C 81/1365/7), have 'especiale', 'avyse' (advice, counsel, used frequently in the poem), 'keping', 'moneth' (month), 'liberte', 'progenitours' (ancestors), 'ayenst' (against), 'entred', 'frendes', 'lyke to', 'semblable' (similar), or 'ensample' (example).

But what does Caudray's authorship of the *Libelle* mean for the poem? The most important consequence of this identification is that it allows us to understand the poem in its immediate context, as a work of the outgoing council administration, produced by one of England's highest-ranking yet not overtly 'political' bureaucrats. The *Libelle* is a parting shot aimed at the new council, and it represents the political views of Lord Hungerford and John Holland, admiral of the fleet, while it professes allegiance to the policies of Henry V. In other words, in its resolute intervention in current policy, the poem declines to affirm or justify Lancastrian authority at a moment when the dynasty was at its weakest point—a teenage Henry VI was coming of age while the feuding council members had already done much irreparable damage to the reputation of the government. In a movement that inverts the trajectory of Hoccleve's *Regement*, the *Libelle* urges the council overseeing the transfer of power to the new king to resuscitate the policy of the old king, Henry V, who had been dead for fourteen years. It is telling that a poem as self-consciously propagandistic and political as the *Libelle* does not engage in any Lancastrian propaganda itself, instead raising as examples Edgar, Edward III, and Henry V.

As with other indexical works, the *Libelle* is not anonymous as an accident of history: as the envoys and deictic references demonstrate, this poem was written for an intimate audience who were personally acquainted with the author's bureaucratic activities. In addition to the council member Lord Hungerford, who is named in the poem as having overseen and approved the work, Warner identified all of the poem's likely intended recipients in the envoy to the second edition,[99] and all of them happened to be members of the council. The audience therefore was in all probability the council itself, perhaps extending to a few persons close to the council, but it was hardly wider than that. In this sense, the *Libelle* assumes the reader to know its author,

[99] Warner, *The Libelle of Englyshe Polycye*, 102–4.

Richard Caudray, and assign his voice to its argument. While the policy advocated by this poem furthers the interests of Duke Humphrey and Caudray's new employer, John Holland, the poem also marks Caudray's withdrawal from the national stage with a political warning shot. It is much less personal, of course, than Gower's Trentham manuscript or Hoccleve's *Series*, but the *Libelle* lays to rest Caudray's public persona just as it performs his political vision, and it does so by articulating his concern for the direction of the council's foreign policy.

4

Lydgate's Kneeling Retraction

The Testament *as a Literary Palinode*

Lydgate's Indexical Self

The *Testament of Dan John Lydgate*, which survives in sixteen manuscripts and in one inscription, is a poem of some 800 lines, broken down into five movements that deploy rhyme royal for the second and fourth parts, and octave stanzas for the remainder.[1] Written toward the end of John Lydgate's life, the autobiographical *Testament* offers a uniquely retrospective angle on the poet's work.[2] At the centre of

[1] The manuscripts are listed in the *Digital Index of Middle English Verse*, ed. Linne R. Mooney, Daniel W. Mosser, and Elizabeth Solopova (www.dimev.net). Certain parts of the poem, in particular parts 1 and 5, circulated independently. This is also the case with the stanzas in John Clopton's chantry chapel at Long Melford, which are limited to part 5. On these fragments, see Shannon Gayk, *Image, Text, and Religious Reform in Fifteenth-Century England* (Cambridge: Cambridge University Press, 2010), 117–20; and Gail McMurray Gibson, *The Theatre of Devotion: East Anglian Drama and Society in the Late Middle Ages* (Chicago, IL: Chicago University Press, 1995).

[2] The generally accepted late dating of the *Testament* is based on the self-referential remarks to old age in the poem. Similar references are contained in 'On De Profundis', 'An Exposition of the Pater Noster', and the 'Prayer in Old Age' (W. H. E. Sweet, 'Lydgate's Retraction and "his resorte to his religyoun"', in *After Arundel: Religious Writing in Fifteenth-Century England*, ed. Vincent Gillespie and Kantik Ghosh (Turnhout: Brepols, 2011), 243–59, at 251). Derek Pearsall, too, places this poem among Lydgate's final years, between 1441 and 1449, by accepting the narrator as the

Last Words: The Public Self and the Social Author in Late Medieval England.
Sebastian Sobecki, Oxford University Press (2019).
DOI: 10.1093/oso/9780198790778.001.0001

this indexical poem is Lydgate's kneeling persona, steeped in prayer and mindful of his advanced age:

> I, that am falle in age,
> Gretly feblysshed of old infirmite,
> . . .
> Age is crope In, calleth me to my grave,
> To make rekenyng how I my tyme haue spent.
> (197–8, 217–18)[3]

Substantial parts of the *Testament* reflect on Lydgate's youth (parts 2, 4) and the speaker's subsequent reconciliation with his religious life (parts 3, 5).

The critical response to the *Testament* has been overshadowed by Lydgate's longer poems. During the last two decades, however, readers have begun to turn to this work as part of a wider surge of interest in Lydgate's writings. In a first significant treatment of the *Testament*, Julia Boffey has shown it to be indebted to the literary convention of the testamentary poem.[4] She sees the work as a careful combination of 'fervently devotional and . . . more reflective, ostensibly autobiographical' elements.[5] These autobiographical features occasionally invite comparisons with similar passages in other works. Specifically, the parallels between Lydgate's account of his misspent youth in the *Testament* and Thomas Hoccleve's less than earnest narrative of his misrule in *Le Male Regle* court generalizations about the shared conventions of moralizing poetry. Yet, while the ironic exploitation of Hoccleve's youth looks like a trap set for readers unaware of the intentional fallacy, there is no such distancing tone in Lydgate's text.[6] James Simpson sees in the *Testament* a

'ageing poet' (*John Lydgate (1371–1449)* (Victoria, BC: University of Victoria, 1997)), 13, 39. Pearsall regards the references to Lydgate's youth as formulaic but generally accurate in detail (13), confirming the biographical information in the poem as plausible.

[3] The *Testament*, in *The Minor Poems of John Lydgate*, ed. Henry N. MacCracken, vol. 1, EETS e.s. 107 (London, 1911). All subsequent references to the *Testament* are to this edition.

[4] Julia Boffey, 'Lydgate, Henryson, and the Literary Testament', *Modern Language Quarterly*, 53 (1992), 41–56.

[5] Boffey, 'Lydgate, Henryson, and the Literary Testament', 48.

[6] The fundamental differences between these two poems were first discussed by Jerome Mitchell, *Thomas Hoccleve: A Study in Early Fifteenth-Century English Poetic* (Urbana, IL: University of Illinois Press, 1968), 5, 8–9.

manifestly documentary work that is marked by a movement from the secular text to the spiritual image, producing a document 'in which Christ deletes Lydgate's biography'.[7] This idea has been taken up by Ruth Nisse, for whom the gradual replacement of the textual 'I' with 'Jesu' marks Lydgate's 'self-erasure' toward the end of the poem.[8] A broader sense of self-erasure informs W. H. E. Sweet's reading of the *Testament* as the centrepiece in a retraction that extends over a number of Lydgate's late poems. Sweet follows Fiona Somerset's appeal to cross-examine Lydgate's 'religious' and 'secular' oeuvres, but he interprets the resulting retraction at face value as 'a rejection of Lydgate's own secular and laureate poems', suggesting that the poet 'revolted against' the writing of 'pagan histories'.[9] Thus, the *Testament* has come to be seen as a genuine attempt by Lydgate either to remove himself from the poem in a textual exercise of piety or to retract his secular writings at the end of his extraordinarily productive literary career.

Yet such a radical break with his deictic self is uncharacteristic of Lydgate's writing, and seems to misread the *Testament* itself, where, if anything, it is precisely the Lydgate persona as a pious, kneeling petitioner that moves into the foreground of the poem. Looking back at his literary career—if Lydgate's choices in terms of scope, tone, genre, and subject matter are anything to go by—then holism and inclusivity emerge as paradigmatic in his life as a writer. For self-erasure to work in the final section of the *Testament*, Lydgate should have avoided writing himself into the poem in the first place. No amount of self-deletion at the end of the text can erase the Lydgate persona from the *Testament*: all the attention paid to his youth and to showcasing his poetry in the rhyme royal stanzas remains fixed both on the page and in the memory of the reader. In order to delete Lydgate from the poem, one would

[7] James Simpson, *Reform and Cultural Revolution, 1350–1547* (Oxford: Oxford University Press, 2002), 456.

[8] Ruth Nisse, 'Was it not routhe to se?', in *John Lydgate: Poetry, Culture, and Lancastrian England*, ed. Larry Scanlon and James Simpson (Notre Dame, IN: University of Notre Dame Press, 2006), 279–98, at 293.

[9] Fiona Somerset, 'Hard is with seyntis for to make affray', in *John Lydgate: Poetry, Culture, and Lancastrian England*, ed. Larry Scanlon and James Simpson (Notre Dame: University of Notre Dame Press, 2006), 258–78, at 258, and Sweet, 'Lydgate's Retraction', 359.

need to delete the sections concerned with him. Such a fragmented reading of the poem has been attempted, as is brought out by the stanzas from the *Testament* that were painted around the cornice of John Clopton's chantry chapel at Long Melford.[10] But to achieve this effect, to extract all traces of Lydgate's indexical self, the text first requires dismembering. Nisse perceptively notes that the *Testament* is remarkable for what it omits, but I do not think that the elision of Lydgate's public life from the poem amounts to a dismissal of the active portion of his life: if Lydgate had wished to distance himself from his younger, worldly alter ego, then why is so much of the poem written in rhyme royal and in the established conventions of his aureate style?

Because Lydgate restricts his allusions to Chaucer to passages dedicated to his own misspent youth, the *Testament* appears to deny secular poetic language the power to capture profound religious experience. I will suggest, however, that the absence of secular forms and allusions in those sections of the poem that portray the kneeling poet-narrator encourage us to read the *Testament* as a literary palinode rather than a genuine rejection of Lydgate's secular and laureate career. I shall argue, therefore, that Lydgate's *male regle* has made possible his spiritual writing at the end of the poem, since the compelling nature of the underlying prayer scene relies on the prior enactment of what has by now become Lydgate's traditional poetic diction. The resulting language of the final section of the poem—a pared-down, highly repetitive litaneutical code—cannot therefore exist by itself. Rather, as the language of conversion, it is dependent on and vindicated by the prior performance of poetic bravado. In short, as Lydgate stages not a withdrawal from but spiritual reconciliation with the world, the poem is a literary palinode that attempts to impress a sense of coherence onto a body of work so diverse that it defies available literary categorization. Central to the poem's palinodal function is the crucial gesture of the poet's kneeling deictic self who presents his life's work to his patron, God.

Because the *Testament* was written toward the end of Lydgate's life and because the poem appears to provide a set of self-reflective

[10] Gayk, *Image, Text, and Religious Reform*, 117–20; Gibson, *The Theatre of Devotion*; and J. B. Trapp, 'Verses by Lydgate at Long Melford', *Review of English Studies*, 6 (1955), 1–11.

comments on Lydgate's work, any discussion of this text bears directly on the evaluation of his oeuvre. The sheer volume of Lydgate's poetry carries with it a catholic range of literary expressions that explodes available frameworks. Given the transcanonical scope of Lydgate's oeuvre, the secular aesthetic and political configurations denoted by 'Chaucerian' and 'Lancastrian', respectively, fall short of explaining such a vast corpus. Although much of Lydgate's work is indebted to Chaucer, much is also independently inspired by Italian and French models, as Stephanie Kamath has shown.[11] Similarly, many of Lydgate's texts seek out public and political spheres, whereas many others are at home in traditionally religious forms and modes that have no antecedent in the extant repertoire of Chaucer. Long ignored, this capacious body of religious writing has led a number of readers to re-evaluate Lydgate as a spiritual writer: Andrew Cole speaks of 'Lydgate the theologian', and Shannon Gayk astutely notes that 'even a cursory examination of Lydgate's religious writing reveals him to be as much "vernacular theologian" as courtly poet laureate'.[12] I suggest that the fruitful tension between the often conflicting demands of the secular and the religious, as recorded in the palinodal *Testament*, offers a unique yet apt conceptual framework for future explorations of the entire body of Lydgate's work.

The significance of this poem for the contemporary reception of Lydgate's oeuvre is brought out by the prominent treatment the *Testament* receives in a number of manuscripts that collect Lydgate's poetry. As Boffey has shown, the poem is the first item in Cambridge, Jesus College MS 56, whereas it has been bound in as a separate item with Leiden University MS Vossius 9.[13] In London, British Library Harley MS 2255, the heading 'Testamentum Johannis lidgate nobilis poete' (fol. 47r) emphasizes his poetic reputation, and Oxford, Bodleian Library MS Laud Misc. 683 may connect the *Testament* to the poet's perhaps recent death: 'Here begynneth the prologe of damp John /

[11] Stephanie A. Viereck Gibbs Kamath, 'John Lydgate and the Curse of Genius', *Chaucer Review*, 45 (2010), 32–58.

[12] Andrew Cole, *Literature and Heresy in the Age of Chaucer* (Cambridge: Cambridge University Press, 2008), 131–52; and Gayk, *Image, Text, and Religious Reform*, 86.

[13] Boffey, 'Lydgate, Henryson, and the Literary Testament', 50.

lydgatys testament monk of Bury. On whos / sowle I beseche Jhesu haue mercy' (fol. 88r).[14]

Secular Traditions and Religious Devotion

For much of its duration, in the learned references to Dante and Chaucer and, perhaps most clearly, in the many allusions to classical myth, the *Testament* acknowledges, celebrates even, the very literary nature of Lydgate's poetry.[15] During its account of the Harrowing of Hell, Christ is said to have rescued 'soules many a peyre / Maugre Cerberus and all his cruelte' (109–10). Here, the presence of Cerberus aligns Christ's descent into Hell with Aeneas's or Orpheus's journeys to the Underworld. Later, the poem confirms this pairing of Christ and Orpheus when it extols Jesus's name:

Our strong Sampsoun, þat strangled the lyoun,
Our lord, our makere, & oure creatoure,
And be his passioun fro deth our redemptour,
Our Orphevs that from captiuyte
Fette Erudice to his celestiall tour,
To whom alle creatures bowe shall ther kne.
(155–60)

In echoing the long-standing conflation of Christ with Orpheus—a conflation that reaches back to the very beginnings of Christianity—Lydgate opts for a sanitized and therefore accepted Christian use of a classical myth. In this context of conventional Christian allegory, 'Erudice', who is delivered by Orpheus to his 'celestiall tour', becomes the Christian soul, resting securely in heaven. But Lydgate was aware of the ambiguity of Orpheus's achievement, for, in the *Fall of Princes*, his Orpheus is doomed:

But Orpheus, fadir off armonye,
Thouhte Erudice, which was his wiff, so fair,

[14] Boffey, 'Lydgate, Henryson, and the Literary Testament', 50.

[15] Discussions of the *Testament*'s religious significance generally do not draw attention to the frequency of such references. Sweet discusses allusions to pagan material in the *Testament* and in some of Lydgate's other late poems but reads these poems as rejecting such concepts ('Lydgate's Retraction').

For hir sake he felte he muste deie,
Because that he, whan he made his repair,
Off hir [in] trouthe enbracid nothyng but hair.
Thus he lost hire, there is no mor to seyne.
(I.5818–23)[16]

The demise of Lydgate's Orpheus in the *Fall of Princes* is sealed when his blissful youth is contrasted with suffering and death at the hands of women in later life:

How Orpheus endured in his lyue
Ioie entirmedlid with aduersite;
In his youthe whan he dede wyue
He felte in wedlok ful gret felicite,
His worldli blisse meynt with duplicite,
As Fortune hir chaungis gan deuyde,
Which from al vertu be set ful ferr a-side.
(I.5881–7)

Nor is it likely that Lydgate forgot about the biblical motif of a wife who looks back at a place of no hope only to turn to stone, for he employs a reference to Lot's wife glancing back at Sodom: commenting on the lack of enthusiasm for his religious vocation as a young man in the *Testament*, he recollects that 'With Lothes wyf I loked often abak' (676).

In the languid spring opening starting at stanza 37, the reader encounters 'Phebus', 'Aurora', and 'Zepherus', and the psalmic prayer to Christ later in the poem has the Lydgate persona pray for deliverance:

That worldly wawes with ther mortall deluge
Ne drowne me nat in the dredfull dongeoun,
Where Caribdes hath domynacioun,
And Circes syngeth songes of disturbaunce.
(537–40)

His vain life as a young monk who simply went through the motions made him into 'the image of Pygmalyon' (696). Is he praying to be rescued from the secular world, we may ask? After all, he speaks of

[16] *Lydgate's Fall of Princes*, ed. Henry Bergen, 4 vols, EETS e.s. 121–24 (London: Oxford University Press, 1924–7). Subsequent references are to this edition and are cited by book and line number.

'worldy wawes'. A provisional answer is provided a little later: 'To veyn fables I did myn eres dresse, / Fals detraccioun among was to me swete' (721–22). The picaresque account of Lydgate's riotous youth, taking up stanzas 31–56, is cast in a matching tone and lexis, replete with clear borrowings from the General Prologue to the *Canterbury Tales*, as has been noted by a number of readers:[17]

> The yeres passed of my tender youthe
> Of my fresshe Age sered the grennesse,
> Lust appalled, thexperience is kouthe,
> The onweldy Ioyntes starked with rudenese,
> The cloudy sight mysted with dirkenesse,
> Without redresse, recure, or amendes,
> To me of death han brought in the kalendes.
> (241–7)

Echoes of the *Canterbury Tales* are perhaps strongest in Lydgate's ensuing description of spring, which is based on the first eleven lines of the General Prologue:

> Whan that Aprill with his shoures soote
> The droghte of March hath perced to the roote,
> And bathed every veyne in swich licour
> Of which vertu engendred is the flour;
> Whan Zephirus eek with his sweete breeth
> Inspired hath in every holt and heeth
> The tendre croppes, and the yonge sonne
>   Hath in the Ram his half cours yronne,
>   And smale foweles maken melodye,
>   That slepen al the nyght with open ye
>   (So priketh hem Nature in hir corages).
> (I.1–11)[18]

In what marks the difference between Chaucer's writing and Lydgate's aureate style, the later poet spreads his allusions to Chaucer's brief passage over the space of almost fifty lines of the *Testament*: 'The bavme vpreysed most souereyne and entere, / Out of the rote doth

[17] See, for instance, Nisse, 'Was It Not Routhe to Se?', 291–2, and, more fully, Sweet, 'Lydgate's Retraction', 347ff.

[18] All citations of Chaucer's works are taken from *The Riverside Chaucer*, ed. Larry D. Benson, 3rd edn (Oxford: Oxford University Press, 1987).

naturally ascende / With new lyffre, the bareyne soil tamende' (280–2), 'prikkes fressh corages' (297), and 'Zepherus with his blastes sote / Enspireth ver with newe buddes grene' (325–6). In effect, this passage becomes Lydgate's most elaborate variation on the beginning of the General Prologue, even when compared to the *Legend of Dan Joos* or the Prologue to the *Siege of Thebes*.[19] This point cannot be overstated: the description of spring in the *Testament* continues for a further seventy lines until, as with line 12 of the General Prologue ('Thanne longen folk to goon on pilgrimages'), Lydgate introduces the concept of pilgrimage as a metaphor: 'Our dwellyng here is but a pilgrymage' (394). Perhaps Lydgate's use of the *Canterbury Tales* in the *Testament* runs deeper still: the almost verbatim use in line 297 ('So priketh hem nature in hir corages') sets an expectation for a religious shift in the subsequent line ('thanne longen folk to goon on pilgrimages'), but Lydgate's audience has to wait almost 100 lines for such a turn. Some of Lydgate's readers must have been familiar with Chaucer's subversive pairing of 'corages' with 'pilgrimages': if, in the *Canterbury Tales*, the mating birds of the secular spring opening undermine the sincerity behind the desire to undertake penitential journeys, thus paving the way for the estates satire that is about to unfold, then Lydgate's suspension to line 394 of a religious counterweight to 'corages' renders this spiritual lacuna awkward.

Formally speaking, of course, the use of rhyme royal in parts 2 and 4 appears to upset the piety of the *Testament*: rhyme royal is Lydgate's preferred choice throughout his oeuvre, and this stanza form predominates in his secular works. Whether Lydgate follows Chaucer or whether he wishes to depart from the earlier poet by using Chaucer's stanza form is not material here because, as Lois Ebin has shown, the aureate Chaucerian-Lydgatian style had gradually become associated with Lydgate by this stage of his career.[20] For Lydgate, Chaucerian elements had become 'public interiorities', to extend David Lawton's term.[21] And the deployment of

[19] Lydgate's use of the General Prologue in *The Legend of Dan Joos* and *The Siege of Thebes* has been treated by Amanda Leff, 'Lydgate Rewrites Chaucer: The *General Prologue* Revisited', *Chaucer Review*, 46 (2012), 472–9.

[20] Dunbar calls him 'Ludgate aureate' in *The Goldyn Targe* (line 262); see Lois A. Ebin, 'The Theme of Poetry in Dunbar's "Goldyn Targe,"' *Chaucer Review*, 7 (1972), 147–59, at 154. The point is reinforced by Sweet ('Lydgate's Retraction', 347–8).

[21] David Lawton, *Voice in Late Medieval English Literature: Public Interiorities* (Oxford: Oxford University Press, 2017), 1–11.

rhyme royal in the *Testament* clearly evokes Lydgate's aureate poetry: the account of his irreverent youth and his allusions to Chaucer are confined to the rhyme royal sections of the poem. As with the opening of Hoccleve's *Complaint*, the allusions to Chaucer and to his own works are too overt and too numerous to be listed here, but they accompany the transition of Lydgate's porous indexical self from unreformed youth to repentant textual 'I'. The language of the sequence and the secular rhyme royal format, all the while, retain their aureate and literary character.

And so, the extensive use of conventional stylistics throughout the poem and the consistent deployment of classical allusions undermine any attempt by the narrator to successfully displace Lydgate's life as a poet. How is the reader to distinguish between appropriate and 'veyn' uses of myth, between Orpheus, Eurydice, and Cerberus, on one hand, and Charybdis, Circe, and Pygmalion, on the other? In some instances, Orpheus prefigures Christ; in others, the Lydgate persona slips into the guise of Pygmalion or Odysseus, harassed by Circe and Charybdis, while the former nimbleness of Lydgate's 'fresshe Age' has been made rigid by his 'onweldy Ioyntes'. These classical allusions and aureate passages belong to and are shaped by those parts of Lydgate's life that have been left out of this poem. Their form and language, however, have been retained.

No such invocations of classical myth and secular sentiments have found their way into the last section of poem, part 5. When the visual and devotional sequence begins at line 754, Lydgate has expended exactly 100 stanzas on his past life.[22] This final part of the poem, marked by plain diction and paratactic syntax, differs sharply from what has come before:

> Behold the paynemes of whom that I was take,
> Behold the cordes with whiche þat I was bounde,
> Behold the Armoures which made my herte to quake,
> Beholde the gardeyn in which þat I was founde,
> Behold how Iudas toke xxx[ti] pens rounde,
> Beholde his tresoun, beholde his couetyse.
> Behold how I with [many a] mortall wounde,
> Was like a lambe offred in sacrifice.
>
> (762–9)

[22] Though likely to be a coincidence, this is the exact amount of cantos in Dante's equally biographically inspired *Divine Comedy*. See Charles S. Singleton, 'The Poet's Number at the Center', *Modern Language Notes*, 8 (1965), 1–10, at 4.

Sustained anaphora and syntactic parallelism are defining attributes of litanies,[23] and these rhetorical devices tend to generate the affective quality characteristic of litaneutical forms. More specifically, the repetition of the exhortative 'Behold' in part 5 (used almost forty times in the next thirteen stanzas) and the frequency of the name 'Jesus' in parts 1 and 3 are elements commonly found in devotions to the Holy Name of Jesus.[24]

Officially recognized during the Second Council of Lyon in 1274, such devotions became particularly widespread in fifteenth-century England where they were adapted as a liturgical rite.[25] To use the injunction 'behold', as Lydgate's persona does, is to invite the audience to visualize the setting:

> For every Middle English poem that calls for its hearers to listen—'lysteth', or 'herkneth'—another begins with the injunction to look—'beholde', 'looke', 'see', or even 'lo, here'. These poems call for a kind of 'looking' in the mind, for their readers' imaginative engagement with visual forms and spatial structures.[26]

The spatial structure Lydgate envisages throughout the poem is that of the kneeling poet-narrator before Christ. As a quintessentially affective

[23] Although focused on pre-Conquest materials, Michael Lapidge, *Anglo-Saxon Litanies of the Saints* (Woodbridge: Boydell Press for the Henry Bradshaw Society, 1991), remains the fullest discussion of English litanies. See also Nigel Morgan's work on English litanies, *English Monastic Litanies of the Saints after 1100*, 2 vols (Woodbridge: Boydell Press for the Henry Bradshaw Society, 2012-13).

[24] On the significance of the word 'behold' in the poem's visual setting, see Gayk, *Image, Text, and Religious Reform*, 115–16. The convention 'behold and see' is discussed by David Mills, '"Look at Me When I'm Speaking to You": The Behold and See Convention in Medieval Drama', *Medieval English Theatre*, 7 (1985), 4–12.

[25] Jessica Brantley, *Reading in the Wilderness: Private Devotion and Public Performance in Late Medieval England* (Chicago, IL: University of Chicago Press, 2007), 179–80; Richard W. Pfaff, *New Liturgical Feasts in Later Medieval England* (Oxford: Oxford University Press, 1970), 77n7; Catherine A. Carsley, 'Devotion to the Holy Name: Late Medieval Piety in England', *Princeton University Library Chronicle*, 53 (1992), 156–72; Denis Renevey, 'The Name Poured Out', in J. Hogg, ed., *The Mystical Tradition and the Carthusians* (Salzburg, 1996), 127–47; and Denis Renevey, '"Name above Names": The Devotion to the Name of Jesus from Richard Rolle to Walter Hilton's *Scale of Perfection I*', in Marion Glasscoe, ed., *The Medieval Mystical Tradition: England, Ireland, and Wales (Exeter Symposium VI)* (Cambridge: Cambridge University Press, 1999), 103–21.

[26] Brantley, *Reading in the Wilderness*, 122.

and submissive gesture,[27] kneeling permits Lydgate already in the first part of the *Testament* to balance the poem's textual nature with a physical and performative dimension. The first thirty stanzas of the poem, constituting part 1, repeat Christ's name and end in the same emphatic 'kne', merging linguistic with physical devotion:

> Ther is no speche nor language can remembre,
> Lettre, sillable, nor word that may expresse,
> Though into tunges were turned euery membre
> Of man, to telle the excellent noblesse,
> Of blessed Iesu, which of his gret mekenesse,
> List suffre deth to make his servant fre;
> Now mercyful Iesu, for thyn hygh goodnesse,
> Haue mercy on alle that bowe to the her kne!
>
> (57–64)

No linguistic system can encompass 'Jesus', just as no component of such a system ('Lettre, sillable, nor word') can articulate the semantic remit of the divine name. And even if our sole purpose were to be articulatory agents ('into tunges were turned euery membre / Of man'), the poem suggests, we would still fail in this task. In line with the incarnational theology of the devotions to the Name of Jesus, it is not language but the reified speech act, the physical name of Christ on parchment, that figures as an object of devotion and becomes the spiritual catalyst for this form of devotion. Brantley explains that,

> The name of Jesus, honored by visual embellishment and decoration, becomes in these prayers as much picture as word. The name exists precisely at the intersection of textual and visual experience, where holy words become 'objects' meaningful beyond their transparent, grammatical sense, and their manifestation in monograms and pictures, often unvoiceable, is imbued with the power to work miracles. For late medieval Christians, no word is more efficacious, 'does' more in an Austinian sense, than the Holy Name of Jesus.[28]

[27] Richard C. Trexler, 'Legitimating Prayer Gestures in the Twelfth Century: The *De penitentia* of Peter the Chanter', *History and Anthropology*, 1 (1984), 97–126; and Jean Claude Schmitt, 'Between Text and Image: The Prayer Gestures of Saint Dominic', *History and Anthropology*, 1 (1984), 127–62.

[28] Brantley, *Reading in the Wilderness*, 179.

The manuscripts containing Lydgate's poem do not necessarily include the extravagant pictures and monograms of Jesus's name found in typical devotions to the Holy Name, but there are attempts in the layout of the *Testament* visibly to distinguish instances of the name. One manuscript, London, British Library Royal MS 18 D II, gives each instance of 'jhesu' in part 3 in red ink.[29] Although not as ornately as in typical devotions to the Name of Jesus, stanzas 22 and 23 of the *Testament* perform Jesus's name, creating not so much an acrostic as a spelling-out of 'Iesus' in a vertical sequence:

I in Iesu sette for iocunditas,
Gynnyng & grounde of all gostly gladnesse,
E. next in ordre is eternitas,
Tokene and signe of eternall bryghtnesse,
S sette for sanitas, socour ageyn sekenesse,
V. for vbertas, of spirituall plente,
S for suauitas, from whom comyth all suetnesse,
To them that knele to Iesu on there kne.
I in lesu, is ioye that neuere shall ende,
E signyfieth euerlastyng suffisaunce,
S our sauacioun when we shall hens wende;
V. his fyve woundes, þat made vs acquietaunce,
Fro Sathanes myght thurgh his meke sufferaunce,
S for the sacrament, which ech day we may se,
In forme of bred, to saue vs fro myschaunce,
Whan we devoutly receyue it on our kne.

(169–84)

This is not an aural experience, but a visual one: the vertically spelled name of Jesus cannot be heard; it must be seen. Jesus's name, invoked a staggering eighty-five times in this poem, amounts to a protective charm: 'Once the invocation is accomplished, the speaker is protected, just as the pronouncement of a couple performed in the marriage ceremony is followed by certain social and legal effects'.[30] The written

[29] Fols 2v–3v. The manuscript, which lacks part 1, was 'commissioned between 1455 and 1469 by [William] Herbert, first earl of Pembroke' (Alexandra Gillespie, *Print Culture and the Medieval Author: Chaucer, Lydgate, and Their Books, 1473–1557* (Oxford: Oxford University Press, 2006), 37).

[30] Brantley, *Reading in the Wilderness*, 179.

name of Jesus, in other words, becomes a contact relic. Lydgate's *Testament* assigns precisely this function to the name:

> And vndir supporte, Iesu, of thy fauour.
> Or I passe hens, this hoolly myn entent,
> To make Iesu to be chief surveiour,
> Of my laste wille sette in my testament,
> Whiche of myself am Insufficient
> To rekene or counte, but mercy & piete
> Be preferryd, or thou do Iugement,
> To alle that calle to Iesu on ther kne.
>
> (209–16)

Once the written name of Jesus is recorded in pen and ink, it becomes a signature, authorizing and underwriting Lydgate's will in this documentary passage. The poem is now a legal testament, with Jesus's signature turning him into its main executor, or 'chief surveiour'.[31] Rob Lutton points to the 'abundance of marginalia indicating devotion to the name of Jesus, in particular, use of the holy monogram or the name of Jesus itself, not just in religious manuscripts but in letters, wills, charters, accounts and other administrative documents from the late fourteenth century'.[32] Such authorizing uses of Jesus's name and 'signature' transcend the already fluid boundaries of practices associated with the devotion to the Name of Jesus and extend especially to legal practice in charters and, crucially, wills. Thus, when Lydgate writes that 'Iesu' is his 'chief surveiour', the *Testament* inserts itself into the emerging broad tradition of writing influenced by the devotion to the Holy Name of Jesus. I do not wish to classify this poem among the devotions to the Holy Name, for such a firm category may not have existed:

> It is probably futile to attempt to define clear boundaries between those works centred on the holy name and the larger body of Christocentric devotional literature in late medieval England. In

[31] Simpson emphasizes the documentary nature of this poem (*Reform and Cultural Revolution*, 455).

[32] Rob Lutton, '"Love This Name That Is IHC": Vernacular Prayers, Hymns and Lyrics to the Holy Name of Jesus in Pre-Reformation England', in Elizabeth Salter and Helen Wicker, eds, *Vernacularity in England and Wales, c. 1300–1550* (Turnhout: Brepols, 2011), 119–45, at 130.

> fact, it is doubtful that it would be possible to define the common features of those literary representations that we might want to describe as being associated with the holy name.[33]

Lutton adds, however, that 'devotion to the holy name had a vital and increasingly significant basis in popular vernacular text, speech and song in the fifteenth and sixteenth centuries'.[34] Lydgate's *Testament* clearly intersects with this development, and the performative character of part 5—and especially its survival in Clopton's chantry chapel at Long Melford—points to the potential liturgical uses of this poem, not least because the devotion to the Holy Name started as a votive mass before it became 'a generally recognised regular feast' in the fifteenth century.[35] It is worth noting that London, British Library Arundel MS 285, which contains part 5 of the *Testament* among twenty other Christocentric and Marian prayers and lyrics, also includes a popular four-line devotion to the Holy Name of Jesus (*NIMEV* 1703/*DIMEV* 2840). Furthermore, the first forty-four stanzas of the *Testament* are contained in London, British Library Add. MS 34193, a collection of mostly Christocentric hymns and prayers.

Lydgate's Kneeling Pose

This devotional staging of Lydgate's piety is unsettled, however, by the prior performance of his poetic skill in the many learned allusions to antiquity, in the overt borrowings from Chaucer's writings, as well as in his own aureate style in the two interwoven rhyme royal sections. Perhaps the duality of Lydgate's written output that is circumscribed by his laureate poetry and his religious verse—a duality never fully reconciled—provides a conceptual frame of reference that allows us to explore his texts without incessant recourse to Chaucer. Unlike Sweet, I stress duality rather than dichotomy, for we cannot assume that Lydgate wished to distance himself from his public writings or, rather, from his laureate persona, even in the *Testament*.[36] What this poem

33 Lutton, 'Love This Name That Is IHC', 120.
34 Lutton, 'Love This Name That Is IHC', 121.
35 Lutton, 'Love This Name That Is IHC', 123.
36 Sweet, 'Lydgate's Retraction', 343–5.

seems to be suggesting is that the courtly mould in which he wrote so many of his works *can* coexist with genuine expressions of devotion.[37] Lydgate's language of personal devotion, which I have shown to be indebted to the tradition of the devotion to the Holy Name of Jesus, is thus paradoxically sustained by the displacement of a prior secular code, a displacement that requires that which has been removed from the poem to remain in the reader's memory.

In the *Testament*, Lydgate establishes the terms of his own reception. Here, the Benedictine poet makes arrangements for his literary as well as his spiritual afterlife. This simultaneity allows us to glean how he would like to be read by others: Lydgate's indexical self wants to be remembered as a pious monk, but one who could write like no other, and who could straddle religious and secular domains. Thus, I argue that his piety takes the shape of the kneeling monk-poet in a deliberate conflation of devotional kneeling and the genuflexion performed before a sovereign.

It is the final envoy to the *Fall of Princes* that most clearly prefigures, I believe, Lydgate's kneeling pose in the *Testament*, as if these two works—the early and ambitious *Fall of Princes* and the final poetic expression in the personal *Testament*—were meant to bookend Lydgate's prolific career:

> And, for my part, of oon hert abidyng,
> Void of chau*n*g and mutabilite,
> I do presente this book with hand shaki*n*g,
> Of hool affecciou*n* knelyng on my kne,
> Praying the Lord, the Lord oon, too & thre,
> Whos magnificence no clerk ca*n* co*m*prehende,
> To sende you miht, grace and prosperite
> Euer in vertu tencresen & ascende.
>
> (IX.3597–604)

In the *Testament*, too, we witness the poet-narrator on his knees halfway through the poem, only this time the book to be presented is

[37] In this point, I depart from Sweet, who maintains that 'Lydgate signals an awareness of the limitations of this language and its ability to convey religious lessons' ('Lydgate's Retraction', 350). It would be worth examining whether Lydgate's stripped religious language in this poem is an attempt to construct a vernacular alternative to Lollard textuality.

his life's work: 'Mekely kneling, Iesu, in thy presence, / I me to purpose to gynne with prayere' (410–11).[38] The prayer he offers is a text, not an oral expression of devotion. This becomes clear in the final, and most visual, section of the poem, entitled *Vide* ('Behold'), which is preceded by a stanza that reminds the reader that what follows is an ekphrastic vignette and therefore, ultimately, a text:

> The which word, whan I dyd vndirstond,
> In my last age takyng the sentence,
> Theron remembryng, my penne I toke in honde,
> Gan to wryte with humble reuerence,
> On this word, 'vide', with humble diligence,
> In remembraunce of Crystes passioun,
> This litel dite, this compilacioun.
>
> (747–53)

In a gestural and iconographic conflation of devotional kneeling and the secular genuflexion before a patron, the kneeling Lydgate presents Christ with a book.

And there is no shortage of manuscripts—possibly either authorized by Lydgate or produced at Bury shortly after his death—that represent a kneeling Lydgate: at least six witnesses of works as diverse as the lives of *Saints Edmund and Fremund*, the *Troy Book*, and the *Fall of Princes* depict a kneeling Lydgate.[39] These are London, British Library Harley MS 2278, fols 6r and 9r (Figs 9 and 10, respectively); London, British Library Harley MS 1766, fol. 5r (Fig. 11); London, British Library Yates Thompson MS 47, fol. 4r (Fig. 12); Manchester, John Rylands Library MS English 1, fol. 1r (Fig. 13); Oxford, Bodleian Library MS Digby 232, fol. 1r (Fig. 14); Oxford, Bodleian Library MS Ashmole 46, fol. 1r (Fig. 15); and the McGill fragment of the *Fall of Princes*, Montreal, McGill University Libraries MS 143, fol. 4r (Fig. 16). The iconography of the kneeling monk-poet as set out during his lifetime, though not necessarily under his direction, in Harley 2278 and Digby 232 continued to influence the next generation of illuminated manuscripts produced at Bury. This tradition, I argue, shows the

[38] Of course, throughout part 1 the narrator is also kneeling.

[39] Sonja Drimmer maintains that most if not all of the kneeling Benedictine figures depicted in Lydgate manuscripts are actually not author portraits but votive images (*The Art of Allusion*, 114–48 (esp. 115)).

The noble story to putte in remembraunce
Of saynt Edmund martir maide & kyng
With his support my style I wil auaunce
Ffirst to compile after my kunnyng
His glorious lif his birthe and his gynnyng
And be discent how that he that was so good
Was in saxonie born of the roial blood

FIG 9 London, British Library Harley MS 2278, fol. 6r.

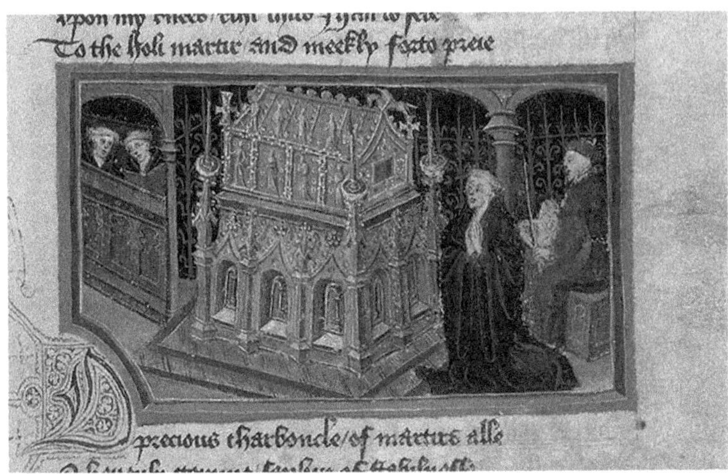

FIG 10 British Library Harley MS 2278, fol. 9r.

extent to which Bury's monks directed Lydgate's reception after his death in a manner consistent with pictorial and textual representations produced during his lifetime. These visual interpretations of the writer, therefore, suggest that his early readers fully understood Lydgate's poetic identity as religious *and* secular.

Harley 2278, which contains the metrical lives of *Saints Edmund and Fremund*, is a superb presentation copy for Henry VI, produced in Bury St Edmunds between 1434 and 1439.[40] William Curteys, abbot of the Benedictine monastery of St Edmund, Bury St Edmunds, commissioned the book as a gift for Henry VI.[41] The manuscript is remarkable

[40] The text has been re-edited in Anthony Bale and A. S. G. Edwards, eds, *John Lydgate's* Lives of SS Edmund and Fremund *and the Extra Miracles of St Edmund* (Heidelberg: Winter, 2009). Edwards has also published a facsimile edition of Harley 2278: *The Life of St Edmund, King and Martyr: John Lydgate's Illustrated Verse Life Presented to Henry VI: A Facsimile of British Library MS Harley 2278* (London: British Library, 2004).

[41] Sonja Drimmer, 'Picturing the King or Picturing the Saint: Two Miniature Programmes for Lydgate's *Lives of Saints Edmund and Fremund*', in *Manuscripts and Printed Books in Europe, 1350–1550: Packaging, Presentation and Consumption*, ed. Sue Powell and Emma Cayley (Exeter: Exeter University Press, 2013), 48–67, at 49; and Edwards, *The Life of St Edmund*, 1–3.

FIG 11 London, British Library Harley MS 1766, fol. 5r.

FIG 12 London, British Library Yates Thompson MS 47, fol. 4r.
© The British Library Board.

FIG 13 Manchester, John Rylands Library MS English 1, fol. 1r.
Copyright of the University of Manchester.

FIG 14 Oxford, Bodleian Library MS Digby 232, fol. 1r.

FIG 15 Oxford, Bodleian Library MS Ashmole 46, fol. 1r.
Reproduced by permission of the Bodleian Libraries, University of Oxford.

FIG 16 Montreal, McGill University Libraries MS 143, fol. 4r.
Reproduced by permission of the Medieval Manuscript Collection, Rare Books and Special Collections, McGill University Library, Montreal.

for a number of reasons, not least because it is the best exponent of what Alexandra Gillespie calls the 'Bury style of book illumination'.[42] Harley 2278, probably produced under Lydgate's supervision,[43] contains not one but two miniatures featuring a kneeling Lydgate. First, on fol. 6r, the poet Lydgate is seen kneeling as he presents his book to the boy-king Henry (Fig. 9), and, later, the monk Lydgate is kneeling before Edmund's shrine on fol. 9r (Fig. 10).[44] In her trenchant analysis of the iconography of Harley 2278, Sonja Drimmer demonstrates that this manuscript 'encourages Henry to envision himself as Edmund and to match both the monarchic and saintly ideals he embodies'.[45] But the parallel kneeling scenes do not only equate Henry with Edmund; Lydgate is displaying the same form of devotion to the saint and to the secular ruler by kneeling in front of both. Elsewhere in her argument, when discussing Yates Thompson 47, Drimmer draws attention to the significance of the type of kneeling: one knee before a worldly patron, but two before God.[46] John Burrow has shown that there is some support for this distinction,[47] but I would like to point out that, on fol. 6r in Harley 2278, where the poet is kneeling before the king, the artist has clearly made an effort to contour both of Lydgate's kneeling legs under his habit (Fig. 9). Just as kneeling on both legs before Henry turns the king into a saint, so the fact that there is no distinction in

[42] Gillespie, *Print Culture*, 39.

[43] 'The original presentation copy of *SS Edmund and Fremund*, BL Harley MS 2278, is one of the few manuscripts that survives that was certainly made in Lydgate's lifetime and in his ambit at Bury' (Gillespie, *Print Culture*, 43).

[44] The apparent youth of Henry corroborates the dating of the manuscript between 1434 and 1439.

[45] Drimmer, 'Picturing the King', 52. Drimmer shows how the presentation scene on fol. 6r is connected to Edmund's coronation scene on fol. 31r (62–3).

[46] Drimmer, 'Picturing the King', 64.

[47] *Dives and Pauper*: 'o God men shuldyn knelyn wyt bothe knees in tokene þat in hym is al oure principal helpe, but to man only wyt þe to [one] knee' (Priscilla Heath Barnum, *Dives and Pauper*, vol. 1, EETS o.s. 275 (London: Oxford University Press for the EETS, 1976), 106). See also *The Book of Curtasye*: 'Be curtayse to God, and knele doun / On bothe knees with grete devocioun. / To mon þou shalle knele opon þe ton, / The toþer to þy self þou halde alon' (Frederick J. Furnivall, ed., *Early English Meals and Manners*, EETS o.s. 32 (London: Humphrey Milford, 1868), 182–3, lines 163–6). Both are quoted by John Burrow, *Gestures and Looks in Medieval Narrative* (Cambridge: Cambridge University Press, 2002), 19–25. Burrow adds, however, that kneeling on both knees is the more common form. On the use of both knees in prayer, see Jean Claude Schmitt, *La raison des gestes dans l'occident médiéval* (Paris: Gallimard, 1990), 295, 300, 306.

Lydgate's manner of kneeling in these two illuminations collapses the distinction between worldly and spiritual iconography. The secular and the religious pose have become one in a Lydgatean gesture.

The afterlife of this 'Bury style' of illumination continues in manuscripts that were produced at Bury in the generation after Lydgate's death. Gillespie has shown that *Edmund and Fremund* in Yates Thompson 47 and Ashmole 46, as well as the two copies of the *Fall of Princes* in Harley 1766 and the McGill fragment, were written by the same scribe, who is also associated with Bury.[48] The indebtedness of Yates Thompson 47 to Harley 2278, discussed by Kathleen Scott but more fully developed by Drimmer,[49] reveals the shared provenance of these manuscripts and the continuation of a particular illumination style that may have been 'authorized' by Lydgate. Harley 1766 (*Fall of Princes*; Fig. 11) and Yates Thompson 47 (Fig. 12) show Lydgate kneeling on both knees before St Edmund, whereas he is kneeling before Henry's father, Henry V, in two copies of the *Troy Book*—John Rylands Library MS English 1 (Fig. 13) and Bodleian Library MS Digby 232 (Fig. 14)—as well as in the McGill fragment of the *Fall of Princes* (Fig. 16).[50] Most interesting here is Digby 232, which features Lydgate kneeling before Henry V on both legs (unlike the McGill fragment, which clearly shows him kneeling on one leg only): unsurprisingly, Digby 232 was copied during Lydgate's lifetime, between 1420 and 1430.[51]

Not only can Lydgatean kneeling turn Henry VI into a saint, but a kneeling Lydgate can also transform St Edmund into Henry's royal father: in Ashmole 46, fol. 1r (*Edmund and Fremund*; Fig. 15), and Harley 1766, fol. 5r (*Fall of Princes*; Fig. 11), Edmund is enthroned, donning the same ermine and blue gown worn by Henry V in the McGill *Fall of*

[48] Gillespie, *Print Culture*, 38–9.

[49] Kathleen L. Scott, 'Lydgate's *Lives of Saints Edmund and Fremund*: A Newly Located Manuscript in Arundel Castle', *Viator*, 13 (1982), 335–66, at 358–9; and Drimmer, 'Picturing the King', *passim*.

[50] The John Rylands Library manuscript was influenced by the 'Bury style' (Gillespie, *Print Culture*, 37). Daniel Wakelin notes that Harley 1766 'plausibly... reflects the special involvement of Lydgate' (*Humanism, Reading, and English Literature, 1430–1530* (Oxford: Oxford University Press, 2007), 40), but since the same scribe was involved in the production of London, British Library MS Yates Thompson 47, which Drimmer convincingly dates to 'between 1461 and 1465' (56), then this scribe was either old when producing Yates Thompson 47 or, more probably, Harley 1766 was written after Lydgate's lifetime.

[51] Gillespie, *Print Culture*, 37.

Princes and in the Digby *Troy Book*.[52] Whether Lydgate is kneeling on both knees in a spiritual fashion before a secular ruler (as in Harley 2278) or whether he is representing St Edmund in the regal attire of Henry V, these manuscripts appear to have made an effort to reconcile the religious and secular dimensions of Lydgate's identity as a monk-poet.

Kneeling was part of a complex 'gestural dialogue in accordance with fixed social rules: kneeling demanded a specific reaction'.[53] Barbara Stollberg-Rilinger notes the structural affinity between secular and spiritual genuflexion:

> Genuflection or kneeling is a symbolic gesture of self-abasement, generally with the intention of obtaining mercy—in the act of penance before God, in the act of submission, *deditio*, before a temporal ruler. It is clear that a close structural affinity exists between the political ritual of apology upon one's bended knee and the Christian ritual of remorse, repentance, and absolution, even that both rituals occasionally formed an inseparable unity.[54]

The deferential act of *deditio*, or submission, by the kneeling person demanded of the ruler that he act in accordance with mercy and magnanimity. 'The social logic of these procedures,' adds Stollberg-Rilinger, 'followed not least from the analogy of penance before God and absolution from sins.'[55] The staged nature of this process leads her to conclude that all such instances of genuflexion were essentially public performances and, thus, fiction. Stollberg-Rilinger concentrates on the influence of the religious pose on secular kneeling, but, given the pervasive use of genuflexion in social contexts, the staged nature of secular kneeling must have created an expectation of mercy in religious contexts. If, therefore, in secular contexts 'the ritual's effect of creating

[52] Drimmer has analysed a further representation of Edmund enthroned in Yates Thompson 47 fol. 1r, which does not include any supplicants. This figural absence, argues Drimmer, 'is a lacuna meant for the reader/viewer to fill' ('Picturing the King', 59).

[53] Barbara Stollberg-Rilinger, 'Kneeling before God, Kneeling before the Emperor: The Transformation of a Ritual During the Confessional Conflict in Germany', in Nils Holger Petersen, Eyolf Østrem, and Andreas Bücker, eds, *Resonances: Historical Essays on Continuity and Change* (Turnhout: Brepols, 2011), 149–72, at 150. On kneeling in contexts of book dedication, see Isabel Davis, '"The Trinite Is Our Everlasting Lover": Marriage and Trinitarian Love in the Later Middle Ages', *Speculum*, 86/4 (2011), 914–63.

[54] Stollberg-Rilinger, 'Kneeling before God', 149.

[54] Stollberg-Rilinger, 'Kneeling before God', 151.

obligation was achieved without reference to the inner conviction of the one who performed it', then something similar must hold true in instances where the believer *is seen* to be kneeling before God. In other words, when Lydgate represents himself in a kneeling pose, he is not only showing the outer signs of remorse, but he is vindicating his life and work by expecting forgiveness and acceptance. Whether he is kneeling before the saint or before the king, or both, Lydgate may have chosen this as the pose in which he wanted to be seen (and read) throughout his career and, particularly, at the end of life.

The *Testament*, therefore, is both an outer and an inner gesture that shows the kneeling Lydgate to be offering his 'litel dite', his 'compilacioun', to Christ. As an inner gesture, the poem throws open the conflicting expectations of public service and spiritual devotion; as an outer gesture, the kneeling pose attempts to reconcile the poet's literary career with his calling—simultaneously expecting forgiveness for his sins as a Christian and acceptance of his life's work as a poet. Lydgate's self-interpretation as a conflicted monk-poet, therefore, establishes a new framework for conceptualizing his work as an ambitious yet ultimately unrealized project of splicing two lives and thus reconciling two literary domains. And even as he rejects his worldly self in the outer gesture of kneeling, the aureate verses of much of the *Testament*—his inner literary conviction—show that he wants to have it both ways.

Retractions and Palinodes

In the end, the success of the *Testament* and, surely, most narrative poems, lies not in one particular section but in the work in its entirety. What precedent is there, after all, for a writer urging his or her audience—in earnest—to discard in terms of content and form a portion of what they have just read? There is Chaucer's well-known Retraction, of course, which continues the tradition of such mock-remorseful palinodes.[56] It is generally agreed that the Retraction,

[56] For important discussions of the Retraction, see Jason Michael Herman, 'Intention, Utility, and Chaucer's Retraction' (PhD dissertation, University of Arizona, 2009); James McNelis, 'Parallel Manuscript Readings in the CT Retraction and Edward of Norwich's *Master of Game*,' *Chaucer Review*, 36 (2001), 87–90; Anita Obermeier, *The History and*

which circulated with those manuscripts of the *Canterbury Tales* that contain the Parson's Tale, may have been the original ending devised by Chaucer for his cycle of tales, even though the Retraction probably also circulated independently in stand-alone copies of the Parson's Tale.[57] There is less agreement, however, on whether Chaucer was sincere in his closing words. Many readers find it difficult to reconcile the literary palinode, usually placed at the end of a single work, with Chaucer's attempt to include all of his writings in the Retraction.[58] Such readings, however, do not fully acknowledge the indexical relationship between the content and its material context. By binding the closing words together with the *Canterbury Tales*, the Retraction performs its paradoxical service of transmitting in manuscript a text rejected by its writer. In other words, the distancing tone of a palinode, however comprehensive or penitential, is silenced by the simultaneous deictic presence of the physical manuscript.

And such retractions need not be limited to a single text: one analogue to Chaucer's authorial humility in his Retraction provides a remarkably complete model for Lydgate's *Testament*: the probably authentic *Le Testament* by Jean de Meun (1291–5), which, to my knowledge, has not been directly associated with Lydgate's poem.[59]

Anatomy of Auctorial Self-Criticism in the European Middle Ages (Amsterdam: Rodopi, 1999), 203–20; Matthew C. Wolfe, 'Placing Chaucer's "Retraction" for a Reception of Closure', *Chaucer Review*, 33 (1999), 427–31; Peter Travis, 'Deconstructing Chaucer's Retraction', *Exemplaria*, 3 (1991), 135–58; and Robert Boenig, 'Taking Leave: Chaucer's Retraction and the Ways of Affirmation and Negation', *Studia Mystica*, 12 (1989), 21–8.

[57] This question has been investigated by Herman, 'Intention'. Challenges to the established view have come from Charles Owen, Jr., 'What the Manuscripts Tell Us about the Parson's Tale', *Medium Aevum*, 63 (1994), 239–49; and Mìceál Vaughan, 'Creating Comfortable Boundaries: Scribes, Editors, and the Invention of the Parson's Tale', in *Rewriting Chaucer: Culture, Authority, and the Idea of the Authentic Text, 1400–1602*, ed. Thomas A. Prendergast and Barbara Kline (Columbus, OH: Ohio University Press, 1999), 45–90, although both 'concede that the textual evidence... is heavily in favour of the Parson's Tale and Retraction as Chaucer's original ending' (Herman, 'Intention', 19). However, both Owen and Vaughan have demonstrated that the Retraction circulated separately with The Parson's Tale.

[58] This specificity of Retraction has been pointed out by Benson in *The Riverside Chaucer*, 22.

[59] On the poem, see the introduction in Silvia Buzzetti Gallarati, *Le testament maistre Jehan de Meun: un caso letterario* (Alessandria: Ed. dell'Orso, 1989). The similarity in the works' common titles, *Le Testament de Maistre Jehan de Meung* and *The Testament of Dan*

Isabel Davis notes that copies of de Meun's *Le Testament* are often accompanied by kneeling figures.[60] Of the 116 surviving copies, one exemplar, London, British Library Royal MS 19 B XII,[61] carries the fifteenth-century inscriptions of Nicholas Upton, who enjoyed Duke Humphrey's patronage at the same time as Lydgate.[62] And just as Chaucer's Retraction was placed at the end of manuscripts containing the *Canterbury Tales*, de Meun's *Testament* was often bound together with copies of the *Roman de la Rose* as a literary palinode. This is certainly the case with Nicholas Upton's manuscript as well as with two of the most celebrated copies of de Meun's *Testament*: the sumptuously illuminated copies in Paris, Bibliothèque nationale MS Bibliothèque de l'Arsenal 3339, and Geneva, Bibliothèque de Genève MS fr. 178. De Meun's palinode is an altogether closer analogue to Lydgate's poem because, unlike Chaucer's Retraction, the French poet makes youth central to his argument. The opening sequence of de Meun's *Testament* already contains the references to 'the youthful literary error' and 'the wish to atone with this *Testament*':[63]

> J'ay fait en ma jeunesce mains dits par vanité
> Ou maintes gens se sont pluseurs fois delité
> Or m'en doint Dieux un faire par vraie charité
> Pour amender les autres qui peu m'ont proufité.
> Bien doit estre escusez jeune cuer en jeunesce
> Quant Diex li donne grace d'estre viel en viellesce;
> Mais moult est granz vertus et tres haute noblesce

John Lydgate, is of course no indicator of influence, as these titles varied from manuscript to manuscript. Anita Obermeier points to de Meun's *Le Testament* in her treatment of Chaucer's Retraction, in Robert M. Correale and Mary Hamel, eds, *Sources and Analogues of the Canterbury Tales II* (Cambridge: Cambridge University Press, 2005), 780–1.

[60] Davis, '"The Trinite Is Our Everlasting Lover"', 945–58.

[61] A second copy is contained in London, British Library Royal MS 19 A IV, also a fifteenth-century manuscript (James P. Carley, *The Libraries of Henry VIII* (London: British Library, 2000), 121). Other copies held in British libraries are listed in Silvia Buzzetti Gallarati, 'Nota bibliografica sulla tradizione manoscritta del Testament di Jean de Meun 1', *Revue Romane*, 13 (1978), 3–33, at 23–6. For the total number of manuscript copies, see Henri-Jean Martin, *The History and Power of Writing* (Chicago, IL: Chicago University Press, 1995), 201.

[62] Boffey, 'Lydgate, Henryson, and the Literary Testament', 41n3.

[63] Obermeier, *The History and Anatomy of Auctorial Self-Criticism*, 124.

Quant cuer en jeune aage a meurté s'adresce.
Maiz li uns et maint autre sont de si grant durté
Qu'en nul estat ne veulent venir a meurté,
Ainz se sont a jeunesce si joint et ahurté
Com se de touzjours vivre eussent seurté.

(5–16)

(In my youth, it is true, I composed a number of works which regularly gave pleasure to a variety of people; may God now allow me to compose one out of real charity to make up for those others which have profited me little.
A young heart in its youth deserves forgiveness when by God's grace it becomes mature in maturity, but it is a signal virtue and most noble act when a heart strives for maturity while still young.
But there are many who are so obdurate that at no point in their career do they wish to achieve maturity, but are attached to youth as if they were sure of living for ever.)[64]

Although Lydgate's tone is more personal and less didactic than de Meun's, the English poet also bemoans the follies of his own youth before asking for forgiveness. In part 2, after thirty-two rhyme royal stanzas dedicated to youth and spring, Lydgate turns to himself:

And for my part, I can remembre weell
Whan I was gladdest in that fresshe sesoun,
Lyke brotel glasse, not stable nor like stell,
Fer out of harre, wilde of condicioun,
Ful geryssh, and voyde of all resoun,
Lyk a phane, ay turnyng to and fro,
Or like an orloge whan the peys is goo.
Youe to onthryfte and dissolucioun,
Stode onbrydeled of all gouernaunce,
Whiche remembryng, be meke confessyoun,
Now with my potent to fynde allegeaunce,
Of olde surfetes, contrite with repentaunce,
To the Iesu, I make my passage,
Rehersyng trespaces don in my tender age.

(395–408)

[64] Text and translation are taken from Tony Hunt, *Villon's Last Will: Language and Authority in the Testament* (Oxford: Oxford University Press, 1996), 22.

De Meun's 'jeune cuer' receives fuller treatment in Lydgate's string of analogies (397–401), whereas the French writer's frequently used 'jeunesce' finds its equivalent in 'tender age' (408) in this passage, and in 'tender youthe' and 'fresshe Age' elsewhere (241–2). Likewise, as if written in response to the conventions laid out by de Meun, Lydgate's appeal to God's grace and forgiveness follows immediately and takes on the form of kneeling:

> But to directe þe grace my matere,
> Mekely knelyng, Iesu, in thy presence,
> I me purpose to gynne with prayere,
> Vnder thi mercyfull fructuous influence,
> So thou Iesu of thy benevolence,
> To my requestes be mercyfull attendaunce,
> Graunt or I deye, shryft, hosel, repentaunce.
> (409–15)

I do not argue that Lydgate modelled his *Testament* on de Meun's poem, although the English poet might very plausibly have seen Upton's copy or one of the manuscripts in circulation, but I wish to show that the movement from the misspent youth of a writer to religious contrition is ultimately a formal device, closely allied to the literary retraction as shaped by de Meun's *Testament*. Most significantly, there is a crucial codicological dimension to Lydgate's palinode: since virtually all of the surviving manuscripts of the *Canterbury Tales* that include the complete Parson's Tale also contain the Retraction,[65] it is unlikely that Lydgate would not have seen Chaucer's palinode. Furthermore, there is good reason to believe that he also may have encountered de Meun's retraction in a similar position in Upton's manuscript or in another copy of the *Roman de la Rose*. As a reader of manuscripts, therefore, Lydgate would have experienced the palinode as a device that physically transmits the very work that it textually rejects.

If the *Testament* is indeed an attempt by Lydgate to close his poetic career with a retraction, then he makes sure that his poetic talents are not overlooked. In other words, the *Testament* is not an attempt by his

[65] Herman, 'Intention', 19; and John M. Manly and Edith Rickert, eds, *The Text of The Canterbury Tales: Studied on the Basis of All Known Manuscripts*, 8 vols (Chicago, IL: University of Chicago Press, 1940), 2:471–2.

indexical self to reject his laureate past but to assign a place to it in an ultimately pious narrative. His use of aureate style and rhyme royal conventions connects the piety of the final sequence with the affected humility invoked in so many of his own envoys and colophons, where the writer asks the reader's forgiveness for errors and omissions.[66] By drawing on and evaluating his own body of work in a single text that is not binary but dualistic—the structure of which is encoded in the enmeshing of octave and rhyme royal sections—Lydgate's *Testament* takes the place of such an authorial palinode, casting his own life as text and presenting it to its ultimate reader—God. Perhaps the fruitful tension between the secular and the religious offers a new conceptual framework for future explorations of the Monk of Bury: the interweaving of his religious vocation and the often conflicting demands of secular patrons characterize the *Testament* and, with hindsight, much of Lydgate's literary production, as Lydgatean.

[66] See, for instance, John Lydgate, *The Siege of Thebes*, ed. Robert A. Edwards (Kalamazoo, MI: Medieval Institute Publications, 2001), 150 (lines 4709–16); John Lydgate, *Saint Austin at Compton, c. 1420–40*, in *Saints' Lives in Middle English Collections*, ed. E. G. Whatley, A. Thompson, and R. Upchurch (Kalamazoo, MI: Medieval Institute Publications, 2004), 224–37, at 237 (lines 403–8); John Lydgate, *The Temple of Glass*, ed. J. Allan Mitchell (Kalamazoo, MI: Medieval Institute Publications, 2007), 53 (lines 1393–1403); and John Lydgate, *Lydgate's Troy Book*, ed. Henry Bergen, 4 vols, EETS s.s. 97, 103, 106, 126 (London: Kegan Paul, 1906–35), 3:879 (Envoy, lines 92–9).

5

The Signet Self

George Ashby's Autograph Writing

George Ashby (d. 1475) was a poet and royal signet clerk during the reign of Henry VI. He is known for three works: the Chaucerian complaint *A Prisoner's Reflections* (henceforth: *Reflections*) and two combined poems dedicated to Edward of Westminster, the mirror for princes *The Active Policy of a Prince* (henceforth: *Active Policy*) and translations of classical epigraphs and political maxims, the *Dicta et opiniones diversorum philosophorum* (henceforth: *Dicta*), which is usually considered to be an unfinished component of the *Active Policy of a Prince.*[1] Ashby's poems survive in two fifteenth-century manuscripts: *Reflections* is preserved in Cambridge, Trinity College, MS

[1] On Ashby, see John Scattergood, 'Ashby, George (b. before 1385?, d. 1475), Administrator and Poet', *ODNB* (Oxford: Oxford University Press, 2004); John Scattergood, 'Peter Idley and George Ashby', in *A Companion to Fifteenth-Century English Poetry*, ed. A. S. G. Edwards and Julia Boffey (Cambridge: D. S. Brewer, 2013), 113–25; Otway-Ruthven, *The King's Secretary and the Signet Office in the XV Century*, 120, 132, 135, 185; and Robert Meyer-Lee, 'Laureates and Beggars in Fifteenth-Century English Poetry: The Case of George Ashby', *Speculum*, 79/3 (2004), *passim*. *A Prisoner's Reflections* has been edited by Linne R. Mooney and Mary-Jo Arn, eds, *The Kingis Quair and Other Prison Poems* (Kalamazoo, MI: Medieval Institute Publications, 2005). For Ashby's *Active Policy of a Prince*, see Mary Bateson's *George Ashby's Poems: From the Fifteenth-Century MSS at Cambridge*, EETS ES 76, Repr. 1965 (London: Kegan Paul, Trench, and Trübner, 1899).

Last Words: The Public Self and the Social Author in Late Medieval England.
Sebastian Sobecki, Oxford University Press (2019).
DOI: 10.1093/oso/9780198790778.001.0001

R.3.19, whereas the other two poems make up Cambridge, University Library, MS Mm.4.42. Both *Reflections* and *Active Policy/Dicta* have received attention in critical discussions of prison writing and political advice literature, respectively.[2]

Ashby is usually studied in the context of fifteenth-century Chaucerian traditions and continuations; he certainly uses material from Chaucer's works, and he explicitly mentions Chaucer, Gower, and Lydgate, though his most extensive, if unacknowledged, literary debt may be to his fellow bureaucrat, Thomas Hoccleve, whose *Series* is echoed in *Reflections* and whose political tract for Henry V, *The Regement of Princes*, appears to have shaped aspects of *Active Policy*.[3] The most obvious connection between Ashby and Hoccleve, and perhaps the conduit for Hoccleve's work, is John Hethe, Hoccleve's colleague in the Privy Seal office who was either temporarily transferred or on loan to the signet office in the 1420s, when he overlapped with Ashby in France.[4] A signet letter signed by Hethe in France in October 1420 survives.[5] Ashby's silent use of Hoccleve is particularly remarkable given the depth and scope of the elder poet's impact on Ashby, so much so that Robert Meyer-Lee sees this omission as symptomatic of the unsung fate of the bureaucrat-poet in the later Middle Ages: 'Hoccleve would go unacknowledged even by George Ashby, the sole fifteenth-century poet who demonstrates close acquaintance with

[2] For *Reflections*: John Scattergood, 'George Ashby's *Prisoner's Reflections* and the Virtue of Patience', *Nottingham Medieval Studies*, 37 (1993), 102–9; Meyer-Lee, 'Laureates and Beggars', 688–726; Julia Boffey, 'Chaucerian Prisoners: The Context *of The Kingis Quair*', in *Chaucer and Fifteenth-Century Poetry*, ed. Julia Boffey and Janet Cowen (London: King's College London, 1991), 84–102; Joanna Summers, *Late-Medieval Prison Writing and the Politics of Autobiography* (Oxford: Clarendon Press, 2004); for the *Active Policy/Dicta*: Curt F. Bühler, 'The *Liber de Dictis Philosophorum Antiquorum* and Common Proverbs in George Ashby's Poems', *PMLA*, 65/2 (1950), 282–9; Margaret Kekewich, 'George Ashby's *The Active Policy of a Prince*: An Additional Source', *Review of English Studies*, 41/164 (1990), 533–5; John Watts, *Henry VI and the Politics of Kingship* (Cambridge: Cambridge University Press, 1996), 41–55; Meyer-Lee, 'Laureates and Beggars', 688–726; and Rosemarie McGerr, *A Lancastrian Mirror for Princes: The Yale Law School New Statutes of England* (Bloomington, IN: Indiana University Press, 2011), 107–12.

[3] Hoccleve's influence on Ashby has been discussed in depth by Meyer-Lee, 'Laureates and Beggars', 688–726, a revised version of which is included in Meyer-Lee, *Poets and Power*, 139–68.

[4] On Hethe, see Chapter 2.

[5] TNA C 81/1365/24.

his work'.[6] What does a clerkly poet need to do to get cited, one may ask? Yet it is too tempting to view bureaucratic poetry as saddled with a poetics of failure, in the sense that such works frequently do not reach their audiences and more often than not fail to register their writer's identity in their subsequent manuscript transmission.[7] Perhaps this fear of irrelevance and slight (paradoxically justified by Ashby helping himself to Hoccleve's work without attribution) underlies the genuine anxiety of influence among bureaucratic poets that leads Ashby to state his name and identity so proudly in his own poems—he does this once in *Reflections* and twice (once in Latin and once in English) in *Active Policy*: 'George Asshby ys my name' (*Reflections*, l. 29); 'So I, George Asshby' (*Active Policy*, l. 22) and 'compilatus, extractus et anglicatus in Balade per Georgium Asshby' (*Active Policy*, proem).[8] But it strikes me as more probable that the borrowings from Hoccleve were deictic rather than silent—much as the words 'I', 'here', and 'now'—in that Ashby did not have to identify Hoccleve because he was writing for an intimate bureaucratic audience familiar not only with himself but also with Hoccleve and his work.

This chapter will adjust Ashby's role in the literary history of political poetry and document his contribution to the dissemination of literary culture. I will establish his autograph hand, based on five extant documents I have discovered that contain his scribal signature. Next, I will identify six additional documents written in his hand. This, in turn, will allow me to show that Cambridge University Library MS Mm.4.42, which contains the sole copy of *Active Policy*, is, in fact, a holograph. I will also identify Ashby as the scribe who may have written the first 220 folios of *The Canterbury Tales* in London, British Library Add. MS 5140. Although the new findings help better to explain Ashby's biography, they also extend the copying of Chaucer's works and the dissemination of literary culture beyond London and Westminster circles, associating them with Henry's signet at Windsor, where Ashby's office was based, and with royal courts elsewhere.

[6] Meyer-Lee, *Poets and Power*, 123.

[7] See, for instance, Rory Critten, '"Her Heed They Caste Awry": The Transmission and Reception of Thomas Hoccleve's Personal Poetry', *Review of English Studies* (2012); Rory Critten, 'The Uses of Self-Publication in Late Medieval England' (unpublished PhD, University of Groningen, 2013).

[8] All quotations from Ashby's *Active Policy* and the *Dicta* are from Bateson, *George Ashby's Poems*.

Ashby's Autograph Hand in Paris, Bibliothèque nationale MS français 4054 and in London, National Archives C 81/1367

In *Reflections* Ashby sums up four decades of a career during which he performed signet duties first for Duke Humphrey of Gloucester, then for Henry VI, and, finally, for Margaret of Anjou, Henry's queen consort:

I gan remembre and revolve in mynde
My bryngyng up from chyldhod hedyrto
In the hyghest court that I coude fynd
With the kyng, quene, and theyre uncle also,
The duk of Gloucetre, God hem rest do!
With whom I have be cherysshed ryght well
In all that was to me nedefull every dell,
Wrytyng to theyre sygnet full fourty yere
As well beyond the see as on thys syde,
Doyng my servyce as well there as here,
Nat sparyng for to go ne for to ryde,
Havyng pen and inke evyr at my syde,
As truly as I coude to theyre entent
Redy to acomplysshe theyre commandment.
(57–70)[9]

Some of this information is confirmed in the Latin proem to *Active Policy*: 'nup*er* Cleric*um* Signeti Supp*reme* d*omi*ne n*ost*re Margarete, dei gra*ti*a Regine Anglie, etc.' (lately clerk of the signet of our supreme lady Margaret, by grace of God Queen of England etc.).[10] The eleven records that I have identified to be in Ashby's hand, gathered from three archives, span the years 1420 to 1447, and confirm his self-description as having written successively for the signets of Duke Humphrey, Henry VI, and Queen Margaret. I should add that some of these eleven

[9] All references to this poem are to Mooney and Arn, *The Kingis Quair and Other Prison Poems.*

[10] The Latin proem has been printed and translated in Jocelyn Wogan-Browne, Jocelyn, Nicholas Watson, Andrew Taylor, and Ruth Evans, *The Idea of the Vernacular: An Anthology of Middle English Literary Theory, 1280–1520* (University Park, PA: Pennsylvania State University Press, 1999), 56–8.

documents are known and have been either reproduced as plates, printed in various sources, or discussed in a number of studies. But the five key documents required for identifying Ashby's hand—three French letters written for Queen Margaret and two English letters written for Henry, all bearing Ashby's autograph signature—have not been reproduced in print and none of the modern readers who has treated these documents appears to have noticed Ashby's signature.

Paris, Bibliothèque nationale MS français 4054 (formerly Ancien 9037(7), *olim* Baluze 474) is a paper and vellum codex preserving a substantial collection of original fifteenth-century documents and contemporary copies in English, French, and Latin connected to the Hundred Years' War. The manuscript features 130 groups of texts, often consisting of multiple letters and documents.[11] As one of the most significant primary sources for Anglo-French relations in the fifteenth century, MS français 4054 is well known to historians of the Hundred Years' War, cross-Channel diplomacy, and the palaeography of foreign correspondence. In fact, the manuscript is a cornucopia of autographs and holographs: in addition to three instances of Ashby's signature and letters, MS français 4054 contains a holograph letter by Prince Edward of Westminster, the scribal signatures of Henry's French secretaries Michel de Paris and Gervais le Vulre, the signs manual of Queen Margaret, Henry, and a number of English noblemen, in addition to an important rediscovery: MS français 4054 includes the only known letter featuring Sir John Fortescue's autograph signature. The signature was reproduced in 1876 by Lord Clermont in his privately circulated edition of Fortescue's works but appears to have been forgotten to the extent that subsequent readers believe that Fortescue's handwriting has been irretrievably lost.[12]

[11] An overview of its contents can be found in the online manuscripts catalogue of the Bibliothèque nationale: http://archivesetmanuscrits.bnf.fr/ark:/12148/cc50473h. The manuscript has been fully digitized and is available at the same online location.

[12] Lord Clermont, *The Works of Sir John Fortescue, Knight: Chief Justice of England and Lord Chancellor to King Henry the Sixth* (London: Chiswick Press, 1869), ii, II: plate between pp. 20 and 21. Perhaps MS français 4054 slipped into oblivion because the shelfmark nomenclature underwent multiple revisions since Lord Clemont's volumes; to him it was known as Baluze 474, and it has since changed names twice. For the impression that Fortescue's handwriting is lost, see Sarah Peverley, 'Adapting to Readeption in 1470–1471: The Scribe as Editor in a Unique Copy of John Hardyng's *Chronicle of England* (Garrett MS. 142)', *Princeton University Library Chronicle*, 66/1 (2004), 165.

Some of the studies that have made use of MS français 4054 even came within touching distance of Ashby's signature: J. Otway-Ruthven, in her pioneering 1939 work *The King's Secretary and the Signet Office in the XVth Century*, refers to types of seals, dating clauses, and the scribal signatures of Henry VI's French secretaries in some of the letters preserved in this manuscript, and although she discusses Ashby's career in detail and appears to be familiar with some of the letters written for Henry VI in the codex, she appears not to have scrutinized Queen Margaret's letters in MS français 4054.[13] John Ferguson's *English Diplomacy, 1422–1461* refers to one of the three letters that contain Ashby's signature, without paying attention to the signature itself,[14] while Helen Maurer, in *Margaret of Anjou: Queenship and Power in Late Medieval England* (2003), discusses and even quotes some of Queen Margaret's letters from this manuscript, again without considering the signatures at the bottom of the letters.[15] Many other studies could be added here.[16] Beyond historical inquiries, palaeographic examination of this manuscript has concentrated solely on the many letters by Henry VI and the work of his French secretaries, which may explain why Ashby's signature has remained overlooked.

MS français 4054 contains five letters and one set of instructions by Margaret of Anjou, each of which is signed with her sign manual.[17] All five letters were written in French between 1445 and 1447, and all are addressed to Charles VII of France. These are the only known original letters of Margaret to Charles to have survived. All five conform in their

[13] Otway-Ruthven, *The King's Secretary*, 54n2, 93n3, and 101n2.

[14] John Ferguson, *English Diplomacy, 1422–1461* (Oxford: Clarendon Press, 1972), 29n4.

[15] Helen E. Maurer, *Margaret of Anjou: Queenship and Power in Late Medieval England* (Woodbridge: Boydell, 2003), 35–8, 96.

[16] See also, for instance, Craig Taylor, '"La querelle Anglaise": Diplomatic and Legal Debate during the Hundred Years' War' (unpublished PhD, Oxford University, 1998), *passim*; Craig Taylor, *Debating the Hundred Years War: Pour ce que plusieurs (La Loy Salicque) and a Declaration of the Trew and Dewe Title of Henry VIII* (Cambridge: Cambridge University Press, 2006), *passim*; and Elizabeth L. Glyn, 'Negotiating Queenship from Malory to Shakespeare' (unpublished PhD, King's College London, 2015), 40.

[17] The five letters have been calendared in Gaston Louis Emmanuel du Fresne Marquis de Beaucourt, *Chronique de Mathieu d'Escouchy. Vol. 3: Pièces justificatives* (Paris: Renouard, 1864), 150–70 (items 32, 56, 71, 76, and 100).

physical shape and textual layout to signet letters,[18] even though only the last three have been written under the queen's signet. These three bear George Ashby's signature and are written in his hand. The earliest of Margaret's five letters in MS français 4054 is dated at Sheen on 17 December 1445 (fol. 37).[19] Although there is no scribal signature below Margaret's sign manual, I am certain that this letter is written in the hand of Michel de Paris, Henry VI's junior French secretary between 1443 and 1449.[20] The hand shares the duct, aspect, and all graphs with Paris's letter-hand, which can be found in a number of original missives marked with his scribal signature, such as that below Margaret's sign manual following the letter on fol. 33. In his signature the name 'Paris' is followed by a paraph with a ballooning heart flourish, similar to the fashionable heart-shaped ascenders of *d* often found in the opening lines of documents and folios in the work of mid-fifteenth-century French and French-trained scribes.[21] The next of Margaret's letters to Charles in MS français 4054 dates from 20 May 1446. The place is given as Windsor and the letter bears Michael de Paris's scribal signature (fol. 33).[22]

Next come the three French signet letters written by George Ashby. As with the two earlier letters written by de Paris, Ashby's three letters have been discussed by Helen Maurer, so there is no need to give their contents here in full. I refer to the page references in Maurer's book:

1. Fol. 94. Margaret of Anjou to Charles VII. Dated at Sheen, 10 December 1446 (Fig. 17). Margaret reassures Charles of Henry's goodwill and of her willingness to be helpful (Maurer, 36).

[18] On the format of signet letters, see Pierre Chaplais, *English Royal Documents: King John–Henry VI, 1199–1461* (Oxford: Clarendon Press, 1971), 34–8.

[19] The letter has been printed and translated in Joseph Stevenson, *Letters and Papers Illustrative of the Wars of the English in France during the Reign of Henry the Sixth, King of England* (London: Longman, Green, Longman, and Roberts, 1861), I: 164–7. For a discussion of its contents, see Maurer, *Margaret of Anjou*, 32–3.

[20] On Michel de Paris, see Otway-Ruthven, *The King's Secretary*, 99–101 and 156.

[21] Richard Franceys (Ricardus Franciscus) uses this feature frequently (e.g. San Marino, Huntington Library MS HM 932, fol. 13v, signature), as does Scribe 1 in Durham University Library MS Cosin V. ii. 13, fol. 27r, or the French scribe in London, British Library Royal MS 16 F VII, fol. 16r. See also Oxford, Bodleian Library MS Ashmole 764, fols 100v and 114. The ballooning heart was so common that the modern calligrapher Marc Drogin even provides a four-step demonstration on how to draw it (*Medieval Calligraphy: Its History and Technique* (New York: Dover, 1980), 160, fig. 38).

[22] A printed version of this letter is in Stevenson, *Letters and Papers*, I: 183–6. On this letter, see Maurer, *Margaret of Anjou*, 36.

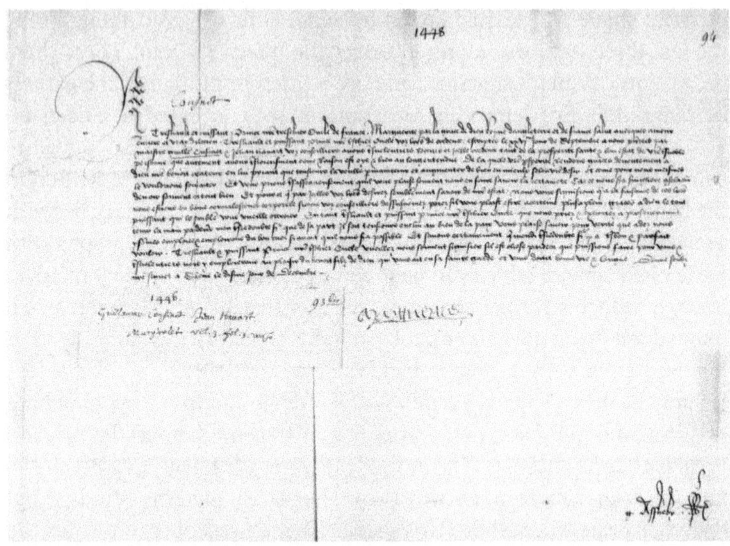

FIG 17 Paris, Bibliothèque nationale MS français 4054, fol. 94. Signed letter by George Ashby. Margaret of Anjou to Charles VII. Dated at Sheen, 10 December 1446. *Source*: gallica.bnf.fr/Bibliothèque nationale de France

2. Fol. 79. Margaret of Anjou to Charles VII. Dated at Windsor, 20 December 1446. Margaret vouches for Adam Moleyns and Lord Dudley (Maurer, 37).
3. Fol. 76. Margaret of Anjou to Charles VII. Dated at Pleasance, 28 July 1447. Margaret recommends a certain Jehan Cambray (Maurer, 37).

I have subsequently discovered two further signed letters by Ashby, this time written in English for Henry VI in January 1440. Both are in the National Archives:

4. TNA C 81/1367/17 (Fig. 18). Henry VI to Chancellor John Stafford. Dated at Windsor, 1 January 1440.
5. TNA C 81/1367/18. Henry VI. Dated at Reading Abbey, 20 January 1440.

Each of Ashby's letters contains three registers of the script used by royal scribes in the mid-fifteenth century, a variety of secretary almost entirely dominated by the lettre courante script used by Henry's French

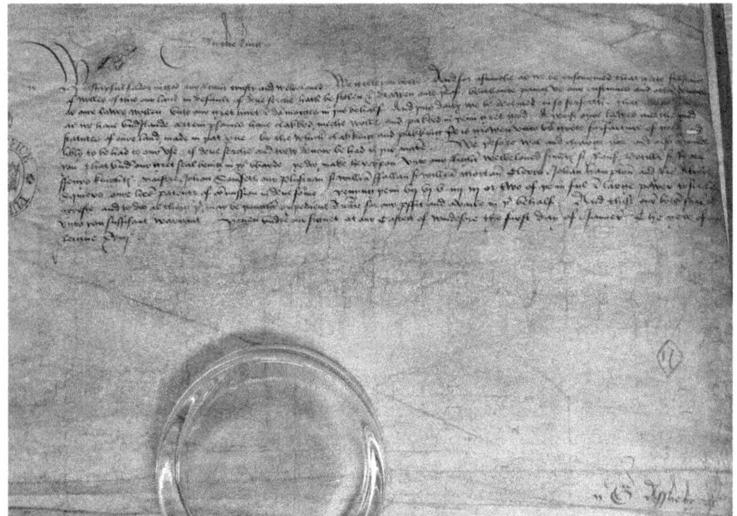

FIG 18 TNA C 81/1367/17. Signed letter by George Ashby. Henry VI to Chancellor John Stafford. Dated at Windsor, 1 January 1440.

secretaries and the Rouen chancery, where a number of English signet, council, and privy seal clerks trained and worked from time to time. To distinguish this insular variety from other forms of secretary, especially that of the Privy Seal, I will refer to this script as 'signet secretary'.

Neither in Ashby's hand nor in any of the surviving signet letters I have examined are there any anglicana forms and, unlike the secretary varieties used in some Privy Seal documents, there are no instances of two-compartment *g* or the more elaborate forms of majuscule and minuscule *w* characteristic of insular hands. The basic set of the script, a quickly written yet angular cursive secretary only slightly inflected by allographs typical for the target language, is used for the body of each missive. Ashby's confident yet swift duct executes a fluent signet script, with an upright appearance setting his descenders at an angle of 80°, extending to 70° for the most slanted letters. Despite the cursive aspect and frequent biting, Ashby's hand follows lettre courante hands in their angular appearance. This is the result of a pointed pen and horned letter forms for *a*, *e*, and *E*, among others. As is the case with other

French and English signet letters at the time, Ashby's secretary hand seems to be modelled on the lettre courante of Henry's French secretaries, a simplified and smaller cousin of lettre bâtarde. The specimen book of Robert of Tours (Paris, Bibliothèque nationale MS latin 8685) offers clear parallels for this script on fols 39r–v and 41r–v. Malcolm Parkes has drawn attention to the influence of lettre courante on commercial scribes working in England,[23] and my research has shown that all letters produced under the signets of Henry and Margaret are modelled on this script rather than on insular secretary. Parkes's description of this script in the hands of English scribes also holds true for Ashby's hand:

> The angle of the exaggerated tapering descenders of *f* and long *s*, was balanced by the angle in the opposite direction in the stems of *c*, *e*, and *r*, and in the broader segment of the broken strokes forming the lobes of letters (especially *a*). The splay also accentuated the difference between the broad strokes traced with the full width of the nib and the hairline strokes traced with the edge, thus altering the profiles of letters.[24]

In addition—and in contrast to lettre bâtarde—lettre courante features a smaller size of script, consistent biting, and simpler letter forms, especially of *d*, where in its plain, non-lobed form lettre courante does not feature the coathanger ascenders common to many lettre bâtarde hands. There is a considerable amount of shading, though it is much less pronounced than in lettre bâtarde hands.

Typical letter forms in Ashby's basic register signet secretary/lettre courante are horned *a* and *e*, secretary *g* with a counterclockwise descender, both the lobed and simple allographs of *d* and *h*, where *h* can also feature an extended limb that points counterclockwise (for a lobed *h* with this feature, see MS français 4054, fol. 76, line 8, '*tre*schierz'). Ashby uses various forms of the tironian sign, both modern and z-shaped *r*, kidney-shaped and long-*s*, and two basic forms of *w*: a plain angular secretary version in his French texts, though in his Latin and English documents this form is sometimes preceded by

[23] M. B. Parkes, *Their Hands before Our Eyes: A Closer Look at Scribes: The Lyell Lectures Delivered in the University of Oxford, 1999* (Aldershot: Ashgate, 2008), 117–19.

[24] Parkes, *Their Hands before Our Eyes*, 118.

straight or curved approach strokes; the second allograph is the curved double v-shaped *w*, a peculiarity he shares not only with the scribe of Oxford, New College MS 314 and Oxford Bodleian Library MS Dugdale 45, but also with Henry's French secretaries when they attempt to write out English place names such as 'Woodstock', 'Westminster', or 'Windsor' (see the French signet letter for Henry VI in MS français 4054, fol. 24, bottom line, 'Woudestok'). This feature is thought to be so rare among scribes producing English literary manuscripts that Linne Mooney named the scribe of New College MS 314 and MS Dugdale 45 'Double-v Scribe', but this allograph is common among French and French-trained scribes working in an English context. It also appears in Hand 1 in Durham University Library MS Cosin V.II.13, whereas Henry's French secretaries Michel de Paris and Jean Rinel use a double straight-fronted *v*, for instance (MS français 4054, fol. 38, bottom line, 'Wyndesore', for de Paris; BN MS Dupuy 760, fol. 161, and BN MS Baluze 11, fol. 25, bottom line in both MSS, 'Westm*instre*', for Rinel).

In line with other signet secretary hands and insular hands influenced by lettre courante, Ashby uses a number of different majuscule forms of *A*. However, his preferred and most elaborate idiograph features a lobed head and is executed using a hairline stroke for the bottom lobe followed by a broken stroke with a reverse movement initiated at the cusp. He uses this letter form for the first letter of his surname in his signature (Figs 17 and 18). This form of *A* is common in northern French chanceries, especially in Normandy. It is current, for instance, in BN MS français 4485, produced between 1423 and 1425 and containing the accounts of Pierre Surreau, Henry VI's receiver general for the duchy of Normandy. Ashby's second most characteristic majuscule is *I*, which appears in a number of usually elaborate forms. In all instances the stem extends to a long tapered descender and supports a flat or curving head stroke which is sometimes accompanied by a vertical hairline stroke of various lengths. In some instances this hairline stroke is short (MS français 4054, fol. 76, line 3, 'Iehan'); in others it is of moderate length (TNA SC 1/44/13, line 8, 'Iuggement') or curves to the left (TNA SC 1/44/13, line 11, 'Iustice'). Ashby also uses different forms for *O*, depending on the size and register of the script. The most common specimens feature a circle with a dot inside or, if space permits, a circular stroke with a superimposed curl that curves to the right in the top-left quarter of the letter (MS français 4054, fol. 76, line 1, 'Oncle'). The direction of this curved stroke is indicative of Ashby's angular duct and it is typical for writers influenced by lettre courante; in insular forms of secretary it is more common for this superimposed stroke to curve to the left. For a similar contemporary register and letter courante hand of a French scribe, see BN, MS français 5519, written between 1411 and 1417.[25]

Ashby's next register of signet secretary is reserved for the address on the dorse of his letters, select words in the first line, and specific letters in the bottom line (for an example of first-line usage, see MS français 4054, fol. 76, 'Marguerite par la'; for letters belonging to this register in bottom lines see *P* in 'Pleasance' or *I* in 'Iuillet' in the same document). In this middle tier the minuscules are slightly larger than in his basic register and there is only little biting. Horned forms of *a*, *e*, and *g* are traced with precision, while descenders in the last line and especially ascenders in the first line receive flourishes and loops (most of his signet missives have looped ornamental ascenders on *h* on the dorse and in first lines).

His third and highest tier of script consists of engrossed forms of majuscules borrowed from lettre bâtarde and other French display varieties. This includes not only his *A* of choice but this register is reserved for certain letters in the addresses on the dorse, the opening lines, and some of the bottom lines. Various calligraphic forms of capital letters, especially *M*, *N*, *P*, *R*, and *W* belong to this register. Within this tier there exist additional registers for particularly extravagant initial letters and paraphs common to lettre courante and lettre bâtarde scripts; these can be found in such specimen and exercise books as BN MS latin 8685 (Robert of Tours) or the opening folios of Oxford, Bodleian Library MS Ashmole 789, sometimes attributed to Richard Franceys. There is also a fourth or zero-register variety of Ashby's hand, a hastily executed cursive note-taking form of signet secretary, visible above the address on the dorse of the French letter for Margaret dated 28 July 1447, MS français 4054, fol. 76.

The two signed letters by Ashby from 1440 that I subsequently found in the National Archives in London (C 81/1367/17 and C 81/1367/18)

[25] On the date of this manuscript, see Marc Bompaire, 'Un exemple de livre de changeur français du XVe siècle, le manuscrit Bibl. nat. de Fr., Nouv. Acq. Fr. 471', *Revue Numismatique*, 6/167 (2011), 110.

follow the same pattern. The main difference to the three letters for Margaret is that the earlier letters are written for Henry VI in English and feature majuscule *G* for Ashby's initial in the signature rather than the miniscule *g* in the three French letters.

Six Further English, French, and Latin Signet Letters by Ashby

In addition to the three letters in MS français 4054 and the two specimens in TNA C 81/1367, I have identified Ashby's hand in six further documents. Only one of Margaret of Anjou's English signet letters is known to have survived in the original. TNA SC 1/44/13 (Fig. 19) is addressed to the chancellor, John Stafford, and is dated at Windsor, 8 January (1446/7).[26] The bottom of the letter is damaged and torn, so no scribal signature is visible. The duct and overall angular aspect are the same as that of the three French letters in MS français 4054, with the basic register of signet secretary being employed for the body of the letter. (For an example of an English signet letter produced for Henry VI that was not written by Ashby but shows the influence of lettre courante see Canterbury Cathedral Archives CCA-DCc-ChAnt/K/4 and the signet letters by Ashby's fellow clerks in TNA C 81/1365-1372.) Throughout TNA SC 1/44/13 there is biting and the consistent presence of lettre courante forms. Ashby's characteristic allographs are used throughout: horned *a* and *e* (l. 12, 'Ianuer' and 'yeuen'); simple and lobed *d* (l. 1, 'fader' and 'god'); both types of *h* (l. 9, 'hiderto' and 'hertly'); secretary *w*/*W* and its double-v form (l. 1 'welbeloued', l. 12 'Windesore'); *g* with a counterclockwise curling descender (l. 1, 'god'); modern- and z-shaped *r* (l. 1, 'fader' and 'right'); and kidney-shaped and long-*s* (l. 2, 'proctours' and 'seruant'). The majuscules throughout are Ashby's (*A*, *B*, *C*, *I*, *O*, *R*, *S*, and *W*, with *E* being supplied by the address on the dorse. Most significantly, Ashby's typical *A* and *I* appear. His preferred *A* with the lobed top can be seen in l. 1 ('And'), executed

[26] The letter has been printed by Fisher et al., *An Anthology of Chancery English*, 185. The date is corroborated by contemporary documents referring to the matter raised by this letter. The references are given at the foot of p. 185.

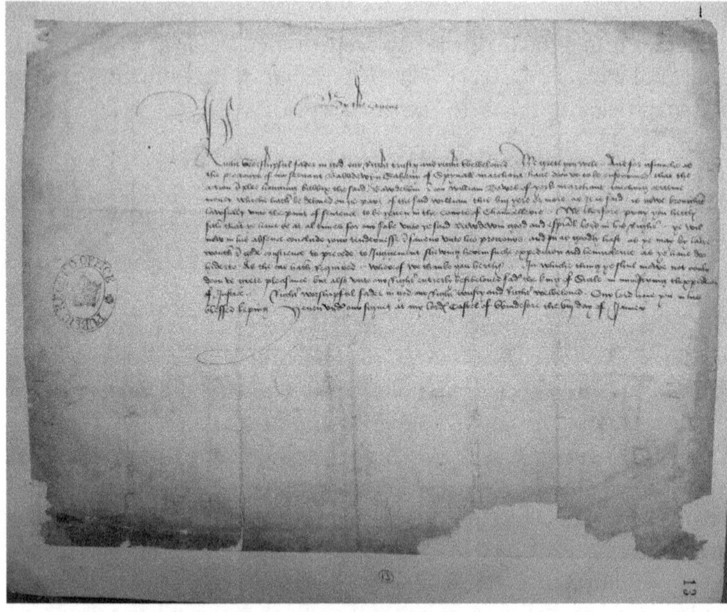

FIG 19 TNA SC 1/44/13. Signet letter, English. Margaret of Anjou to the chancellor, John Stafford. Windsor, 8 January 1446/7.

as in his signature, with the broken stroke at its cusp. Similarly, *I* includes the vertical hairline stroke reaching down from the left end of the head stroke (l. 8, 'Iuggement'), though this signet letter also contains another allograph in which the hairline stroke curls to the left (l. 9, 'In'). Unlike the French letters, where the tironian sign is wrapped by a downward right-curling stroke starting at the left end of the upper bar, the English signet letter features a form where the curling stroke starts at the right end of the lower bar and curls upward to the left (l. 3). However, elsewhere in his writing Ashby employs both forms. Specimen books of secretary and lettre courante scripts frequently list both allographs side by side (Bodleian Library, MS Ashmole 789, fol. 4v, gives both variants in the bottom rows of the specimen paragraphs headed 'B' and 'C'; since the upward-curling form coincides with similar-looking Latin and English suspension marks, scribes appear to have opted for the downward-curling tironian sign to disambiguate it from the suspension mark).

In TNA SC 1/44/13 Ashby also follows the principle of using three registers of signet secretary. The middle register is again found in the address on the dorse and certain words in the first line ['We grete', 'And']. The difference between the registers is particularly visible when comparing 'grete' in l. 10 with 'grete' in l. 1: the first instance is more carefully traced, giving it an angular appearance buffered by more generous spacing, while 'grete' in l. 10 is rounder and compact, generating biting between the rounded limb of *r* and *e* while connecting *e* to *t* by means of a ligature. The first line and the address on the dorse feature lobed ascenders on *h*, while the bottom line has exaggerated descenders, most notably Ashby's characteristic hairline stroke on *I* which touches the descender before it curls upward to the left ('Ianuer'). Finally, the same upper-register majuscules are chosen for certain letters in the initial line—*W* and the Ashby-*A*—accompanied by higher-register initials for the first majuscule of the address (*R*), the floating description above ('By the Quene'), and the first letter of the address on the dorse ('T', of which only part of the lower stem is visible). Three further signet letters, written for Henry between 1440 and 1443, share the above characteristics and, although unsigned, have also been written by Ashby: they are TNA C 81/1367/20, C 81/1368/20, and C 81/1367/18.

The four signet letters written between 1440 and 1447 for Queen Margaret certainly confirm the external information preserved in a copied letter, from about 1446, which 'Queen Margaret later wrote to an unidentified lady thanking her "for service to George Ashby, Clerk of Our Signet"'.[27] Ashby's identification as the writer of TNA SC 1/44/13 is further confirmed by the circumstantial evidence that he was Margaret's (only) signet clerk at the time.[28] In addition to these four French and English letters for Margaret's signet, Ashby's hand not only appears in the five English signet letters for Henry (two of which are signed) but also in one of Henry's Latin signet letters. The letter,

[27] Scattergood, 'George Ashby's *Prisoner's Reflections*', 104; Scattergood, 'Ashby, George'; Meyer-Lee, 'Laureates and Beggars', 717n54.

[28] Margaret's accounts for 1452–3 (31 Henry VI) show that she only employed one clerk, Ashby, in this function (A. Myers, 'The Household of Queen Margaret of Anjou, 1452–3', *Bulletin of the John Rylands Library*, 40/1 (1957), 91).

Urkunde Kurköln no 1927, is preserved in the Hauptstaatsarchiv Düsseldorf, and has been reproduced and transcribed by Pierre Chaplais.[29] It is addressed to Dietrich, archbishop of Cologne, and is dated at Windsor, 15 July 1438. Again, the duct and aspect are characteristic of Ashby, and all his minuscule and majuscule letter forms make an appearance, including the lobed Ashby-*A* and *I* with a hairline stroke (bottom line, 'Iulij', 'Anno'). Given the nature of diplomatic Latin, this letter features more abbreviations than Ashby's French and English missives, and a range of tironian signs is in use, including one of his two preferred forms, the downward-curling form of *et* (l. 2). The absence of the upward-curling shape can be explained by his decision to distinguish it from the suspension mark for *-aternita-*, which is identical to the upward-curling *et* (l. 15, 'p*aternita*ti').

This letter carries the signature of Thomas Beckington, Henry's secretary and head of the royal signet office. However, Beckington's hand differs from the letter, and Pierre Chaplais correctly states that this letter 'was written by a signet clerk, under the supervision of Thomas Beckington . . . whose name ("Bekynton"), written by the scribe of the document, appears in the bottom right-hand corner; this name is followed by Beckington's autograph signature in monogrammatic form ("TB")'.[30] The date of this letter, 1438, falls into the period during which Ashby is believed to have written for Henry's signet, under Beckington's supervision. Otway-Ruthven believes that Ashby first wrote for Duke Humphrey's signet, where Beckington served as chancellor, and was transferred in 1437 to the reorganized signet office, before becoming clerk of the signet to Queen Margaret on her marriage to Henry.[31] In all likelihood, Beckington appears to have had a hand in Ashby's transfer since both of them enjoyed an association that went back to Ashby's time in Duke Humphrey's signet.[32] Ashby's hand in a

[29] A facsimile of the letter and address on the dorse are printed in Pierre Chaplais, *English Medieval Diplomatic Practice: Part II, Plates* (London: H. M. Stationery Office, 1975), ii, plates 54a and 54b, with a description on pp. 19–20; the entire letter has been transcribed and edited in Chaplais, *English Medieval Diplomatic Practice: Part I*, i, 41–3.

[30] Chaplais, *English Medieval Diplomatic Practice: Part II*, ii, 20.

[31] Otway-Ruthven, *The King's Secretary*, 120.

[32] In *Reflections* Ashby states that he wrote for 'The duk of Gloucetre, God hem rest do!' (l. 61). This was during Beckington's tenure as Humphrey's chancellor. In 1439, Ashby was sent with Beckington to Calais (Otway-Ruthven, *The King's Secretary*, 120n1); Scattergood, 'George Ashby's *Prisoner's Reflections*', 104; Scattergood, 'Ashby, George'.

letter signed by Beckington shows that the clerk did work for Henry VI during this period. In addition, given Beckington's patronage of Thomas Chaundler and his ownership of books, including a thoroughly glossed copy of Boethius's *Consolation of Philosophy* given to him by Chaundler,[33] it is not unlikely that Ashby's literary (and Boethian) interests were encouraged by Beckington.

I have also located a document dating from the earlier part of Ashby's career that confirms his role as a signet clerk for Duke Humphrey. This signet letter close, TNA C 81/1537/4, was written in French and is dated at York, 8 August 1420. It is addressed to the chancellor, Thomas Langley. This letter has also been printed and transcribed by Chaplais.[34] The letter shows Ashby's characteristic duct, the angular appearance of his signet secretary, and the presence of his favoured letter forms for *a*, *e*, *g*, and *k* with both forms of *r* and *s* being present. The tironian sign features a downward-curling stroke, while *w* is of the double-v type throughout. Ashby loses the double-v in the course of his career: no secretary *w* is present in this letter from 1420, while no double-v forms appear in his later writing, as I will show below. It is noteworthy that the simpler, unlobed form of *d*—the standard allograph in lettre courante—is not yet present, nor are the looped ascenders on *h* in the first line. These features are borrowings from continental varieties of lettre courante, and it appears that Ashby's work for Duke Humphrey had not yet brought him into contact with Henry's French secretaries, with whom, as the letters of 1440–7 show, he occasionally overlapped geographically when the king and the queen were in the same place. Additionally, his documented stays in France would have brought him into contact with the work of continental scribes in French and English service. The majuscules throughout are Ashby's, and this includes *A*, *B*, *D*, *E*, *G*, *L*, and *R*.

Ashby wrote this letter and the floating description above it in his basic register of signet secretary, with three engrossed forms drawn from his highest register reserved for initial words in the description

[33] Daniel Wakelin examines Beckington's patronage of Chaundler in *Humanism, Reading, and English Literature*, 163ff. For Chaundler's copy of Boethius, now BL Harley MS 43, see p. 14.

[34] Chaplais prints a facsimile in *English Royal Documents*, plate 22b. The transcription is on p. 75.

and first line ('Le', 'Reu*er*end'), as wells as for 'Nous'. He had not yet adopted the style of the English chancery at Rouen and of Henry's French secretaries later in the century which featured an intermediate register of the script for certain majuscules and for selected words in the first line and certain letters in the final line. The date of this letter confirms that Ashby was already working for Duke Humphrey in 1420, and not from about 1423.[35] So when Ashby states in 1463 that he wrote for the royal family's signet 'full fourty yere' (*Reflections*, l 64), 'full' actually means more than forty, in this case at least forty-two or forty-three years.

Ashby was part of the delegation that initially escorted Margaret to England,[36] and he became her signet clerk some time in 1445 when Henry married her. The new evidence makes it likely that Ashby's established fluency in French may have been one of the reasons why he was selected not only for this mission but also to become the signet clerk for a francophone queen consort who spoke no English. Henry's personal French letters, on the other hand, appear to have been handled by his French secretaries, primarily Jean Rinel, Gervais le Vulre, and Michel de Paris.[37] The letters de Paris wrote for Margaret are dated at Sheen and Windsor, while two of Ashby's letters are also dated at the same locations. While this does not necessarily mean that all four letters were actually written there, it does suggest that de Paris wrote French letters for Margaret on the occasions when she was present or when the king and the queen were in the same place. As the clerk of Margaret's signet, Ashby always accompanied the queen; he was expected to be with her at all times: 'Havyng pen and inke evyr at my syde' (*Reflections*, l. 68). Since de Paris wrote two of Margaret's five letters to Charles in MS français 4054, it is possible that Ashby took over this particular task when de Paris was not available, most likely when the latter was in France. (De Paris's two letters are dated six months apart, so it is unlikely that he was filling in for Ashby during the latter's illness).

[35] The later date is suggested by Meyer-Lee, 'Laureates and Beggars', 700.

[36] Otway-Ruthven, *The King's Secretary*, 135.

[37] For a list of these letters, most of which have survived in BN MSS français 4054 and Dupuy 760, see the calendar in de Beaucourt, *Chronique de Mathieu d'Escouchy. Vol. 3: Pièces justificatives*. To these I would add Jean Rinel's letter for Henry of 22 July 1447 in BN MS Baluze 11, fol. 25.

I have also examined all other surviving letters sent by Margaret that I could identify. In addition to the five letters in MS français 4054, there exist three further missives signed by Margaret, one of which (TNA SC 1/44/13)—the only surviving original English letter by Margaret—I have discussed above.[38] MS français 4054 also contains a set of letters by Prince Edward and Sir John Fortescue, together with Margaret's instructions for Alfonso V, King of Portugal, sent from St Mihiel in Bar in December 1464. These documents had been intercepted by the French, and although Margaret's sign manual is found on the instructions (fol. 174), the scribe of this set of documents, who wrote everything in the file except for Edward's autograph letter, is not identified, but it is not Ashby. In his letter Fortescue describes the material contained in the parcel and states that his letter, as well as that by the queen and an additional letter by Edward, were 'writyn with the hande of the clerke that hath writyn [Edward's and Margaret's] lettres' (MS français 4054, fol. 175). And indeed, Fortescue's English letter, Margaret's instructions (fol. 174), and Edward's formal letter to Lord Ormond (fol. 172) are in the same hand, while Edward's shorter English letter to Lord Ormond (fol. 173) is in his untrained autograph hand. Since the clerk whom Fortescue mentions here is not Ashby, it is safe to say that Ashby did not join Queen Margaret's party in exile, not least because he may still have been in prison. Another of Margaret's letters, addressed to the Lord of Bouchage and dated after her father's death in 1480 and featuring her sign manual, has survived in BN, MS français 2909, fol. 34, but Ashby had of course died by that time.[39]

Cambridge University Library MS Mm. 4.42, Ashby's Holograph Manuscript

Alone among Ashby's writing, his own poetry receives the most privileged scribal attention in the shape of his highest tier of script, a combination of calligraphically executed minuscules and three

[38] There also survives in the National Archives another letter of Margaret's, SC 1/63/305, dated to 6 November 1453, but it is a draft or transcript.

[39] On this letter, see Margaret L. Kekewich, *The Good King: René of Anjou and Fifteenth Century Europe* (London: Palgrave, 2008), 236.

components found in his letters: ornamental ascenders and descenders usually gracing the opening and closing lines of signet letters; capital letters for opening sentences and the first line of signet letters; and flourishes and paraphs. I will argue that Cambridge University Library, MS Mm. 4.42, the sole copy of Ashby's *Active Policy/Dicta*, is a holograph manuscript written entirely by him. The slim vellum booklet contains forty-eight folios in six quires of eight leaves (wanting the final quire), with twenty-eight lines per page for the *Active Policy* (fols 2v–18v) and between twenty-eight and thirty-two lines per page for the *Dicta* (19r–48v). The manuscript was once part of the library of John Moore, Bishop of Ely.[40] The *Active Policy*, written in English, is preceded by an instructive Latin prose dedication to Prince Edward of Westminster on fol. 2r; the prosimetrum *Dicta* alternates English verse and Latin prose. The entire manuscript is written in a single hand.

CUL MS Mm. 4.42 has been executed in a consistent signet secretary hand modelled on lettre courante (Fig. 20). Throughout, the register corresponds to Ashby's middle tier, usually reserved for addresses on the dorse and selected words in the first line. The duct, angle, and appearance match Ashby's hand, with descenders written at 80°, tilting for the most slanted to a 70° angle. As in Ashby's middle register there is little biting and the text is angular and crafted with precision. On many folios the hand slumps to a slightly smaller and more compact form that in some instances is clearly Ashby's basic register, best visible on fols 4v (Fig. 20) and 15r, bottom two stanzas; 19v, bottom stanza; 31v, bottom five lines; or 43r, bottom three lines. In these instances the writing becomes smaller, the spacing between lines diminishes, biting occurs, and the appearance is that of the body of Ashby's letters. Throughout, all letter forms are consistently Ashby's. Horned *a* and *e* appear (fol. 4v, l. 25, 'attendance'; l. 5, 'were'), next to both simple and lobed forms of *d* (fol. 4v, l. 4, 'daily'; l. 1, 'goodnesse'); on some occasions even a lettre bâtarde *d* with a hooked ascender is employed (fol. 4v, l.1, 'God'; this display-register *d* is common on the opening folio of *Active Policy*, 2v); the standard form of *g* features a long counterclockwise curling descender (fol. 4v, l. 1, 'goodnesse'), though a larger display-type *g* with a left-curling descender also appears

[40] Frederic Madden, Bulkeley Bandinel, and John Gough Nichols, *Collectanea Topographica et Genealogica* (London: Nichols, 1838), v, 5:132.

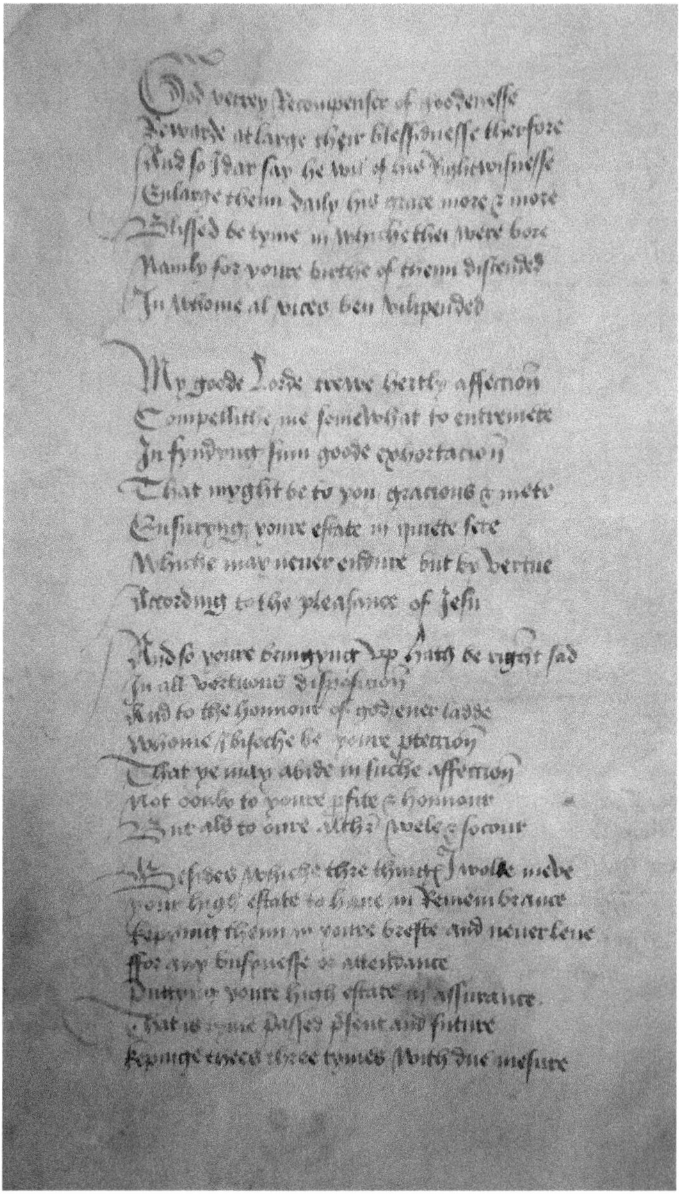
God verrey Recompenser of goodenesse
Rewarde at large theire blessydnesse therfore
And so I dar say he wol of his Rightewisnesse
Enlarge theim daily his grace more & more
Blissed be tyme in whiche thei were bore
Namely for youre birthe of theim discended
In whome al vices ben vilipended

My goode Lorde trewe hertly affection
Compellith me somewhat to entremette
In fyndyng sum goode exhortacion
That myght be to you gracious & mete
Ensuryng youre estate in quiete sete
Whiche may neuer endure but by vertue
According to the pleasance of Jesu

And so youre begynnyng up growth be right sad
In all vertuous disposicion
And to the honour of god euer ladde
Whome I biseche be youre protection
That ye may abide in suche affection
Not oonly to youre profite & honour
But also to oure althir wele & socour

Besides whiche thre thinges I wolde meve
Your high estate to haue in Remembrance
Kepyng theim in youre breste and neuer leue
For any busynesse or attendance
Puttyng youre high estate in assurance
That is tyme passed present and future
Kepyng these thre tymes with due mesure

FIG 20 Cambridge University Library MS Mm. 4.42, fol. 4v. *The Active Policy of a Prince*, by George Ashby.

(fol. 4v, l. 12, 'Ensuryng'); both modern- and z-shaped *r* are in use in the same places as in Ashby's signet letters (fol. 4v, l. 2, 'therfore' features both forms); kidney-shaped and long-*s* appear (fol. 4v, l. 7, 'vices', l. 3, 'so'); *h* is present in its simpler and lobed forms (fol. 4v, l. 8, 'hertly' and l. 6, 'birthe'); while *w* can be seen throughout in a secretary variant, mostly with an approach stroke that is predominately straight though sometimes also curved. Furthermore, as in his Latin signet letter, both types of the tironian sign appear. Ashby's preferred version with the downward right-curling stroke is visible on fol. 4v, l. 4, though, matching his Latin signet letter of 1438, the upward-curling form is reserved to mark a suspension (fol. 4v, l. 21 (Fig. 20)).

All of Ashby's majuscule forms are used in CUL MS Mm. 4.42, including every variation of his characteristic *I* with both a straight and curling hairline stroke descending from the left end of the top: fol. 4v, l. 3, 'I'; l. 18, 'I' (Fig. 20); for a version with a straight stem, see fol. 44v, l. 21, 'Insipida'. Mm. 4.42 features numerous forms of *A*, all of which appear elsewhere in Ashby's signet letters, but his preferred Ashby-*A* is in use both in the text (39v, l. 11, 'Aristotiles' and l. 24, 'Arcules') as well as in its larger engrossed form at the beginning of a line (fol. 38r, l. 10, 'Amonges'). Fol. 39v offers good examples of many of Ashby's typical capital letters, including *T* with a simple and doubled stem (l. 2, 'To' and l. 6, 'These') and *D* and *S* (ll. 9 and 20, respectively), while his tironian form of *E*, which resembles a superscript tironian sign with a downward-curling stroke marking the lower end of the x-height (typical for lettre courante and signet secretary) appears in the final line ('Er'). Significant also is Ashby's *O*, executed as a circle with a superimposed stroke curling to the right (l. 16, 'Of'; l. 8, 'Oportet' features the engrossed form).

Particularly striking about Mm. 4.42 is the consistent presence of majuscules sourced from Ashby's top register of signet secretary, often belonging to the highest engrossing register for the initial letters of a stanza: the effect is that each stanza resembles one of Ashby's signet missives. These engrossed letter forms are often accompanied by flourishes and paraphs, visible consistently throughout the manuscript. All of Ashby's engrossed majuscules are accounted for in Mm. 4.42. For instance, *M* on fol. 4v, l. 8, 'My' is identical to that reserved for 'Marguerite' in the opening lines of his three French signets letters, while *B* with a doubled stem (fol. 4v, l. 22, 'Besides' and fol. 8r, l. 10, 'Be') echoes that of the floating description ('By') in Ashby's English signet letter from 1446/7, TNA SC 1/44/13. The engrossed form of *T* used on fol. 4v, l. 19, 'That' (Fig. 20) has the same shape as that faintly visible on the address of the dorse of TNA SC 1/44/13 (Fig. 19). Other engrossed variants also offer identical matches: the sail-like *L* in 'Libellus' in the first line of the Latin dedication on fol. 2r is the same as 'Le' in the floating description in the 1420 signet letter for Duke Humphrey; *R* on fol. 18r, l. 1, 'Retoriq*ue*', with a slightly simpler upper limb, corresponds to initial *R* in l. 1, 'Reu*er*end' in the 1420 signet letter for Duke Humphrey. More examples could be added, such as *W* in l. 3 on fol. 36v, where 'Why' is the same as 'We' in l. 1 in TNA SC 1/44/13, while *Y* in 'Yeue' on the same page (fol. 36v, l. 13) matches the shape and the long descender of 'yeven' in the last line of TNA SC 1/44/13. The basic shape of engrossed *H* in l. 8 of fol. 21r, 'Honoranti' and l. 1 or 21v, 'Howe', is the same as the deluxe engrossed *H* in l. 1 of the Latin signet letter for the archbishop of Düsseldorf, while the engrossed initial *A* on fol. 34v, 'Associe', has an identical underlying shape as all six deluxe engrossed initials in the opening word, 'A', in the three French signet letters and addresses on the dorses in MS français 4054. A slightly less exaggerated version of *N* in 'Nous' (TNA C 81/1537/4, l. 1) occurs on fol. 25v, l. 17, 'Non'.

In the first half of the manuscript Ashby has left spaces for illuminated initials on fols 2r–2v, 4r, 5r, 6v, 9v, and 19r, but this objective has been abandoned after 19r. Finally, the consistent use of deluxe majuscules for the initial letters of English stanzas and Latin paragraphs is consistent with the pattern in signet letters produced by Ashby and his contemporaries. As with Ashby's English signet letter, there are no dialectal features in Mm. 4.42. This manuscript as well as the English letter (TNA SC 1/44/13) fit the *LALME* profiles for the London region and documents produced in Westminster and Windsor. A good example of this is the persistence of 'yeve/yeven', the standard signet form.[41]

Critical opinion about the quality and execution of Mm. 4.42 has been generally dismissive, with most readers not willing to entertain the possibility that this is a holograph. Henry Luard's *Catalogue of the Manuscripts Preserved in the Library of the University of Cambridge*

41 Fisher calls this the Chancery 'y' (Fisher et al., *An Anthology of Chancery English*, 17).

and Mary Bateson, Ashby's first editor, are silent on this aspect.[42] Ferdinand Holthausen remarked in 1921 that all three of Ashby's surviving works have been 'stark entstellt' (heavily disfigured) by its scribes, implying that Mm. 4.42 could not be a holograph.[43] This assumption transpires again when he disagrees with Bateson's emendation to ll. 385–6 of *Active Policy*, claiming that the repetition of the rhyme 'preseruing'/'preseruyng' was 'obviously' caused by a scribal error (beruht offenbar auf einem Schreiberversehen).[44] In 1950, Curt Bühler offered a first consideration of this question in passing, leaving open the possibility of Mm. 4.42 having been written in Ashby's hand. Bühler was primarily interested in Ashby's use of Latin quotations and the *Dicta* tradition, and he notes that neither Ashby nor 'some inattentive professional scribe (if MS. Mm. 4.42 of Cambridge University Library is not autograph)' should be held accountable for the various misattributions of classical material in the *Dicta*.[45]

John Scattergood was the first to offer a discussion of this question. In arguing for the *Active Policy* and the *Dicta* as one work, Scattergood assumes that the poems were copied by a scribe: 'the copyist thought he was dealing with material which constituted a single work'.[46] He adds that the manuscript was written 'in a single professional hand of the late fifteenth century', noting that although room was left for a rubricator, the manuscript 'was never rubricated'.[47] To be fair, Scattergood is primarily interested in dating the *Active Policy*, yet each of his subsequent observations that the alleged copyist 'thought he was simply moving on to a new division of the same work' gains in force if the manuscript is indeed a holograph. In other words, Scattergood's argument that 'Ashby should be regarded as being the author of

[42] C. Hardwick and H. R. Luard, *A Catalogue of the Manuscripts Preserved in the Library of the University of Cambridge* (Cambridge: Cambridge University Press, 1861), iv, 4:299–300; Bateson, *George Ashby's Poems.*

[43] F. Holthausen, 'Ashby-Studien III', *Anglia*, 1921/45 (1921), 92.

[44] Holthausen, 'Ashby-Studien III', 95.

[45] Bühler, 'The *Liber de Dictis Philosophorum Antiquorum* and Common Proverbs in George Ashby's Poems', 285.

[46] John Scattergood, 'The Date and Composition of George Ashby's Poems', *Leeds Studies in English*, 21 (1990), 172.

[47] Scattergood, 'The Date and Composition', 172.

two, not three, extant works—*A Prisoner's Reflections* and the *Active Policy*'—can now be verified as correct.[48]

In an important article on Ashby published in 2004, Robert Meyer-Lee shares Scattergood's assessment of the manuscript and the combined nature of the *Active Policy* and the *Dicta*.[49] In the revised version of this article, which appeared as a chapter in *Poets and Power from Chaucer to Wyatt* (2007), Meyer-Lee proposes that although Ashby's *Active Policy* and the *Dicta* were composed for 'a Lancastrian prince and heir apparent', they 'survive only in a manuscript so humble (Cambridge University Library MS Mm.4.42) that one would like to congratulate its original collector for deciding it fit for preservation'.[50] Daniel Wakelin, in turn, observes that 'Ashby's *The Active Policy of a Prince* survives in a scruffy booklet that was surely never given to the Prince Edward whom Ashby professes to teach'.[51]

Despite its modest size and lack of illuminations, Ashby's choice of his middle-register script and the pervasive use of higher-register majuscules and their engrossed variants bespeak the careful execution of the signet secretary/lettre courante variety. Mm. 4.42 may look like a scruffy booklet now—unfinished, unlineated, and bearing witness to a programme of illuminated initials that was abandoned less than halfway through—but this manuscript is nevertheless a careful production characterized by Ashby's use of only the finest majuscules and the best display lettering available to a trained signet scribe around the middle of the fifteenth century. Given the range of tiers of script employed in English and French signet and other royal letters, there is no doubt to my mind that Mm. 4.42 was written for Prince Edward and that this copy was intended to reach him either in Edinburgh or at St Mihiel. It was actually fairly common in the late fifteenth and early sixteenth century to present monarchs with 'humble' copies of works; in fact, if the author closely knew the monarch, an unpretentious holograph was perhaps even considered to be appropriate: John Skelton's modest booklet holograph of *A Lawde and Prayse Made for Our Sovereigne Lord the Kyng* (TNA E 36/228), presented by Skelton to Henry VIII in

48 Scattergood, 'The Date and Composition', 174.
49 Meyer-Lee, 'Laureates and Beggars', 707.
50 Meyer-Lee, *Poets and Power*, 140.
51 Wakelin, *Humanism, Reading, and English Literature*, 37.

1509, is one such example.[52] We know that Queen Margaret's party struggled in their French exile, both financially and logistically. Communication with Lancastrian loyalists was difficult and dangerous—the fact that the parcel with the letters of Edward, Margaret, and John Fortescue, from December 1464,[53] has found its way into MS français 4054 means that it was intercepted by the French and that these letters never reached their addressees, Lord Ormond and Alfonso of Portugal. In his own letter, Fortescue speaks of the queen's despondent financial situation, urging Ormond to curb his own spending and preserve his resources to aid the queen when she joins him, a passage prefaced by the frank admission that 'We buthe alle in grete pou*er*te' (MS français 4054, fol. 175). That this is not a trivial statement is borne out by Fortescue's closing instructions in the final line in which he admits that his fellow exiles did not have enough money to pay the messenger appropriately: 'Item, the berer hereof hadde of vs but iij. Scutes for alle his costes towardes you by cause wee hadde no more money'. A prince and a queen in such dire straits do not seem to be far-fetched recipients of a modest but expertly and carefully written manuscript, such as Mm. 4.42.

Since this manuscript was written entirely by Ashby himself, it is worth reconsidering the dating question. There is no need here to go again over the persuasive arguments advanced by Scattergood that move this poem closer to the first deposition of Henry in 1461 and the Yorkist takeover,[54] but it is worth looking once more at the Latin dedication against the background that it was not only composed by but also physically written by Ashby. The Latin passage opens with the following sentence:

> [P]resens Libellus compilatus, extractus, et anglicatus in Balade per Georgium Asshby, nuper Clericum Signeti Suppreme domine nostre Margarete, dei gratia Regine Anglie, etc. ex bona voluntate, Amore et cordiali affeccione, quos ipse naturali iure gerit, tam erga celsitudinem et regiam maiestatem suam et prepotissimum et excellentissimum dominum suum Edwardum.

[52] I am grateful to John Scattergood for drawing my attention to this practice. For slightly later examples, and Thomas More in particular, see David R. Carlson, *English Humanist Books: Writers and Patrons, Manuscript and Print, 1475–1525* (Toronto: University of Toronto Press, 1993), 146–8.

[53] Maurer, *Margaret of Anjou*, 207.

[54] Scattergood, 'The Date and Composition', 167.

(This little book has been compiled, extracted, and turned into English verse by George Ashby, lately clerk of the signet of our supreme lady Margaret, by grace of God, Queen of England, etc., because of the goodwill, love, and cordial affection that he naturally bears both toward her Highness and Royal Majesty and toward the most mighty and excellent lord her Edward.)[55]

Since Ashby physically wrote this copy, the word 'nuper' [lately] carries some weight: Ashby would not have written that he had 'lately' been Margaret's clerk of the signet if a number of years had passed since that time. The circumstance that Mm. 4.42 is a holograph strengthens Scattergood's dating of this poem closer to 1461, though perhaps not specifically to 1463, since, as Rosemary McGerr notes, he is unlikely to have composed the poem while in Yorkist custody.[56] The other suggested date ranges, 1470–1 (proposed by Mary Bateson, Margaret Kekewich, and David Lawton) or during the 1450s (advanced by Paul Strohm),[57] are highly improbable given that Mm. 4.42 is a holograph and that Ashby did not join the Lancastrians in exile. A date of nine to ten years after Edward IV's accession is too late for the word 'nuper' [lately], while there is no reason to imagine a fine presentation copy with an unfinished programme of decorated initials during Ashby's employment for Margaret in the 1450s. As a third option, Meyer-Lee proposes a date in the late 1460s but before 1471 on the grounds that by that stage 'the prince was reasonably old enough to be a credible recipient of its advice' and that in 1463 'Prince Edward was only nine or ten',[58] but as Edward's holograph letter of 1464 shows—written when he was ten years old—the boy was already expected to be tutored and participate in politics.

[55] The proem has been printed in Bateson, *George Ashby's Poems*; and, with a translation by Andrew Taylor, in Wogan-Browne et al., *The Idea of the Vernacular*, 57–8. The translation quoted here is Taylor's.

[56] McGerr, *A Lancastrian Mirror for Princes*, 114–15.

[57] See, in turn, Bateson, *George Ashby's Poems*, vi; Kekewich, 'George Ashby's *The Active Policy of a Prince*', 553; Lawton, 'Dullness and the Fifteenth Century', 772; Paul Strohm, *Politique: Languages of Statecraft between Chaucer and Shakespeare* (Notre Dame, IN: University of Notre Dame Press, 2005), 125. See also McGerr, *A Lancastrian Mirror for Princes*, 113–14.

[58] Meyer-Lee, 'Laureates and Beggars', 709–10.

At the heart of Ashby's dedication is the education and nurture of the young prince: 'pro cuius amore et complacencia fit ista compilacio... suum nobilem sanguinem, sub quo ipse a iuventute sua hucusque, et nunquam tota vita sua in alio servicio fuit tentus, nutritus' (for whose love and goodwill he made this compilation... his noble blood, under which he, from his youth was raised up to this time and never placed in all his life in other's service). The remainder of the dedication is equally didactic, urging the boy to draw lessons from the past and follow basic reading: 'Tempus preteritum exortatur, sepius memin[iss]e de rebus preteritis, ita bene in legendo sacram scripturam et Cronica, sicut alias sp[e]culaciones et experiencias' (Time past urges us often to remember things past, both by reading sacred Scripture and chronicles, and other accounts and retellings). While Laurence Bothe was appointed Edward's tutor in 1457, Ashby was an integral part of the queen's household,[59] certainly until the royal family went into exile following Henry's deposition in 1461. A. Myers notes that Ashby was paid more than Elizabeth Woodville's signet clerk and performed a more dedicated role: 'Thus whereas John Aleyn seems to have acted both as clerk of the signet and secretary in the household of Queen Elizabeth, and at a fee of only £4 (which was disallowed), George Ashby was clerk of the signet, at a fee of £6 13s. 4d., and Nicholas Carent was her "secretarius"'.[60] Myers adds that 'Carent does not seem to have been as important as Ashby'.[61] We also know that one signet clerk always accompanied the person of the king: Margaret only had one signet clerk. At the same time, Edward was with Margaret at all times, and she took personal care of his education.[62] So between Edward's birth in 1453 and the flight of Margaret and her son to Edinburgh in 1461/2, Ashby was always in the same place as Edward. Unlike Bothe, Ashby may not have been the person primarily responsible for Edward's intellectual development, but no one was better equipped, trained, nor readily available to instruct Edward in writing than Ashby, certainly until the prince turned nine years old.

59 Myers, 'The Household of Queen Margaret of Anjou, 1452–3', 92.

60 Myers, 'The Household of Queen Margaret of Anjou, 1452–3', 91. See also Otway-Ruthven, *The King's Secretary*, 135.

61 Myers, 'The Household of Queen Margaret of Anjou, 1452–3', 91n2.

62 R. A. Griffiths, 'Edward [Edward of Westminster], Prince of Wales (1453–1471)', *ODNB* (Oxford: Oxford University Press, 2004).

Ashby's script and letter forms in Mm. 4.42 are striking in two respects: they match the highest register of the signet secretary hand and they represent selected allographs familiar to Edward, whose holograph writing has also survived in MS français 4054 among the group of intercepted Lancastrian letters from December 1464, when Prince Edward had just turned ten years old. Both the wording of the prince's autograph letter to Lord Ormond as well as the script of the letter reveal Ashby's influence. Fortescue closes his letter in the same parcel with the note that 'my lord Prince sendithe to you nowe a lettre writyne withe his awne hande' (MS français 4054, fol. 175). Edward's holograph letter on fol. 173 shows the same untrained child-like secretary script that features in his sign manual elsewhere (for instance, in MS français 4054, fol. 172) which affirms its status as a holograph: 'Writen at seynt mychael in barr, *with* myn awn hand that ye mey se how gode a wrytare I ame'. His inexperienced angular hand is reminiscent of Ashby's upright duct and captures all the hallmarks of a signet secretary hand, with long- and kidney-shaped *s*, modern- and z-shaped *r*, and simple and lobed *d*.

Furthermore, although parts of the text were surely drafted by Margaret or her advisors, there are verbal echoes of Ashby's *Active Policy/Dicta* in the letter. Edward invokes the 'cruel malice' of Ormond's 'adversaries' (ll. 6–7), while *Active Policy*, ll. 707–8, has 'Neither in malice, ne in Cruelte, / Nor owte of tempre for aduersite'.[63] Ashby reiterates in *Active Policy* his central concern to suppress rebels (l. 227), and l. 388 reads 'To subdewe al maner rebellyon', a phrase that has its equivalent in Edward's letter: 'subduing of his rebellis' (l. 11). The phrase 'put you . . . in devoir' (make a committed effort), used by Edward in l. 9, echoes l. 543 of the *Dicta*: 'Put you in . . . deuour'. Edward thanks Lord Ormond for his 'manly gyding'; the word 'guyding' is used a number of times by Ashby in the *Active Policy/Dicta* (*AP* 775, 830; *Dicta* 2, 249, 628, 644; there are some combined fifteen more uses of its antonym 'misguyding' and the verb 'to guyde'), whereas 'manly' appears twice in Ashby's bipartite poem (*AP* 741, *Dicta* 1148). Other shared echoes of abstract or conceptual terms can be included here (Ashby's form is given first): purchased/purcheased;

[63] All quotations from the *Active Policy* and *Dicta* are from Bateson, *George Ashby's Poems*.

perpetuite/perpetually; proteccione; recouerable/recuvering; Royalme/ royalme. This is not to say that Edward may ever have received Mm. 4.42 (nor do I think it likely that another copy was prepared, given the high-grade execution of the surviving manuscript), but, taken together, the care used to write Mm. 4.42, the didactic dedication to Edward, Ashby's proven physical proximity and access to Edward for the first nine years of the prince's life, Margaret's high regard for her best and most professional writer, the signet secretary model behind Edward's holograph letter, the verbal echoes between Ashby's political verses for Edward, and, finally, Edward's own writing suggest that Ashby did have a hand in the prince's education, and that he may have instructed Edward how to write. Meyer-Lee argues that because 'he was the Lancastrians' final poet', Ashby's work, perhaps in mirroring the underwhelming condition of MS Mm. 4.42, 'baldly exhibits the tensions inherent in the politico-literary experiment that, under the circumstances, was stressed to the breaking point'.[64] But Ashby could not have known that the dynasty was about to expire—his closeness to the queen and to Edward suggests that he was not so much a laureate, self-interested beggar poet, but someone directly and intimately involved in Edward's education and the most qualified and likely person to have instructed the young prince in the basic skill of writing. Once again, the bespoke and deictic aspects of the manuscript and its text point toward the indexical value of the sole *Active Policy* specimen as a gift composed and written out by its author whom the recipient knew personally.

There is, I believe, a connection between MS Mm. 4.42 and Ashby's prison poem. In *Reflections* Ashby's deictic voice claims to have composed this poem in prison in 1463.[65] Taking into account that the new year began on Lady Day, 25 March, this information and the remaining biographical references in the poem strongly suggest that Ashby started his prison term in 1462, not 1461. Towards the end of *Reflections* Ashby's persona states that the work was 'Wretyn in pryson in oure Lordes date / A thowsand, foure hundryd, syxty and thre' (ll. 337–8), while earlier in the poem, at l. 30, he discloses that he has been imprisoned 'a hoole yere and more'. The opening two stanzas establish

[64] Meyer-Lee, *Poets and Power*, 140.
[65] Ll. 337–8.

that Ashby—assuming here as elsewhere in his works that the author conflates himself with the textual George—was incarcerated in the Fleet prison at the 'ende of somere' but before Michaelmas (29 September). Even if Ashby wrote the poem on the first day of 1463, that is on 25 March, his imprisonment could hardly have taken place before Michaelmas (29 September) 1461, because the difference in the time elapsed between the two closest dates—28 September 1461 and 25 March 1463—would have been eighteen months, a year and a half, which is probably longer than the idiom 'a hoole yere and more' would suggest. But in any case, eighteen months is only the very minimum for placing the start of his prison term in 1461. With any day, week, or month beyond a composition date of 25 March 1463, the time elapsed exceeds eighteen months and thus tilts toward 'almost two years' rather than 'a hole yere and more'. This means that his imprisonment began between late summer and 28 September 1462. Adding to this date range 'a hoole yere and more' means that this poem can be dated to between some time after Michaelmas 1463 and 24 March 1464 (which was still 1463 to Ashby).

Since the Battle of Towton, in the aftermath of which Henry and Margaret fled to Scotland, was fought during the first week of 1461 (on 29 March), Ashby was in all likelihood not imprisoned for another sixteen to eighteen months; that is, his imprisonment was therefore probably not part of the immediate Yorkist purges. Given his role as Margaret's signet clerk, he may have spent 29 March 1461, the day of the Battle of Towton, in York with the queen. But because of the considerable financial burden sudden exile placed on the queen and the royal party it is improbable that Margaret could have been able to retain a signet clerk paid at £6 13s. 4d. if not more at this stage. Ashby would have left Margaret's retinue either shortly after the Battle of Towton or in the course of the coming year, but certainly before her short-lived invasion of Northumberland in October 1462 since he was in prison by that time. During the period between the Battle of Towton and Ashby's earliest possible date of imprisonment, Edward and the queen were in Edinburgh. One probable cause for Ashby's imprisonment is therefore Mm. 4.42, a manuscript clearly produced to be given to Edward, yet unfinished and never presented. Betrayal and the importance of clandestine operations seem to have been at the forefront of Ashby's mind when writing this work. Already R. A. Griffiths noted that *Active Policy* 'is shot through with a fear of treason, which colours much of the advice which Ashby has to offer'.[66] In *Active Policy* Edward is encouraged to restrict the carrying of weapons,[67] while there are some fifteen instances of 'secret', 'secretary', and '*secretum*'—'secrecy' thus becomes one of the central words of this work. Because Ashby includes his name twice and provides identifying biographical details he could not have disavowed this manuscript. As an indexical text carrying self-referential remarks and his name, Mm. 4.42 was therefore an unusually incriminating piece of evidence in the wrong hands. It would appear that Ashby's decision to inscribe himself and his public identity into this poetical tract may very well have resulted in his imprisonment.

Ashby's surviving poems—the *Active Policy* (which ought to be seen as synonymous with the Cambridge manuscript) and *Reflections*—mark his provisional withdrawal from public life and a profession that, as with Hoccleve, shaped his indexical self. The uprootedness and bitterness with which he characterizes his fall in *Reflections* is not the voice of a cantankerous octogenarian who gambled on the Lancastrians, but an assiduous sociocentric person who has been socialized by the bureaucratic environment with which Ashby has been associated. *Reflections* shows, I believe, that Ashby read and understood Hoccleve's *Series* as a work motivated by loss and rupture that was designed to reconcile the authorial self with its altered reality. The personal references in both the *Series* and *Reflections* are indexical references to the author behind the text, just as Thomas and George are deictic selves that rely on an intimate audience familiar with the author. In a way, the circumstance that Ashby wrote *Reflections* as a deictic poem in the mode of a complaint tied to the Exchequer calendar is a remarkable instance of the reception of Hoccleve's *Complaint* as an indexical poem.

Ashby died on 20 February 1475, and his last decade is actually well documented: I have found no less than six new life records ranging

[66] Ralph A. Griffiths, *The Reign of King Henry VI: The Exercise of Royal Authority, 1422–1461* (Berkeley, CA: University of California Press, 1981), 42.

[67] *Active Policy*, ll. 541–7. The most detailed discussions of the poem are found in McGerr, *A Lancastrian Mirror for Princes*, 110–17; Meyer-Lee, 'Laureates and Beggars', 688–726.

from 1437 to 1474, with most dating after 1465.[68] The density of records related to his Middlesex estate in Harefield, not far from his former work place, the signet's *scriptory* in Windsor Castle,[69] corroborates the notion that he had indeed lost his taste for the public life at this stage. Ashby's son John was also a signet scribe,[70] and his grandson, called George, became a signet clerk for Henry VII and for Henry VIII,[71] and given Ashby's longevity—he died in his nineties—he may have instructed not only his son but also his grandson in his craft.

[68] For the date of his death see Scattergood, 'Ashby, George'. The new life records are as follows: (1) 1 March 1439, demise by Lady Margaret Catesby, lady of Lapworth, to George Assheby, Margaret his wife and John their son (TNA E 40/4494); (2) Easter term 1440, a plea of trespass brought by Walter Roger against George Ashby of Harefield, Court of Common Pleas (TNA CP 40/707); (3) 1 March 1465/66, Witness of Livery of Seisin, of a tenement called Beale Haketes, Harefield, by John Godfrey of Harefield to George Assheby and co-feoffees and assigns (TNA ACC/0852/003); (4) a quitclaim of 10 December 1469 by Ashby's son John to Ashby himself (TNA ACC/0312/96); (5) a dispute of 8 May 1469 settled by Ashby with John Gage and involving Gage's son William, his daughter Eleanor and Ashby's son John (TNA SAS/G21/1); (6) 1474, Memorandum of sale by George Ashby to William Catesby of lands in Lapworth (TNA E 163/29/8). There are also records associated with Ashby's son while Ashby was still alive: (1) 22 August 1472, grant by William Welder of Hillingdon and Dionisia his wife to John Assheby of Herfeld of lands (TNA ACC/0312/98); (2) (TNA ACC/0312/99 (1472); and (3) *c.* 11 November 1474, Indenture of Fine, Octave of St Martin's, 14 Edw. IV., between Joan Kent, plaintiff and John Assheby and William Welder and his wife Dionisia, deforciants (TNA ACC/0312/101).

[69] The *Liber Niger Dominus Regis Angliae*, dating to Edward IV's reign, speaks of a 'scriptory' in Windsor in which signet clerks may take their 'dynners and soupers' if their 'business requireth' it (Otway-Ruthven, *The King's Secretary*, 110 See also Parkes, *Their Hands before Our Eyes*, 50n117).

[70] There are two signet letters signed by his son in TNA C 81/1375/11 and 15, and C 81/1376 contains a number of unsigned letters in John Ashby's hand.

[71] Scattergood, 'Ashby, George'.

Afterword

Pragmatic Selves

Perhaps one way of understanding the textual 'I' in late medieval narratives is to think of it as the pragmatic self of the author. Never quite divorced from the porous indexical self of the writer, the textual 'I' is the authentic guise sociocentric persons assume in public contexts. To some extent, the public selves we ourselves project are real and certainly reliable, yet they are rarely exact extensions of our private selves. But unlike medieval persons, we can actively construct and use our public selves as means through which we influence and control our environment. For the indexical self such an operation is fraught with danger. Their identity is not self-contained or even clearly separated from the environment: they are at the mercy of the spiritual and politicized forces exerting pressure on them. Such persons construct pragmatic selves much less consciously than we do, and their textual selves are closely tied to themselves, so closely, in fact, that they are exposed to their surroundings, just as their authors were. To effect change through the textual 'I' asked of the premodern writer to invest much of their personal reality in their textual reflection. The thinner the membrane separating the respective personae of Thomas, George, and Geoffrey from those of Hoccleve, Ashby, and Chaucer, the more propitious the likely public consequences of their creative efforts.

Last Words: The Public Self and the Social Author in Late Medieval England.
Sebastian Sobecki, Oxford University Press (2019).
DOI: 10.1093/oso/9780198790778.001.0001

That the textual 'I' of medieval writers is deeply tied to the authorial self finds support in much of the archival evidence that has recently come to light. Many of the discoveries I have made in the last few years—John Bailey's will, a letter by Margery Kempe's son, or Ashby's signature missives—were not initiated by exploring historical references to these writers.[1] Instead, in each case my point of departure was a formalist position of testing the reliability of what their textual deictic selves communicate about themselves: Hoccleve lists Bailey's name next to his own in a poem requesting payment to his fellow Privy Seal clerks; in her *Book* Margery speaks of her son living in Gdańsk/Danzig; while Ashby's textual 'I' tells us that he (and, thus, Ashby) wrote for the signets of Humphrey, Margaret, and Henry. Each discovery was therefore made *because* of a writer's textual persona, not despite it. All findings resulted from the rigorous pursuit of close reading and allowing the text—not the context—to lead me. This assumption of proximity between author and audience, and of the indexical nature of these texts and their manuscript instances, always opened up the shortest possible route to the new archival documents that, in turn, confirmed the reliability of the textual self. Not only is the named textual 'I' of the late medieval writer not fictional, but as the pragmatic, public extension of the author's sociocentric, porous, and indexical self it is real and thus reliable. The burden of proof, then, does not fall on arguments that hope to show that pragmatic selves in late medieval literature are reliable but on those that wish to deny it.

[1] For the Kempe letter, see Sebastian Sobecki, '"The Writyng of This Tretys": Margery Kempe's Son and the Authorship of Her Book', *Studies in the Age of Chaucer*, 37 (2015), 257–83.

BIBLIOGRAPHY

Manuscripts and Archival Documents

Cambridge, Jesus College MS 56
Cambridge, Trinity College, MS R.3.19
Cambridge, University Library MS Mm.2.21
Cambridge University Library MS Mm.4.42
Canterbury Cathedral Archives CCA-DCc-ChAnt/K/4
Düsseldorf, Hauptstaatsarchiv, Urkunde Kurköln no 1927
Durham University Library MS Cosin V. ii. 13
Durham University Library MS Cosin V. iii. 9
Edinburgh University Library MS 183
Geneva, Bibliothèque de Genève MS fr. 178
Leiden University MS Vossius 9
London, British Library Add. MS 5140
London, British Library Add. MS 24062
London, British Library Add. MS 34193
London, British Library Add. MS 59495
London, British Library Arundel MS 285
London, British Library Cotton MS Caligula D V
London, British Library Cotton MS Cleopatra F III
London, British Library Cotton MS Cleopatra F IV
London, British Library Cotton MS Tiberius A IV
London, British Library Cotton MS Vitellius A XV
London, British Library Harley MS 43
London, British Library Harley MS 1766
London, British Library Harley MS 2255
London, British Library Harley MS 2278
London, British Library Royal MS 16 F VII
London, British Library Royal MS 18 D II
London, British Library Royal MS 19 A IV
London, British Library Royal MS 19 B XII
London, British Library Yates Thompson MS 47
London, Guildhall MS 25125/32
London, TNA ACC/0312/96
London, TNA ACC/0312/98
London, TNA ACC/0312/99
London, TNA ACC/0312/101

London, TNA ACC/0852/003
London, TNA C 64/11, m. 4d
London, TNA C 76/102, m. 5
London, TNA C 81/557/910
London, TNA C 81/669/1204
London, TNA, C81/729/5907B
London, TNA C 81/729/5913
London, TNA, C 81/729/5915
London, TNA, C 81/729/5916
London, TNA, C 81/729/5919
London, TNA, C 81/729/5920
London, TNA, C 81/729/5922
London, TNA, C 81/729/5925B
London, TNA, C 81/729/5927
London, TNA, C 81/729/5955
London, TNA, C 81/729/5956
London, TNA, C 81/729/5959
London, TNA, C 81/729/5963
London, TNA C 81/729/5964
London, TNA, C 81/729/5969A
London, TNA, C 81/729/5969B
London, TNA, C 81/729/5970
London, TNA C 81/1365/7
London, TNA C 81/1365/24
London, TNA C 81/1367/17
London, TNA C 81/1367/18
London, TNA C 81/1367/20
London, TNA C 81/1368/20
London, TNA C 81/1375/11
London, TNA C 81/1375/15
London, TNA C 81/1376
London, TNA C 81/1537/4
London, TNA C 81/1543/21
London, TNA C 81/1544/1, *olim* C 81/669/1204
London, TNA CP 40/707
London, TNA E 28/29
London, TNA E 36/228
London, TNA E 40/4494
London, TNA E 163/29/8
London, TNA HCA 12
London, TNA PROB 11/2B/363

London, TNA PROB 11/6/37
London, TNA PROB 11/53/491
London, TNA SAS/G21/1
London, TNA SC 1/44/13
London, TNA SC 1/63/305
London, TNA SC 8/270/13497
London, University of London Library, MS 1
London, Westminster Abbey Muniments WAM 5
London, Westminster Abbey Muniments WAM 6643
Manchester, John Rylands Library MS English 1
Manchester, John Rylands Library MS English 955
Montreal, McGill University Libraries MS 143
Oxford, Bodleian Library MS Ashmole 46
Oxford, Bodleian Library MS Ashmole 61
Oxford, Bodleian Library MS Ashmole 764
Oxford, Bodleian Library MS Ashmole 789
Oxford, Bodleian Library MS Digby 232
Oxford, Bodleian Library MS Dugdale 45
Oxford, Bodleian Library MS Laud 704
Oxford, Bodleian Library MS Laud Misc. 683
Oxford, New College MS 314
Paris, Archives nationales, AE III 254 (*olim* J 646 15)
Paris, Bibliothèque nationale MS Baluze 11
Paris, Bibliothèque nationale MS Bibliothèque de l'Arsenal 3339
Paris, Bibliothèque nationale MS Dupuy 760
Paris, Bibliothèque nationale MS français 2909
Paris, Bibliothèque nationale MS français 4054 (formerly Ancien 9037(7), *olim* Baluze 474)
Paris, Bibliothèque nationale MS français 4485
Paris, Bibliothèque nationale MS français 5519
Paris, Bibliothèque nationale MS latin 8685
San Marino, Huntington Library MS HM 111
San Marino, Huntington Library MS HM 932

Primary Sources

Bale, Anthony, and A. S. G. Edwards, eds, *John Lydgate's Lives of SS Edmund and Fremund and the Extra Miracles of St Edmund* (Heidelberg: Winter, 2009)

Bale, Anthony, and Sebastian Sobecki, eds, *Medieval English Travel: A Critical Anthology* (Oxford: Oxford University Press, 2019)

Barnum, Priscilla Heath, *Dives and Pauper*, EETS O.S., 275, 2 vols (London: Oxford University Press for the EETS, 1976)

Bateson, Mary, ed., *George Ashby's Poems: From the Fifteenth-Century MSS at Cambridge*, EETS ES 76, Repr. 1965 (London: Kegan Paul, Trench, and Trübner, 1899)

de Beaucourt, Gaston Louis Emmanuel du Fresne Marquis, *Chronique de Mathieu d'Escouchy. Vol. 3: Pièces justificatives* (Paris: Renouard, 1864)

Benson, Larry D., gen. ed., *The Riverside Chaucer*, 3rd edn (Oxford: Oxford University Press, 1987)

Bolland, William Craddock, *Select Bills in Eyre, AD 1292–1333* (London: Quaritch, 1914)

Brewer, J. S., and James Gairdner, *Letters and Papers, Foreign and Domestic, Henry VIII*, 18 vols (London: H. M. Stationery Office, 1862–1901)

Burrow, J. A., ed., *Thomas Hoccleve's Complaint and Dialogue*, EETS OS 313 (Oxford: Oxford University Press, 1999)

Burrow, J. A., and A. I. Doyle, eds, *Thomas Hoccleve: A Facsimile of the Autograph Verse Manuscripts*, EETS SS 19 (Oxford: Oxford University Press for EETS, 2002)

Calendar of the Patent Rolls: Henry IV, 1399–1401 (London: H. M. Stationery Office, 1903)

Carlson, David R., *The Deposition of Richard II: The Record and Process of the Renunciation and Deposition of Richard II (1399) and Related Writings* (Toronto: Pontifical Institute of Mediaeval Studies, 2007)

Chaplais, Pierre, *English Medieval Diplomatic Practice: Part I, Documents and Interpretation* (London: H. M. Stationery Office, 1982)

Chaplais, Pierre, *English Medieval Diplomatic Practice: Part II, Plates* (London: H. M. Stationery Office, 1975)

Chaplais, Pierre, *English Royal Documents: King John–Henry VI, 1199–1461* (Oxford: Clarendon Press, 1971)

The Chronica Maiora of Thomas Walsingham, 1376–1422, ed. D. Preest and J. G. Clark (Woodbridge: Boydell, 2005)

Clermont, Lord, *The Works of Sir John Fortescue, Knight: Chief Justice of England and Lord Chancellor to King Henry the Sixth* (London: Chiswick Press, 1869)

The Complete Works of Geoffrey Chaucer: Chaucerian and Other Pieces, ed. Walter W. Skeat, 7 vols (Oxford: Clarendon Press, 1894–7)

Correale, Robert M., and Mary Hamel, *Sources and Analogues of the Canterbury Tales II* (Cambridge: D. S. Brewer, 2005)

Daniel-Tyssen, J. R., 'Inventories of the Goods and Ornaments of the Churches in the County of Surrey in the Reign of Edward VI,' *Surrey Archaeological Collections*, 4 (1869), 1–189

Dean, James M., *Medieval English Political Writings* (Kalamazoo, MI: Medieval Institute Publications, 1996)

Devon, Frederick, ed., *Issues of the Exchequer* (London: Murray, 1837)

Edwards, A. S. G., *The Life of St Edmund, King and Martyr: John Lydgate's Illustrated Verse Life Presented to Henry VI: A Facsimile of British Library MS Harley 2278* (London: British Library, 2004)

Edwards, Robert A., *John Lydgate, Troy Book: Selections* (Kalamazoo, MI: Medieval Institute Publications, 1998)

Edwards, Robert A., *The Siege of Thebes* (Kalamazoo, MI: Medieval Institute Publications, 2001)

Eliot, T. S., *Selected Poems* (London: Faber and Faber, 1961)

Fisher, John H., Malcolm Richardson, and Jane L. Fisher, *An Anthology of Chancery English* (Knoxville, TN: University of Tennessee Press, 1984)

Forni, Kathleen, ed., *The Chaucerian Apocrypha: A Selection* (Kalamazoo, MI: Medieval Institute Publications, 2005)

Furnivall, Frederick J., *Early English Meals and Manners: John Russell's Boke of Nurture, Wynkyn de Worde's Boke of Keruynge, the Boke of Curtasye, R. Weste's Booke of Demeanor, Seager's Schoole of Vertue, the Babees Book, Aristotle's ABC, Urbanitatis, Stans puer ad mensam*, EETS O.S., 32 (London: Humphrey Milford, 1868)

Given-Wilson, Chris, *The Parliament Rolls of Medieval England, 1275–1504* (Woodbridge: Boydell Press and the National Archives, 2005)

Gough, Richard, *Sepulchral Monuments of Great Britain*, 2 vols (London: the author, 1786–96)

Gower, John, *Confessio Amantis*, ed. Russell A. Peck and trans. Andrew Galloway (Kalamazoo, MI: Medieval Institute Publications, 2006)

Hardwick, C., and H. R. Luard, *A Catalogue of the Manuscripts Preserved in the Library of the University of Cambridge* (Cambridge: Cambridge University Press, 1861)

Harriss, G. L., and M. A. Harriss, 'III: John Benet's Chronicle for the Years 1400 to 1462', *Camden Fourth Series*, 9 (1972), 151–233

Héron, Alexandre, ed., *Oeuvres de Robert Blondel*, 2 vols (Rouen: Lestringant, 1891–93)

Hertzberg, Wilhelm Adolf Boguslaw, and Reinhold Pauli, eds, *The Libell of Englishe Policye, 1436: Text und metrische Übersetzung* (Leipzig: Hirzel, 1878)

Hoccleve, Thomas, *Hoccleve's Works: The Minor Works*, ed. Frederick J. Furnivall and others, EETS ES 61, 73, 2 vols (Oxford: EETS, 1970)

Hoccleve, Thomas, *Selections from Hoccleve*, ed. M. C. Seymour (Oxford: Clarendon Press, 1981)

Hoccleve, Thomas, *The Regiment of Princes*, ed. Charles Ramsay Blyth (Kalamazoo, MI: Medieval Institute Publications, 1999)

Kennedy, Ruth, '"A Bird in Bishopswood": Some Newly-Discovered Lines of Alliterative Verse from the Late Fourteenth Century', in *Medieval Literature and Antiquities: Studies in Honour of Basil Cottle*, ed. Myra Stokes and T. L. Burton (Woodbridge: D. S. Brewer, 1987), 71–87

Kingsford, C. L., 'Additional Material for the History of the Grey Friars, London', in *Collectanea Franciscana II*, ed. C. L. Kingsford (Manchester: Manchester University Press, 1922), 61–149

Kingsford, C. L., *The Grey Friars of London: Their History with the Register of Their Convent and an Appendix of Documents* (Manchester: Manchester University Press, 1915)

Kirby, John Lavan, *Calendar of Signet Letters of Henry IV and Henry V (1399–1422)* (London: H. M. Stationery Office, 1978)

Lapidge, Michael, *Anglo-Saxon Litanies of the Saints* (Woodbridge: Boydell Press for the Henry Bradshaw Society, 1991)

Lester, G. A., 'The Books of a Fifteenth-Century English Gentleman: Sir John Paston', *Neuphilologische Mitteilungen*, 88 (1987), 200–17

Livingston, Michael, and R. F. Yeager, eds, *The Minor Latin Works with In Praise of Peace* (Kalamazoo, MI: Medieval Institute Publications, 2005)

Lydgate, John, *Lydgate's Fall of Princes*, ed. Henry Bergen, EETS E.S., 121, 4 vols (London: Oxford University Press, 1924–27)

Lydgate, John, *Lydgate's Troy Book*, ed. Henry Bergen, 4 vols, EETS s.s. 97, 103, 106, 126 (London: Kegan Paul, 1906–35)

Lydgate, John, *Saint Austin at Compton, c. 1420–40*, in *Saints' Lives in Middle English Collections*, ed. E. G. Whatley, A. Thompson, and R. Upchurch (Kalamazoo, MI: Medieval Institute Publications, 2004)

Lydgate, John, *The Minor Poems of John Lydgate I*, ed. Henry N. Maccracken, EETS E.S., 107 (Oxford: Oxford University Press, 1911)

Lydgate, John, *The Siege of Thebes*, ed. Robert A. Edwards (Kalamazoo, MI: Medieval Institute Publications, 2001)

Lydgate, John, *The Temple of Glass*, ed. J. Allan Mitchell (Kalamazoo, MI: Medieval Institute Publications, 2007)

Macaulay, G. C., ed., *The Complete Works of John Gower: The French Works* (Oxford: Clarendon Press, 1899)

Madden, Frederic, Bulkeley Bandinel, and John Gough Nichols, *Collectanea Topographica et Genealogica* (London: Nichols, 1838)

Manly, John M., and Edith Rickert, eds, *The Text of The Canterbury Tales: Studied on the Basis of All Known Manuscripts*, 8 vols (Chicago, IL: University of Chicago Press, 1940)

Mitchell, J. Allan, *The Temple of Glas* (Kalamazoo, MI: Medieval Institute Publications, 2007)

Mooney, Linne R., and Mary-Jo Arn, eds, *The Kingis Quair and Other Prison Poems* (Kalamazoo, MI: Medieval Institute Publications, 2005)

Morgan, Nigel John, *English Monastic Litanies of the Saints after 1100*. 2 vols (Woodbridge: Boydell Press for the Henry Bradshaw Society, 2012–13)

Nicolas, Harris, ed., *Proceedings and Ordinances of the Privy Council of England 4* (London: Record Commission, 1835)

Rymer, Thomas, *Foedera*, ed. George Holmes, 3rd edn (The Hague: J. Neaulme, 1743)

Shakespeare, William, *King Henry V*, ed. Andrew Gurr (Cambridge: Cambridge University Press, 1992)

Shakespeare, William, *Shakespeare's History of King Henry the Fifth*, ed. Samuel Neil (Glasgow and London: Collins, 1878)

Shuffelton, George, ed., *Codex Ashmole 61: A Compilation of Popular Middle English Verse* (Kalamazoo, MI: Medieval Institute Publications, 2008)

Stamp, A. E., ed., *Calendar of the Close Rolls, Henry VI: Vol. 2, 1429–1435* (London: H. M. Stationery Office, 1933)

Stevenson, Joseph, *Letters and Papers Illustrative of the Wars of the English in France during the Reign of Henry the Sixth, King of England* (London: Longman, Green, Longman, and Roberts, 1861)

Strong, P., and F. Strong, 'The Last Will and Codicils of Henry V', *English Historical Review*, 96/378 (1981), 79–102

Taylor, Frank, and John S. Roskell, eds, *Gesta Henrici Quinti, Deeds of Henry the Fifth* (Oxford: Clarendon Press, 1975)

Testamenta Eboracensia (London: J. B. Nichols, 1836)

Twiss, Travers, ed., *The Black Book of the Admiralty*, Monumenta Juridica, 4 vols (London: Longman and Trübner, 1871)

Warner, George F., ed., *The Libelle of Englyshe Polycye: A Poem on the Use of Sea-Power, 1436* (Oxford: Clarendon Press, 1926)

Warner, George F., and J. P. Gilson, *Catalogue of Western Manuscripts in the Old Royal and King's Collections* (London: Trustees of the British Museum, 1921)

Waurin, Jean de, *A Collection of the Chronicles and Ancient Histories of Great Britain, Now Called England: From AD 1399 to AD 1422*, trans. William Hardy and Edward Hardy (London: Longman, Roberts, and Green, 1887)

Webb, John, 'Translation of a French Metrical History of the Deposition of King Richard the Second', *Archaeologia*, 20 (1824), 1–423

Whatley, E. G., A. Thompson, and R. Upchurch, *Saints' Lives in Middle English Collections* (Kalamazoo, MI: Medieval Institute Publications, 2004)

William Marx, C., ed., *An English Chronicle, 1377–1461: Edited from Aberystwyth, National Library of Wales MS 21068 and Oxford, Bodleian Library MS Lyell 34* (Woodbridge: Boydell Press, 2003)

Williams, Benjamin, ed., *Chronique de la traïson et mort de Richart Deux Roy d'Engleterre* (London: English Historical Society, 1846)

Wogan-Browne, Jocelyn, Nicholas Watson, Andrew Taylor, and Ruth Evans, *The Idea of the Vernacular: An Anthology of Middle English Literary Theory, 1280–1520* (University Park, PA: Pennsylvania State University Press, 1999)

Wright, Thomas, *Political Poems and Songs Relating to English History*, Volume 2 (London: Longman, Green, Longman, and Roberts, 1861)

Yeager, R. F., ed., *John Gower: The French Balades* (Kalamazoo, MI: Medieval Institute Publications, 2011)

Secondary Sources

Allmand, Christopher, *The Hundred Years War: England and France at War, c. 1300–c. 1450* (Cambridge: Cambridge University Press, 1988)

'Appendix', *Archaeologia*, 18 (1817), 417–48

Appleford, Amy, *Learning to Die in London, 1380–1540* (Philadelphia, PA: University of Pennsylvania Press, 2015)

Bahr, Arthur W., *Fragments and Assemblages: Forming Compilations of Medieval London* (Chicago, IL: University of Chicago Press, 2013)

Bahr, Arthur W., 'Reading Codicological Form in John Gower's Trentham Manuscript', *Studies in the Age of Chaucer*, 33 (2011), 219–62

Barker, Juliet, *Conquest* (Cambridge, MA: Harvard University Press, 2012)

Barrington, Candace, 'John Gower's Legal Advocacy and "In Praise of Peace"', in *John Gower, Trilingual Poet: Language, Translation, and Tradition*, ed. Elizabeth Dutton (Cambridge: D. S. Brewer, 2010)

Barrington, Candace, 'The Trentham Manuscript as Broken Prosthesis: Wholeness and Disability in Lancastrian England', *Accessus*, 1/1 (2013), 1–33

Bawcutt, Priscilla, and Janet Hadley Williams, 'Introduction: "Poets of This Natioun"', in *A Companion to Medieval Scottish Poetry*, ed. Priscilla Bawcutt and Janet Hadley Williams (Cambridge: D. S. Brewer, 2006), 1–18

Bennett, Michael, '*The Libelle of English Policy*: The Matter of Ireland', in *The Fifteenth Century XV*, ed. Linda Clark (Woodbridge: Boydell Press, 2017), 1–22

Bessinger, Jess B., Philip H. Smith, and Michael W. Twomey, *A Concordance to the Anglo-Saxon Poetic Records* (Ithaca, NY: Cornell University Press, 1978)

Boenig, Robert, 'Taking Leave: Chaucer's Retraction and the Ways of Affirmation and Negation', *Studia Mystica*, 12 (1989), 21–8

Boffey, Julia, 'Chaucerian Prisoners: The Context of *The Kingis Quair*', in *Chaucer and Fifteenth-Century Poetry*, ed. Julia Boffey and Janet Cowen (London: King's College London, 1991), 84–102

Boffey, Julia, 'Lydgate, Henryson, and the Literary Testament', *Modern Language Quarterly*, 53 (1992), 41–56

Boger, Charlotte G., *Southwark and Its Story* (London: H. H. G. Grattan, 1881)

Bompaire, Marc, 'Un exemple de livre de changeur français du XVe siècle, le manuscrit Bibl. nat. de Fr., Nouv. Acq. Fr. 471', *Revue Numismatique*, 6/167 (2011), 105–11

Brantley, Jessica, *Reading in the Wilderness: Private Devotion and Public Performance in Late Medieval England* (Chicago, IL: University of Chicago Press, 2007)

Brewer, Thomas, *Memoir of the Life and Times of John Carpenter* (London: Taylor, 1856)

Brown, A. L., *The Early History of the Clerkship of the Council* (Glasgow: University of Glasgow, 1969)

Brown, A. L., 'The Privy Seal Clerks in the Early Fifteenth Century', in *The Study of Medieval Records: Essays in Honor of Kathleen Major*, ed. D. A. Bullough and R. L. Storey (Oxford: Clarendon Press, 1971), 260–81

Brown, Matthew Clifton, '"Lo, Heer the Fourme": Hoccleve's *Series*, Formulary, and Bureaucratic Textuality', *Exemplaria*, 23/1 (2011), 27–49

Brownbill, John, and William Farrer, *A History of the County of Lancaster* (London: Constable, 1912)

Bryan, Jennifer E., 'Hoccleve, the Virgin, and the Politics of Complaint', *PMLA*, 117/5 (2002), 1172–87

Bryan, Jennifer E., *Looking Inward: Devotional Reading and the Private Self in Late Medieval England* (Philadelphia, PA: University of Pennsylvania Press, 2013)

Bühler, Curt F., 'The *Liber de Dictis Philosophorum Antiquorum* and Common Proverbs in George Ashby's Poems', *PMLA*, 65/2 (1950), 282–9

Burckhardt, Jacob, *The Civilization of the Renaissance in Italy: An Essay*, trans. S. G. C. Middlemore (London: Allen and Unwin, 1878)

Burrow, J. A., *Gestures and Looks in Medieval Narrative* (Cambridge: Cambridge University Press, 2002)

Burrow, J. A., *Thomas Hoccleve* (Aldershot: Variorum, 1994)

Butterfield, Ardis, 'Chaucerian Vernaculars', *Studies in the Age of Chaucer*, 31 (2009), 25–51

Butterfield, Ardis, The Familiar Enemy: Chaucer, Language, and Nation in the Hundred Years War (Oxford: Oxford University Press, 2010)

Buzzetti, Gallarati Silvia, *Le testament maistre Jehan de Meun: un caso letterario* (Alessandria: Ed. dell'Orso, 1989)

Buzzetti, Gallarati Silvia, 'Nota bibliografica sulla tradizione manoscritta del Testament di Jean de Meun 1', *Revue Romane*, 13 (1978), 3–33

Cannon, Christopher, 'Class Distinction and the French of England', in *Traditions and Innovations in the Study of Medieval English Literature: The Influence of Derek Brewer*, ed. Charlotte Brewer and Barry Windeatt (Cambridge: D. S. Brewer, 2013), 48–59

Carley, James P., *The Libraries of Henry VIII* (London: British Library, 2000)

Carlson, David R., *English Humanist Books: Writers and Patrons, Manuscript and Print, 1475–1525* (Toronto: University of Toronto Press, 1993)

Carlson, David R., 'Gower *pia vota bibit* and Henry IV in 1399 November', *English* Studies, 89 (2008), 377–84

Carlson, David R., *John Gower: Poetry and Propaganda in Fourteenth-Century England* (Cambridge: D. S. Brewer, 2012)

Carsley, Catherine A., 'Devotion to the Holy Name: Late Medieval Piety in England', *Princeton University Library Chronicle*, 53 (1992), 156–72

Cole, Andrew, *Literature and Heresy in the Age of Chaucer* (Cambridge: Cambridge University Press, 2008)

Copeland, Rita, *Rhetoric, Hermeneutics, and Translation in the Middle Ages: Academic Traditions and Vernacular Texts* (Cambridge: Cambridge University Press, 1995)

Critten, Rory G., *Author, Scribe, and Book in Late Medieval English Literature* (Cambridge: D. S. Brewer, 2018)

Critten, Rory G., '"Her Heed They Caste Awry": The Transmission and Reception of Thomas Hoccleve's Personal Poetry', *Review of English Studies* (2012)

Critten, Rory G., 'The Uses of Self-Publication in Late Medieval England' (PhD dissertation, University of Groningen, 2013)

Crowder, C. M. D., 'Correspondence between England and the Council of Constance, 1414–1418', *Studies in Church History*, 1 (1964), 184–205

Curry, Anne, *The Hundred Years War* (London: Macmillan, 1993)

Daniell, Christopher, *Death and Burial in Medieval England, 1066–1550* (London: Routledge, 1997)

Davis, Isabel, '"The Trinite Is Our Everlasting Lover": Marriage and Trinitarian Love in the Later Middle Ages', *Speculum*, 86/4 (2011), 914–63

Dean, James M., 'Gower, Chaucer, and Rhyme Royal', *Studies in Philology*, 88 (1991), 251–75

Déprez, Eugène, *Études de diplomatique anglaise: de l'avènement d'Édouard 1erà celui de Henri VII (1272–1485)* (Paris: H. Champion, 1908)

Dickinson, Joycelyne Gledhill, *The Congress of Arras, 1435: A Study in Medieval Diplomacy* (Oxford: Clarendon Press, 1955)

Dodd, Gwilym, 'Was Thomas Favent a Political Pamphleteer? Faction and Politics in Later Fourteenth-Century London', *Journal of Medieval History*, 30 (2011), 1–22

Dodd, Gwilym, and Sophie Petit-Renaud, 'Grace and Favour: The Petition and Its Mechanisms', in *Government and Political Life in England and France, c. 1300–c. 1500*, ed. Christopher Fletcher, Jean-Philippe Genet, and John Watts (Cambridge: Cambridge University Press, 2015), 240–78

Doig, James A., 'A New Source for the Siege of Calais in 1436', *English Historical Review*, 110/436 (1995), 404–16

Doig, James A., 'Political Propaganda and Royal Proclamations in Late Medieval England', *Historical Research*, 71/176 (1998), 253–80

Doig, James A., 'Propaganda, Public Opinion and the Siege of Calais in 1436', in *Crown, Government and People in the Fifteenth Century*, ed. Rowena Archer (Stroud: Sutton, 1995), 79–106

Donavin, Georgiana, 'Rhetorical Gower: Aristotelianism in the *Confessio Amantis*'s Treatment of "Rethorique"', in *John Gower: Manuscripts, Readers, Contexts*, ed. Malte Urban (Turnhout: Brepols, 2009), 155–73

Drimmer, Sonja, 'Picturing the King or Picturing the Saint: Two Miniature Programmes for Lydgate's *Lives of Saints Edmund and Fremund*', in *Picturing the King or Picturing the Saint: Two Miniature Programmes for Lydgate's Lives of Saints Edmund and Fremund*, ed. Powell Sue and Emma Cayley (Exeter: Exeter University Press, 2013), 48–67

Drimmer, Sonja, *The Art of Allusion: Illuminators and the Making of English Literature, 1403–1476* (Philadelphia, PA: University of Pennsylvania Press, 2018)

Drimmer, Sonja, 'The Manuscript as an Ambigraphic Medium: Hoccleve's Scribes, Illuminators, and Their Problems', *Exemplaria*, 29/3 (2017), 175–94

Drogin, Marc, *Medieval Calligraphy: Its History and Technique* (New York: Dover, 1980)

Dugdale, William, *Monasticon Anglicanum: A History of the Abbies and Other Monasteries and Cathedral and Collegiate Churches with Their Dependencies in England and Wales* (London: Bohn, 1846)

Ebin, Lois A., 'The Theme of Poetry in Dunbar's "Goldyn Targe"', *Chaucer Review*, 7 (1972), 147–59

Echard, Siân, 'Last Words: Latin at the End of the *Confessio Amantis*', in *Interstices: Studies in Late Middle English and Anglo-Latin Texts in Honour of A. G. Rigg*, ed. Richard Firth Green and Linne Mooney (Toronto: University of Toronto Press, 2004)

Echard, Siân, *Printing the Middle Ages* (Philadelphia, PA: University of Pennsylvania Press, 2008)

Edwards, A. S. G., 'A New Manuscript of *The Libelle of English Policy*', *Notes and Queries*, 46/244 (1999), 444–5

Emden, A. B., *A Biographical Register of the University of Cambridge to 1500* (Cambridge: Cambridge University Press, 1963)

Edwards, Robert R., *Invention and Authorship in Medieval England* (Comunbus, OH: Ohio State University Press, 2017)

Ferguson, John, *English Diplomacy, 1422–1461* (Oxford: Clarendon Press, 1972)

Fisher, John H., *John Gower, Moral Philosopher and Friend of Chaucer* (New York: New York University Press, 1964)

Fox, Denton, 'Chaucer and Chaucerians', in *Chaucer and Chaucerians: Critical Studies in Middle English Literature*, ed. Derek Brewer (London: Thomas Nelson, 1966), 164–200

Gaines, Atwood D., 'Cultural Definitions, Behavior and the Person in American Psychiatry', in Anthony Marsella and Geoffrey White (eds), *Cultural Conceptions of Mental Health and Therapy* (New York: Springer, 1982)

Gayk, Shannon, *Image, Text, and Religious Reform in Fifteenth-Century England* (Cambridge: Cambridge University Press, 2010)

Giancarlo, Matthew, *Parliament and Literature in Late Medieval England* (Cambridge: Cambridge University Press, 2007)

Gibson, Gail McMurray, *The Theatre of Devotion: East Anglian Drama and Society in the Late Middle Ages* (Chicago, IL: University of Chicago Press, 1995)

Gillespie, Alexandra, *Print Culture and the Medieval Author: Chaucer, Lydgate, and Their Books, 1473–1557* (Oxford: Oxford University Press, 2006)

Gillespie, Vincent, 'Chichele's Church: Vernacular Theology in England after Thomas Arundel', in *After Arundel: Religious Writing in Fifteenth-Century England*, ed. Vincent Gillespie and Kantik Ghosh (Turnhout: Brepols, 2011), 3–42

Glyn, Elizabeth L., 'Negotiating Queenship from Malory to Shakespeare' (unpublished PhD, King's College London, 2015)

Goldie, Matthew Boyd, 'Psychosomatic Illness and Identity in London, 1416–1421: Hoccleve's *Complaint* and *Dialogue with a Friend*', *Exemplaria*, 11/1 (1999), 23–52

Gordon-Kelter, Janice, 'The Lay Presence: Chancery and Privy Seal Personnel in the Bureaucracy of Henry VI', *Medieval Prosopography*, 10/1 (1989), 53–74

Grady, Frank, 'The Lancastrian Gower and the Limits of Exemplarity', *Speculum*, 70 (1995), 552–75

Griffiths, Jane, '"In Bookes Thus Writen I Fynde": Hoccleve's Self-Glossing in the *Regiment of Princes* and the *Series*', *Medium Aevum*, 86/1 (2017), 91–107

Griffiths, R. A., 'Edward [Edward of Westminster], Prince of Wales (1453–1471)', *Oxford Dictionary of National Biography* (Oxford: Oxford University Press, 2004)

Griffiths, R. A., 'Holland, John, First Duke of Exeter (1395–1447)', *Oxford Dictionary of National Biography* (Oxford: Oxford University Press, 2006)

Griffiths, R. A., *The Reign of King Henry VI: The Exercise of Royal Authority, 1422–1461* (Berkeley, CA: University of California Press, 1981)

Hanna, Ralph, *London Literature, 1300–1380* (Cambridge: Cambridge University Press, 2005)

Harriss, G. L., Shaping the Nation: England, 1360–1461 (Oxford: Clarendon Press, 2005)

Helmholz, R. H., 'Bastardy Litigation in Medieval England', *American Journal of Legal History*, 13/4 (1969), 360–83

Henn, Volker, '*The Libelle of Englyshe Polycye*: Politik und Wirtschaft in England in den 30er Jahren des 15. Jahrhunderts', *Hansische Geschichtsblätter*, 101 (1983), 43–65

Herman, Jason Michael, 'Intention, Utility, and Chaucer's Retraction' (PhD dissertation, University of Arizona, 2009)

Hines, John, Natalie Cohen, and Simon Roffey, 'Iohannes Gower, Armiger, Poeta: Records and Memorials of His Life and Death,' in *A Companion to Gower*, ed. Siân Echard (Cambridge: Brewer, 2004), 23–42

Hisashi, Sugito, 'The Limits of Language and Experience', *Journal of Medieval Religious Cultures*, 39/1 (2013), 43–59

Hogg, Oliver Frederick Gillilan, *English Artillery, 1326–1716: Being the History of Artillery in This Country Prior to the Formation of the Royal Regiment of Artillery* (London: Royal Artillery Institution, 1963)

Holmes, G. A., '*The Libel of English Policy*', *English Historical Review*, 76/299 (1961), 193–216

Holthausen, F., 'Ashby-Studien III', *Anglia*, 1921/45 (1921), 92–104

Horobin, Simon, and Linne R. Mooney, ed., *Middle English Texts in Transition: A Festschrift Dedicated to Toshiyuki Takamiya on His 70th Birthday* (Woodbridge: York Medieval Press and Brewer, 2014)

Hsy, Jonathan, 'Blind Advocacy: Blind Readers, Disability Theory, and Accessing John Gower,' *Accessus*, 1/1 (2013), 2

Huber, R. A., and A. M. Headrick, *Handwriting Identification: Facts and Fundamentals* (London: Taylor and Francis, 1999)

Hunt, Tony, *Villon's Last Will: Language and Authority in the Testament* (Oxford: Oxford University Press, 1996)

Irvin, Matthew W., *The Poetic Voices of John Gower: Politics and Personae in the* Confessio Amantis (Cambridge: D. S. Brewer, 2014)

Jajdelska, Elspeth, *Silent Reading and the Birth of the Narrator* (Toronto: University of Toronto Press, 2007)

Jehl, Rainer E., 'Acedia and Burn-Out Syndrome: From an Occupational Vice of the Early Monks to a Psychological Concept in Secularized Professional Life', in *In the Garden of Evil: The Vices and Culture in the Middle Ages*, ed. Richard Newhauser (Toronto: Pontifical Institute of Medieval Studies, 2005), 455–76

Johnson, S. R., 'Saunders, William (by 1497–1570), of Ewell, Surr', in *The History of Parliament: The House of Commons, 1509–1558*, ed. Stanley T. Bindoff (London, 1982), iii, 276–8

Judd, Arnold, *The Life of Thomas Bekynton, Secretary to King Henry VI and Bishop of Bath and Wells 1443–1465* (Chichester: Moore and Tillyer for the Regnum Press, 1961)

Kamath, Stephanie A. and Viereck Gibbs, 'John Lydgate and the Curse of Genius', *Chaucer Review*, 45 (2010), 32–58

Keen, Maurice Hugh, England in the Later Middle Ages: A Political History (London: Methuen, 1973)

Kekewich, Margaret L., 'George Ashby's *The Active Policy of a Prince*: An Additional Source', *Review of English Studies*, 41/164 (1990), 533–5

Kekewich, Margaret L., *The Good King: René of Anjou and Fifteenth Century Europe* (London: Palgrave, 2008)

Kempe, Alfred J., *Historical Notices of the Collegiate Church or Royal Free Chapel and Sanctuary of St Martin-Le-Grand, London* (London: Longman, 1825)

Kern, J. H., 'Der Schreiber Offorde', *Anglia*, 1916/40 (1916), 374

Kern, J. H., 'Die Datierung von Hoccleve's *Dialog*', *Anglia*, 1916/40 (1916), 370–3

Kightly, Charles, 'Hungerford, Walter, First Baron Hungerford (1378–1449)', *Oxford Dictionary of National Biography* (Oxford: Oxford University Press, 2006)

Killick, H. K. S., 'Thomas Hoccleve as Poet and Clerk' (unpublished PhD, University of York, 2010)

Knapp, Ethan, *The Bureaucratic Muse: Thomas Hoccleve and the Literature of Late Medieval England* (Philadelphia, PA: Pennsylvania State University Press, 1997)

Knowles, David, David Smith, Christopher Brooke, and Vera London, *The Heads of Religious Houses: England and Wales, III. 1377–1540* (Cambridge: Cambridge University Press, 2008)

Kruger, Steven F., 'Dialogue, Debate, and Dream Vision', in *The Cambridge Companion to Medieval English Literature 1100–1500*, ed. Larry Scanlon (Cambridge: Cambridge University Press, 2009), 71–82

Kurath, Hans, Sherman M. Kuhn, and R. E. Lewis, eds, *The Middle English Dictionary*, 19 vols (Ann Arbor, MI: University of Michigan Press, 1952)

Landrine, Hope, 'Clinical Implications of Cultural Differences: The Referential versus the Indexical Self', *Clinical Psychology Review*, 12/4 (1992), 401–15

Langdell, Sebastian James, '"What World Is This? How Vndirstande Am I?": A Reappraisal of Poetic Authority in Thomas Hoccleve's Series', *Medium Aevum*, 78/2 (2009), 282–99

Lawton, David, 'Dullness and the Fifteenth Century', *English Literature History*, 54/4 (1987), 761–99

Lawton, David, *Voice in Later Medieval English Literature: Public Interiorities* (Oxford: Oxford University Press, 2017)

Leff, Amanda, 'Lydgate Rewrites Chaucer: The General Prologue Revisited', *Chaucer Review*, 46 (2012), 472–9

Lowe, Ben, *Imagining Peace: A History of Early English Pacifist Ideas, 1340–1560* (University Park, PA: Pennsylvania State University Press, 1997)

Lutton, Rob, '"Love This Name That Is IHC:" Vernacular Prayers, Hymns and Lyrics to the Holy Name of Jesus in Pre-Reformation England', in *Vernacularity in England and Wales, c. 1300–1550*, ed. Elizabeth Salter and Helen Wicker, Utrecht Studies in Medieval Literacy, 17 (Turnhout: Brepols, 2011), 119–45

MacDonald, A. A., 'Lyrics in Middle Scots', in *A Companion to the Middle English Lyric*, ed. Thomas G. Duncan (Cambridge: Brewer, 2005), 242–61

Machan, Tim W., 'Textual Authority and the Works of Hoccleve, Lydgate and Henryson', *Viator*, 23 (1992), 281–99

Machan, Tim W., 'The Visual Pragmatics of Code-Switching in Late Middle English Literature', in *Code-Switching in Early English*, ed. Herbert Schendl and Laura Wright (Berlin: de Gruyter, 2011), 303–33

Malden, H. E., *A History of the County of Surrey*, 4 vols (London: Constable, 1902–12; reprint 1967)

Malo, Robyn, 'Penitential Discourse in Hoccleve's *Series*', *Studies in the Age of Chaucer*, 34 (2012), 277–305

Martin, Henri-Jean, *The History and Power of Writing* (Chicago, IL: University of Chicago Press, 1995)

Maurer, Helen E., *Margaret of Anjou: Queenship and Power in Late Medieval England* (Woodbridge: Boydell Press, 2003)

McGerr, Rosemarie, *A Lancastrian Mirror for Princes: The Yale Law School New Statutes of England* (Bloomington, IN: Indiana University Press, 2011)

McHardy, Alison K., 'Religion, Court Culture and Propaganda: The Chapel Royal in the Reign of Henry V', in *Henry V: New Interpretations*, ed. Gwilym Dodd (Woodbridge: Boydell, 2013), 131–56

McNelis, James, 'Parallel Manuscript Readings in the CT Retraction and Edward of Norwich's Master of Game', *Chaucer Review*, 36 (2001), 87–90

McSheffrey, Shannon, 'Richard Caudray (c. 1390–1458): Fifteenth-Century Churchman, Academic, and Ruthless Politician', *Medieval Prosopography*, 33 (2018), 167–79

McSheffrey, Shannon, *Seeking Sanctuary: Crime, Mercy, and Politics in English Courts, 1400–1550* (Oxford: Oxford University Press, 2017)

Meale, Carol M., '"...Alle the Bokes That I Haue of Latyn, Englisch, and Frensch": Laywomen and Their Books in Late Medieval England', in *Women and Literature in Britain, 1150–1500*, ed. Carol M. Meale (Cambridge: Cambridge University Press, 1993), 128–58

Meale, Carol M., '*The Libelle of Englyshe Polycye* and Mercantile Culture in Late-Medieval London', in *London and Europe in the Later Middle Ages*, ed. Julia Boffey and Pamela King (London: Centre for Medieval and Renaissance Studies, Queen Mary and Westfield College, 1995), 181–228

Meyer-Lee, Robert J., 'Hoccleve and the Apprehension of Money', *Exemplaria*, 13/1 (2001), 173–214

Meyer-Lee, Robert J., 'Laureates and Beggars in Fifteenth-Century English Poetry: The Case of George Ashby', *Speculum*, 79/3 (2004), 688–726

Meyer-Lee, Robert J., *Poets and Power from Chaucer to Wyatt* (Cambridge: Cambridge University Press, 2007)

Mills, David, '"Look at Me When I'm Speaking to You:" The Behold and See Convention in Medieval Drama', *Medieval English Theatre*, 7 (1985), 4–12

Minnis, Alastair J., *Medieval Theory of Authorship: Scholastic Literary Attitudes in the Later Middle Ages* (London: Scolar Press, 1984)

Minnis, Alastair J., 'The Author's Two Bodies? Authority and Fallibility in Late-Medieval Textual Theory', in *Of the Making of Books: Medieval Manuscripts, Their Scribes and Readers: Essays Presented to M. B. Parkes*, ed. P. R. Robinson and Rivkah Zim (Aldershot: Scolar, 1997), 259–79

Mitchell, Christina L., *Scottish Chaucerians: Transforming and Reclaiming a Discarded Category* (Williamsburg, VA: College of William and Mary, 2011)

Mitchell, Jerome, *Thomas Hoccleve: A Study in Early Fifteenth-Century English Poetic* (Urbana, IL, 1968)

Mooney, Linne R., 'A New Holograph Copy of Hoccleve's *Regiment of Princes*', *Studies in the Age of Chaucer*, 33 (2011), 263–6

Mooney, Linne R., 'A Woman's Reply to Her Lover' and Four Other New Courtly Love Lyrics in Cambridge, Trinity College MS R.3.19', *Medium Aevum*, 67 (1998), 235–56

Mooney, Linne R., 'Some New Light on Thomas Hoccleve', *Studies in the Age of Chaucer*, 29 (2007), 293–340

Mooney, Linne R., and Estelle Stubbs, Scribes and the City: London Guildhall Clerks and the Dissemination of Middle English Literature, 1375–1425 (Woodbridge: York Medieval Press and Brewer, 2013)

Mortimer, Ian, *The Fears of Henry IV: The Life of England's Self-Made King* (London: Random House, 2013)

Myers, A., 'The Household of Queen Margaret of Anjou, 1452–3', *Bulletin of the John Rylands Library*, 40/1 (1957), 79–113

Newdigate, C. A., 'The Chantry of St. John Baptist at Bailey', *Transactions of the Historic Society of Lancashire and Cheshire*, 68 (1916), 118–58

Nisse, Ruth, 'Was it not routhe to se?', in *John Lydgate: Poetry, Culture, and Lancastrian England*, ed. Larry Scanlon and James Simpson (Notre Dame, IN: University of Notre Dame Press, 2006), 279–98

von Nolcken, Christina, '"O, why ne had Y lerned for to die?": Lerne for to Dye and the Author's Death in Thomas Hoccleve's *Series*', *Essays in Medieval Studies*, 10 (1993), 27–51

Nuttall, Jenni, *The Creation of Lancastrian Kingship: Literature, Language and Politics in Late Medieval England* (Cambridge: Cambridge University Press, 2007)

Nuttall, Jenni, 'Thomas Hoccleve's Poems for Henry V', in *Oxford Handbooks Online* (Oxford: Oxford University Press, 2015)

Obermeier, Anita, *The History and Anatomy of Auctorial Self-Criticism in the European Middle Ages* (Amsterdam: Rodopi, 1999)

Otway-Ruthven, J., *The King's Secretary and the Signet Office in the XV Century* (Cambridge: Cambridge University Press, 1939)

Owen, Jr., Charles, 'What the Manuscripts Tell Us about the Parson's Tale', *Medium Aevum*, 63 (1994), 239–49

Parkes, M. B., 'Patterns of Scribal Activity and Revisions of the Text in Early Copies of Works by John Gower,' in *New Science out of Old Books: Manuscripts and Early Printed Books: Essays in Honour of A. I. Doyle.*, ed. Richard Beadle and A. J. Piper (Aldershot: Scolar, 1995), 81–121

Parkes, M. B., *Their Hands before Our Eyes: A Closer Look at Scribes: The Lyell Lectures Delivered in the University of Oxford, 1999* (Aldershot: Ashgate, 2008)

Patterson, Lee, '"What Is Me?": Self and Society in the Poetry of Thomas Hoccleve', *Studies in the Age of Chaucer*, 23/1 (2001), 437–70

Pearsall, Derek, *John Lydgate (1371–1449)* (Victoria, BC: University of Victoria, 1997)

Pearsall, Derek, 'The English Chaucerians', in *Chaucer and Chaucerians: Critical Studies in Middle English Literature*, ed. Derek Brewer (London: Thomas Nelson, 1966), 201–39

Peverley, Sarah, 'Adapting to Readeption in 1470–1471: The Scribe as Editor in a Unique Copy of John Hardyng's *Chronicle of England* (Garrett MS. 142)', *Princeton University Library Chronicle*, 66/1 (2004), 140–72

Pfaff, Richard W., *New Liturgical Feasts in Later Medieval England* (Oxford: Clarendon Press, 1970)

Pistono, S. P., 'Henry IV and Charles VI: The Confirmation of the Twenty-Eight-Year Truce,' *Journal of Medieval History*, 3/4 (1977), 353–65

Pollard, A. J., *Late Medieval England 1399–1509* (London: Longman, 2000)

Raybin, David, 'Critical Approaches', in *A Companion to Medieval English Literature and Culture, c. 1350–c. 1500*, ed. Peter Brown (Oxford: Blackwell, 2007), 9–24

Renevey, Denis, '"Name above Names: The Devotion to the Name of Jesus from Richard Rolle to Walter Hilton's *Scale of Perfection I*"', in *The Medieval*

Mystical Tradition: England, Ireland, and Wales (Exeter Symposium VI), ed. Marion Glasscoe (Cambridge: D. S. Brewer, 1999), 103–21

Renevey, Denis, 'The Name Poured Out', in *The Mystical Tradition and the Carthusians*, ed. J. Hogg (Salzburg: Institut für Anglistik und Amerikanistik, 1996), 127–47

Richardson, Douglas, *Royal Ancestry* (Salt Lake City, UT: the Author, 2013)

Richardson, Malcolm, 'Hoccleve in His Social Context', *Chaucer Review*, 20/4 (1986), 313–22

Richardson, Walter Cecil, *History of the Court of Augmentations, 1536–1554* (Baton Rouge, LA: Louisiana State University Press, 1961)

Rowse, Alfred Leslie, *Bosworth Field, from Medieval to Tudor England* (Garden City, NY: Doubleday, 1966)

Sanders, Ralph, Peggy Sanders Van der Heide, and Carole Sanders, *Generations: A Thousand-Year Family History* (Philadelphia, PA: Xlibris, 2007)

Sayles, G. O., 'The Manner of King Richard's Renunciation: A "Lancastrian Narrative"?', *English Historical Review*, 108 (1993), 365–70

Scanlon, Larry, 'Lydgate's Poetics', in *John Lydgate: Poetry, Culture, and Lancastrian England*, ed. Larry Scanlon and James Simpson (Notre Dame, IN: University of Notre Dame Press, 2006), 61–97

Scase, Wendy, *Literature and Complaint in England, 1272–1553* (Oxford: Oxford University Press, 2007)

Scattergood, John, 'Ashby, George (b. before 1385?, D. 1475), Administrator and Poet', *Oxford Dictionary of National Biography* (Oxford: Oxford University Press, 2004)

Scattergood, John, 'George Ashby's *Prisoner's Reflections* and the Virtue of Patience', *Nottingham Medieval Studies*, 37 (1993), 102–9

Scattergood, John, 'Peter Idley and George Ashby', in *A Companion to Fifteenth-Century English Poetry*, ed. A. S. G. Edwards and Julia Boffey (Cambridge: D. S. Brewer, 2013), 113–25

Scattergood, John, 'The Date and Composition of George Ashby's Poems', *Leeds Studies in English*, 21 (1990), 167

Scattergood, John, '*The Libelle of Englyshe Polycye*: The Nation and Its Place', in *Nation, Court and Culture: New Essays on Fifteenth-Century English Poetry*, ed. Helen Cooney (Dublin: Four Courts Press, 2001), 28–49

Schaffner, Anna K., *Exhaustion: A History* (New York: Columbia University Press, 2016)

Schmitt, Jean Claude, 'Between Text and Image: The Prayer Gestures of Saint Dominic', *History and Anthropology*, 1 (1984), 127–62

Schmitt, Jean Claude, *Ghosts in the Middle Ages: The Living and the Dead in Medieval Society* (Chicago, IL: University of Chicago Press, 1998)

Schmitt, Jean Claude, *La raison des gestes dans l'Occident médiéval* (Paris: Gallimard, 1990)

Scott, Kathleen L, 'Lydgate's *Lives of Saints Edmund and Fremund*: A Newly Located Manuscript in Arundel Castle', *Viator* (1982), 335–66

Shagan, Ethan H., *Popular Politics and the English Reformation* (Cambridge: Cambridge University Press, 2003)

Sherborn, Charles Davies, *A History of the Family of Sherborn* (London: Mitchell and Hughes, 1901)

Simpson, James, 'Madness and Texts: Hoccleve's *Series*', in *Chaucer and Fifteenth-Century Poetry*, ed. Julia Boffey and Janet Cowen (London: King's College London, Centre for Late Antique and Medieval Studies, 1991), 15–29

Simpson, James, *Reform and Cultural Revolution, 1350–1547* (Oxford: Oxford University Press, 2002)

Singleton, Charles S., 'The Poet's Number at the Center', in *Essays in the Numerical Criticism of Medieval Literature*, ed. Caroline D. Eckhardt (Lewisburg, PA: Bucknell University Press, 1980), 79–90

Smith, Bill, 'Moleyns, Adam (d. 1450)', *Oxford Dictionary of National Biography* (Oxford: Oxford University Press, 2004), <https://doi-org.proxy-ub.rug.nl/10.1093/ref:odnb/18918>

Sobecki, Sebastian, 'A Southwark Tale: Gower, the Poll Tax of 1381, and Chaucer's *The Canterbury Tales*', *Speculum*, 92/3 (2017), 630–60

Sobecki, Sebastian, 'Bureaucratic Verse: William Lyndwood, the Privy Seal, and the Form of *The Libelle of Englyshe Polycye*', *New Medieval Literatures*, 12/1 (2011), 251–88

Sobecki, Sebastian, 'Ecce Patet Tensus: The Trentham Manuscript, *In Praise of Peace*, and John Gower's Autograph Hand', *Speculum*, 90/4 (2015), 925–59

Sobecki, Sebastian, 'Lydgate's Kneeling Retraction: The *Testament* as a Literary Palinode', *Chaucer Review*, 49/3 (2015), 265–93

Sobecki, Sebastian, *The Sea and Medieval English Literature* (Cambridge: D. S. Brewer, 2008)

Sobecki, Sebastian, '"The Writyng of This Tretys": Margery Kempe's Son and the Authorship of Her Book', *Studies in the Age of Chaucer*, 37 (2015), 257–83

Sobecki, Sebastian, *Unwritten Verities: The Making of England's Vernacular Legal Culture, 1463–1549* (Notre Dame, IN: University of Notre Dame Press, 2015)

Somerset, Fiona, 'Hard is with weyntis for to make affray', in *John Lydgate: Poetry, Culture, and Lancastrian England*, ed. Larry Scanlon and James Simpson (Notre Dame, IN: University of Notre Dame Press, 2006), 258–78

Spearing, A. C., *Medieval Autographies: The 'I' of the Text* (Notre Dame, IN: University of Notre Dame Press, 2012)

Spearing, A. C., *Textual Subjectivity: The Encoding of Subjectivity in Medieval Narratives and Lyrics* (Oxford: Oxford University Press, 2005)

Spies, Heinrich, 'Bisherige Ergebnisse und weitere Aufgaben der Gower-Forschung', *Englische Studien*, 28 (1900), 163–208

St John Hope, William, and E. G. Cuthbert, *English Liturgical Colors* (London: SPCK, 1918)

Staley, Lynn, *Languages of Power in the Age of Richard II* (Philadelphia, PA: Pennsylvania State University Press, 2006)

Staley, Lynn, 'Margery Kempe: Social Critic', *Journal of Medieval and Renaissance Studies*, 22 (1992), 159–84

Staley, Lynn, *Margery Kempe's Dissenting Fictions* (University Park, PA: Penn State Press, 1994)

Stansfield, Michael, 'The Holland Family, Dukes of Exeter, Earls of Kent and Huntingdon, 1352–1475' (unpublished DPhil., University of Oxford, 1987)

Starkey, David, *The English Court: From the Wars of the Roses to the Civil War* (London: Longman, 1987)

Stollberg-Rilinger, Barbara, 'Kneeling before God, Kneeling before the Emperor: The Transformation of a Ritual during the Confessional Conflict in Germany', in *Resonances Historical Essays on Continuity and Change*, ed. Nils Holger Petersen, Eyolf Østrem, and Andreas Bücker (Turnhout: Brepols, 2011), 149–72

Storer, James, *Select Views of London and Its Environs* (London: Vernor, Hood, Storer, and Greig, 1804)

Strohm, Paul, *England's Empty Throne: Usurpation and the Language of Legitimation, 1399–1422* (Notre Dame, IN: University of Notre Dame Press, 2006)

Strohm, Paul, *Hochon's Arrow: The Social Imagination of Fourteenth-Century Texts* (Princeton, NJ: Princeton University Press, 1992)

Strohm, Paul, *Politique: Languages of Statecraft between Chaucer and Shakespeare* (Notre Dame, IN: University of Notre Dame Press, 2005)

Strohm, Paul, *Social Chaucer* (Cambridge, MA: Harvard University Press, 1989)

Strohm, Paul, 'The Trouble with Richard: The Reburial of Richard II and Lancastrian Symbolic Strategy', *Speculum*, 71 (1996), 87–111

Strohm, Paul, *Theory and the Premodern Text* (Minneapolis, MN: University of Minnesota Press, 2000)

Stubbs, Estelle, and Linne Mooney, 'A Record Identifying Thomas Hoccleve's Father', *Journal of the Early Book Society*, 14 (2011), 233–7

Summers, Joanna, *Late-Medieval Prison Writing and the Politics of Autobiography* (Oxford: Clarendon Press, 2004)

Summit, Jennifer, *Memory's Library: Medieval Books in Early Modern England* (Chicago, IL: University of Chicago Press, 2008)

Sumption, Jonathan, *The Hundred Years War, Volume 4: Cursed Kings* (London: Faber and Faber, 2017)

Sweet, W. H. E., 'Lydgate's Retraction and "His Resorte to His Religyoun"', in *After Arundel: Religious Writing in Fifteenth-Century England*, ed. Vincent Gillespie and Kantik Ghosh, Medieval Church Studies, 21 (Turnhout: Brepols, 2011), 343–60

Taylor, Charles, *A Secular Age* (Cambridge, MA: Belknap Press of Harvard University Press, 2007)

Taylor, Charles, 'An Issue about Language', in *Language, Culture, and Society: Key Topics in Linguistic Anthropology* (Cambridge: Cambridge University Press, 2006), 16–46

Taylor, Craig, *Debating the Hundred Years War: Pour ce que plusieurs (La Loy Salicque) and a Declaration of the Trew and Dewe Title of Henry VIII* (Cambridge: Cambridge University Press, 2006)

Taylor, Craig, 'Henry V, Flower of Chivalry', in *Henry V: New Interpretations*, ed. Gwilym Dodd (Woodbridge: Boydell Press, 2013), 217–48

Taylor, Craig, '"La Querelle Anglaise": Diplomatic and Legal Debate during the Hundred Years' War' (Unpublished PhD, Oxford University, 1998)

Taylor, Craig, '"Weep Thou for Me in France": French Views of the Deposition of Richard II,' in *Fourteenth Century England III*, ed. W. M. Ormrod (Woodbridge: Boydell, 2004), 207–22

Taylor, Frank, 'Some Manuscripts of the *Libelle of Englyshe Polycye*', *Bulletin of the John Rylands Library*, 24/2 (1940), 376–418

Trapp, J. B., 'Verses by Lydgate at Long Melford', Review of English Studies, 6 (1955), 1–11

Travis, Peter, 'Deconstructing Chaucer's Retraction', *Exemplaria*, 3 (1991), 135–58

Trexler, Richard C., 'Legitimating Prayer Gestures in the Twelfth Century: The *De Penitentia* of Peter the Chanter', *History and Anthropology*, 1 (1984), 97–126

Turner, Marion, *Chaucerian Conflict: Languages of Antagonism in Late Fourteenth-Century London* (Oxford: Oxford University Press, 2007)

Vaughan, Mìceál, 'Creating Comfortable Boundaries: Scribes, Editors, and the Invention of the Parson's Tale', in *Rewriting Chaucer: Culture, Authority, and the Idea of the Authentic Text, 1400–1602*, ed. Thomas A. Prendergast and Barbara Kline (Columbus, OH: Ohio University Press, 1999), 45–90

Wagner, John A., *Encyclopaedia of the Hundred Years War* (Westport, CT: Greenwood, 2006)

Wakelin, Daniel, *Humanism, Reading, and English Literature, 1430–1530* (Oxford: Oxford University Press, 2007)

Walker, Michael L., 'The Manor of Batailles and the Family of Saunder in Ewell during the 16th and 17th Centuries,' *Surrey Archaeological Collections*, 54 (1955), 76–101

Walker, Greg, Writing under Tyranny: English Literature and the Henrician Reformation (Oxford: Oxford University Press, 2007)

Wallace, David, *Chaucerian Polity: Absolutist Lineages and Associational Forms in England and Italy* (Stanford, CA: Stanford University Press, 1997)

Wallace, David, *Premodern Places: Calais to Surinam, Chaucer to Aphra Behn* (Oxford: Blackwell, 2006)

Warner, George F., 'Wilhelm Hertzberg, Ed., *The Libell of Englishe Policye, 1436: Text und metrische Uebersetzung von W. Hertzberg* (Leipzig, 1878)', *Academy*, 14 (1878), 491–2

Warner, Lawrence, 'Scribes, Misattributed: Hoccleve and Pinkhurst', *Studies in the Age of Chaucer*, 37/1 (2015), 55–100

Watt, David, *The Making of Thomas Hoccleve's Series* (Liverpool: Liverpool University Press, 2013)

Watts, John, *Henry VI and the Politics of Kingship* (Cambridge: Cambridge University Press, 1996)

Werner, Janelle, '"Just as the Priests Have Their Wives": Priests and Concubines in England, 1375–1549' (PhD dissertation, University of North Carolina at Chapel Hill, 2009)

Werner, Janelle, 'Living in Suspicion: Priests and Female Servants in Late Medieval England', *Journal of British Studies*, 55/4 (2016), 658–79

Wertheimer, Laura, 'Children of Disorder: Clerical Parentage, Illegitimacy, and Reform in the Middle Ages', *Journal of the History of Sexuality*, 15/3 (2006), 382–407

Wertheimer, Laura, 'Illegitimate Birth and the English Clergy, 1198–1348', *Journal of Medieval History*, 31/2 (2005), 211–29

Whitaker, Thomas Dunham, *The History and Antiquities of the Deanery of Craven, in the County of York*, 2nd edn (Dubuque, IA: Nichols, 1812)

Wolfe, Matthew C., 'Placing Chaucer's "Retraction" for a Reception of Closure', *Chaucer Review*, 33 (1999), 427–31

Yeager, R. F., 'Gower in Winter: Last Poems', in *The Medieval Python: The Purposive and Provocative Work of Terry Jones*, ed. R. F. Yeager and Toshiyuki Takamiya (New York: Palgrave Macmillan, 2012), 87–103

Yeager, R. F., 'John Gower's Audience: The Ballades', *Chaucer Review*, 40/1 (2005), 81–104

Yeager, R. F., 'John Gower's French,' in *A Companion to Gower*, ed. Siân Echard (Cambridge: Brewer, 2004), 137–52

Yeager, R. F., 'Pax Poetica: On the Pacifism of Chaucer and Gower', *Studies in the Age of Chaucer*, 9 (1987), 97–121

Yeager, R. F., 'Politics and the French Language in England during the Hundred Years' Way: The Case of John Gower', in *Inscribing the Hundred Years' War in French and English Cultures*, ed. Denise Baker (Albany, NY: University of New York Press, 2000), 127–57

INDEX OF MANUSCRIPTS AND RECORDS

Note: The Index below concerns discussion of individual manuscripts and contemporary records. Figures are indicated by an italic *f* following the page number.

For the benefit of digital users, indexed terms that span two pages (e.g., 52–53) may, on occasion, appear on only one of those pages.

GENERAL INDEX

References to manuscripts and archival records appear in a separate index. Figures are indicated by an italic *f* following the page number.

For the benefit of digital users, indexed terms that span two pages (e.g., 52–53) may, on occasion, appear on only one of those pages.